SERVICE-LED GROWTH

The Role of the Service Sector in World Development

Dorothy I. Riddle

PRAEGER SPECIAL STUDIES • PRAEGER SCIENTIFIC

New York • Philadelphia • Eastbourne, UK
Toronto • Hong Kong • Tokyo • Sydney

Library of Congress Cataloging-in-Publication Data

Riddle, Dorothy I.
  Service-led growth.

  Bibliography: p.
  Includes index.
  1. Service industries.   2. Economic development.
I. Title.
HD9980.5.R53   1985   338.4'6   85-16743
ISBN 0-03-005664-0 (alk. paper)

Published in 1986 by Praeger Publishers
CBS Educational and Professional Publishing, a Division of CBS Inc.
521 Fifth Avenue, New York, NY 10175 USA

© 1986 by Praeger Publishers

6789 052 987654321

Printed in the United States of America on acid-free paper

INTERNATIONAL OFFICES

Orders from outside the United States should be sent to the appropriate address listed below. Orders from areas not listed below should be placed through CBS International Publishing, 383 Madison Ave., New York, NY 10175 USA

Australia, New Zealand
Holt Saunders, Pty, Ltd., 9 Waltham St., Artarmon, N.S.W. 2064, Sydney, Australia

Canada
Holt, Rinehart & Winston of Canada, 55 Horner Ave., Toronto, Ontario, Canada M8Z 4X6

Europe, the Middle East, & Africa
Holt Saunders, Ltd., 1 St. Anne's Road, Eastbourne, East Sussex, England BN21 3UN

Japan
Holt Saunders, Ltd., Ichibancho Central Building, 22-1 Ichibancho, 3rd Floor, Chiyodaku, Tokyo, Japan

Hong Kong, Southeast Asia
Holt Saunders Asia, Ltd., 10 Fl, Intercontinental Plaza, 94 Granville Road, Tsim Sha Tsui East, Kowloon, Hong Kong

Manuscript submissions should be sent to the Editorial Director, Praeger Publishers, 521 Fifth Avenue, New York, NY 10175 USA

Published and Distributed by the
Praeger Publishers Division
(ISBN Prefix 0-275)
of Greenwood Press, Inc.,
Westport, Connecticut

PREFACE

In working on the material for this volume, I have frequently been challenged to justify focusing on one particular sector—the service sector—as the major explanatory variable for economic development and growth. Why services? cry the critics. Can we really say that one sector of an economy is more important than the others? Aren't economic sectors interdependent and all necessary? Even though agricultural production is not a major portion of Gross Domestic Product (GDP), where would we be without it?

It is precisely because *all* sectors are important that I first began research on the role of services in GDP growth. In trying to "internationalize" the marketing and management literature which was developing in the United States in the early 1980s, I discovered that little comparative data existed *from an output perspective* about service sectors in various countries. Prior studies focused almost exclusively on patterns of employment—one of the inputs to the production process. Other inputs, such as fixed capital formation, had not been studied by sector, and only a few had looked systematically at the relationship between GDP from services and economic growth.

As I began to analyze sectoral patterns in economic growth, I became impressed by two phenomena: (1) how pervasive the biases were that only manufacturing activities stimulated growth; and (2) how difficult it was to do comparative economic research even at the most general level. The first phenomenon has resulted in what may appear to some to be a "pro-services" bias in this book, a setting up of straw "manufacturing-biased" men and knocking them down. For those who are already well aware of the crucial role played by services, I apologize for any repetitiveness in reviewing and discrediting pervasive myths about manufacturing. Having taught service-related issues to graduate students for over four years and presented service sector research at numerous professional conferences, I am keenly aware of how resistant our manufacturing biases are to change; hence, the detailed attention to demythifying our economic assumptions.

The second phenomenon has made me more compassionate toward my colleagues who have opted to ignore the service sector. Disaggregated economic data—i.e., broken down by International Standard Industry Classifications—are hard to come by for developing countries. Reasonably accurate disaggregated data are even more difficult to find. The GDP data I have used come from the data banks of the United Nations and the World

v

Bank. While I cannot vouch for their accuracy, I believe them to be the best available. By using constant currency data whenever possible and then looking primarily at sectoral percentages rather than at absolute figures, I have tried to reduce distortions. I offer the suggestion that since the service sector has not been valued as a sign of "development," its data are more likely to be understated than those of the manufacturing sector.

Some reviewers of my work have felt that my data are not as current as they could be. At the time of the analysis—the winter of 1984—there were 1982 and 1983 available on some countries, notably the industrialized countries. In order to have comparable data across nations at all levels of development, however, I found it necessary to go back to 1981 data. If, as I believe to be the case, the trends reported here are accurate, then the latest year makes less difference. What I have tried to describe are general principles of development and growth, grounded in analyses of data from 1965 to 1981 for 81 countries at four levels of economic development. Samples of 1983 data verify the trends already uncovered.

Those familiar with previous research on the service sector may be surprised that I have used factor analysis rather than the more usual multiple regression. May I remind my colleagues, as I was myself reminded initially, that multiple regression is not appropriate when the independent variables are correlated with each other (as is the case with most economic data). For the interested reader, a detailed description of methodology appears in Appendix A, with detailed statistics on the country data appearing in Appendix C. For those with more general, conceptual interests, what is important to know is that the country groupings that I have used are based on the categorizations by per capita GNP used in the 1984 World Bank *World Development Report.*

As the national studies on trade in services for submission to the General Agreement on Tariffs and Trade (GATT) have begun to appear, the results have underscored the data reported in this volume. It is clear from the discussions that have occurred in the GATT as well as in the United Nations Conference on Trade and Development (UNCTAD) that data are desperately needed in order for responsible policy setting, trade negotiations, and investment decisions to occur. My hope is that this volume can contribute some of those needed data and point the way for further research.

A work of this magnitude cannot be undertaken without support and encouragement from a wide variety of sources. I wish to thank first the International Studies Department and its chairman, Joaquim Duarte, of the

American Graduate School of International Management for allowing me to develop the course, Global Service Delivery, in 1982 which was the initial impetus for this work. I am also grateful for the funding from AGSIM which allowed me to present various portions of this work at professional conferences and for the valuable criticism that I received from colleagues who heard or read those papers. A special word of thanks goes to the students I have taught for their patience in studying a yet-uncharted area, and particularly to the students who have worked on building the data base—David Burks, Joe Cash, Dwaine Freeman, Matt Mosher, Lim Seuw-Lian, Catherine Tripp, Gary Van der Hoof. I am deeply indebted to staff members—too numerous to list—of the U.S. Office of the Trade Representative, the U.S. Department of Commerce, the U.S. Chamber of Commerce, the World Bank, ESCAP, LOTIS, OECD, GATT, UNCTAD, and many national governments. Rita Mae Kelly, Martin Sours, and Beverly Springer have been particularly helpful in critiquing my work. My thanks to Miriam Axelrod and Dawn Napolitan for the illustrations, as well as to all other colleagues, friends, and family members who have helped with the manuscript. Finally, I am particularly grateful to Lyn Salmon for her many hours of support and encouragement and her patience in editing drafts of this work.

CONTENTS

LIST OF TABLES AND FIGURES

TABLES

FIGURES

LIST OF ACRONYMS
AND ABBREVIATIONS

ASEAN	Association of Southeast Asian Nations
CAPTAIN	Character and Pattern Telephone Access Information Network
CARECOM	Caribbean Common Market
EC	European Communities
EEC	European Economic Community
ESCAP	Economic and Social Committee for Asia and the Pacific
GDP	Gross Domestic Product
GNP	Gross National Product
GATT	General Agreement on Tariffs and Trade
ILO	International Labour Organisation
IMF	International Monetary Fund
INS	Information Network System
ISIC	International Standard Industry Classification
LAFTA	Latin American Free Trade Association
NICs	Newly Industrializing Countries
OECD	Organisation for Economic Co-operation and Development
PRC	People's Republic of China
UN	United Nations
UNCTAD	United Nations Conference on Trade and Development

INTRODUCTION

1

UNDERSTANDING SERVICES

Agriculture, mining, and manufacturing are the bricks of economic development. The mortar that binds them together is the service industry (Shelp et al. 1984, p. 1).

In the end, the wealth-producing forces of an economy are its immaterial resources—not oil or gas, copper or iron ore, but rather the intellectual and organizational skills that are the very core of the services. And what is a manufactured good but a service in a packaged form? . . . In a real economy, goods and services are interdependent and mutually supportive (Krommenacker 1984, p. 9).

Services lie at the very hub of economic activity in any society. In 1980, service sector trade was valued at US $350 billion, or about 20 percent of world trade; and the contribution of the service sector to Gross Domestic Product[1] (GDP) worldwide averaged 58 percent. People are spending an ever-increasing percentage of their disposable income on services, and over half of all fixed capital formation has been occurring in the service sector. Services provide a variety of crucial functions—the distributive infrastructure for extractive and manufactured goods, the capital markets for financing enterprises, the administrative functions that enable a society to exist, the maintenance and recycling (renting/leasing) facilities for durable goods, and the activities (health, education, recreation) that enhance the quality of the labor force.

Yet the service sector is one of the least understood portions of our global economy. The service sector receives only minimal attention in country analyses, policy deliberations, or development funding strategies.

1

Many feel they know all they need to know about services, without recognizing that our common services mythology is just that—a myth with little basis in fact. Typically, prejudices include beliefs that services are labor-intensive, not very productive, and characteristic of "post-industrial" (often used to mean stagnant) societies. Development economists characteristically view services as a "developed country" issue, of little concern to developing nations. The excitement, the dynamism, the key to growth is believed to lie in the manufacturing sector.

Researchers who have analyzed the service sector in developing economies have usually examined primarily employment trends—i.e., the sectoral distribution of labor inputs. The service sector has therefore been viewed as existing to absorb excess labor no longer needed for agricultural production—a useful, but passive, role. Kuznets, one of the few economists to examine sectoral *output*, restricted his studies for the most part to the "developed" or "industrialized" economies.[2] It was not until Shelp's crucial volume, *Beyond Industrialization*, that we could see clearly the importance of the service sector in the Gross Domestic Product of both developed and developing economies. In this volume, we will be analyzing simultaneously countries at differing levels of economic development.[3] We will be concerned with both the commonalities across economies regarding the service sector and the different roles played by service industries as an economy develops.

The service sector plays a seldom recognized role as a necessary and critical ingredient in all economic growth. Please note the choice of words: "necessary and critical," not "necessary and sufficient." All functioning economies require a productive interplay among the three economic sectors—extractive (agriculture and mining), manufacturing, and services. All three sectors are important. In a global economy, however, nations can survive using primarily imported agricultural products—Hong Kong, Singapore, and Japan are all cases in point. Countries can also survive and thrive using imported manufactured products, with more rapid growth in services than in manufactures. Egypt, for example, has had an average annual growth rate of 6.3 percent between 1965 and 1981 with a US $2.06 billion 1981 merchandise trade deficit; however, it also had a total trade surplus of US $234 million (due to service exports), and 57.4 percent of its GDP originated in services.

No economy, though, can survive without a service sector. There would be no transportation or communications infrastructure, no financial markets, no government structure. "Even fully agricultural economies need the services of public administration and defense, trade, transport and credit" (Ezekiel and Pavaskar 1976, p. 3).

Why we are so loathe to recognize the centrality of services remains a mystery. Perhaps the traditional values placed in Western economic thought on self-sufficiency rather than interdependence, on static rather than dynamic systems, are responsible. We will return to the issue of historical bias in the next chapter. For now, our task is to clarify what exactly services are, first recognizing that many biases need to be overcome and many inaccurate assumptions brought into question.

EXAMINING ASSUMPTIONS ABOUT SERVICES

Assumptions about services have multiplied over the years, embedded in our language, and for the most part remain unchecked by rigorous examination. For example, "industrialization" ususally refers to manufacturing operations, implying that these are the only large-scale, mechanized productive activities. Overlooked is the fact that services are industries, that the Industrial Revolution involved changes not only in production methods but also in financial structures and the transportation and communication networks available for distribution of goods.

The words that are chosen to label concepts are more powerful than is often recognized in determining assumptions that are made. If we wish to understand the misconceptions that have developed around services, we must first recognize the role played by the three most common labels for the service sector—"tertiary," "residual," and "post-industrial"—in perpetuating misconceptions about services.

Services As "Tertiary"

Fisher coined the term "tertiary" in 1935 to refer to the service sector. As he explained in a later paper (1939), Fisher chose the term "tertiary" as parallel in construction to the terms "primary" and "secondary" then in use in Australia and New Zealand to refer, respectively, to the agricultural/pastoral and manufacturing sectors. Unfortunately, in selecting the term "tertiary," Fisher positioned services in people's minds as economic activities of lesser importance. "Tertiary" is a term denoting relative rank or position—third in importance.

Fisher's intention, though, was to point out that there was, in fact, a third group of economic activities in addition to the two traditionally analyzed by economists—i.e., agriculture and manufacturing. As is unfortunately still the case, data on economic activity were restricted to measures such as agricultural output and factory inventory. None of the macroeconomic indicators reflected service sector activity.

In selecting terminology, "primary sector" is an appropriate term to use in reference to agriculture, fishing, hunting, forestry, mining, and quarrying. Without the extractive process, there would be no raw materials to use either for basic survival or for the creation of other products. These activities, then, are necessary, though not sufficient, for existence.

Even in the most primitive of societies, though, simple extraction and consumption are insufficient to form a community. A community or society is based fundamentally on a web of social activities that create and sustain common traditions. At both the family and community levels, social consciousness is created through socialization in educational, religious, and legal precepts. All of these functions are service sector functions—what are commonly thought of as social overhead or public services.

The distributive or trade services—wholesaling and retailing—are also fundamental to the formation of a society out of a collection of individuals. A sense of community develops in part from the creation of interdependence. Rather than each individual or family unit having to meet all its own needs, certain extractive goods and/or services in which the family has a "comparative advantage" can then be produced in excess of the family's own needs and exchanged for those extractive goods and/or services that the family cannot produce for itself.

Manufactured goods function to facilitate extraction and service delivery. The term "durable consumer good" in actuality denotes a manufactured good that the ultimate consumer can use for the production of a service—e.g., food services, laundry services, transportation services. Hence, the term "secondary sector" to refer to the manufacturing of tangible goods is accurate in implying that the creation of tangible objects is of secondary importance. After all, such goods have little value in and of themselves; they are important only to the extent that they serve as the equipment and supplies for the extraction or service production processes.

The appropriate term for services is not as apparent. They are in many ways as "primary" to societies as are the extractive industries. While extractive activities are essential to physical survival, service activities are essential to social well-being. Indeed, one could argue that once one shifts from individual survival to economic interdependence, service industries form the primary sector, extractive industries the secondary sector, and manufacturing the tertiary sector.

Services As "Residual"

In 1940, Clark wrote, "There remains an important residual which we may describe for convenience as 'service industries'" (p. 375). As had Fisher, Clark was trying to point out that there *were* economic activities other than agriculture and manufacturing. His terminology has persisted in macroeconomics as the most usual description of services—that is, as the "residual" after agriculture, mining, and manufacturing. We see here again the unintended implication that services are not important in their own right, but only in relation to the extractive and manufacturing processes.

In addition, the term "residual" has another more misleading implication—that of size. A "residual" is usually thought of as that little bit which is left over. Nothing could be further from the truth in the case of the service sector. As we can see in Table 1.1, the service sector is, on the average, the largest of the three economic sectors at *all* levels of economic development—ranging from an average of 48 percent of GDP in Low-income developing countries to an average of 66 percent of GDP in industrialized market economies. Clark himself was aware of the size of the service sector from an employment perspective at least as early as 1938 when he pointed out in lectures that Australia and New Zealand already had over 50 percent of their populations employed in service industries, which "may come as a surprise to some".[4]

Services As "Post-Industrial"

Bell began the use of the term "post-industrial sector" in 1973 to refer to the service sector, and the term "post-industrial society" to refer to one in which the service sector is dominant. His choice of terminology reflected the common assumption that service industries did not develop until after "industrialization"—i.e., manufacturing development—had occurred. His terminology is based on the apparent development process of the economies of Western Europe from large agrarian societies to manufacturing-based societies, with service industries assumed to become important only in the present century.

As have other prominent writers, Bell based his arguments regarding economic development on changes in sectoral employment (a production

TABLE 1.1
Percentage of GDP and Employment
by Economic Sector: 1977 and 1981

| | Development Category | | | | | | | |
| | Low Income | | Lower Middle | | Upper Middle | | Industrial | |
Economic Sector	1977	1981	1977	1981	1977	1981	1977	1981
GDP								
Extractive Sector	42%	42%	30%	27%	16%	15%	9%	7%
Manufacturing Sector	11	10	15	16	21	21	24	27
Service Sector	47	48	55	57	63	64	67	66
Employment								
Extractive Sector	59%	72%	46%	53%	24%	25%	14%	9%
Manufacturing Sector	14	10	15	14	22	22	30	24
Service Sector	27	18	39	33	54	53	56	67

Calculations based on data from the International Labour Office, *Yearbook of Labour Statistics* (Geneva: ILO, 1983); the World Bank, *World Tables*, 3rd. ed. (Baltimore, MD: Johns Hopkins University Press, 1983).

input), rather than on sectoral Gross Domestic Product (a production output). Even so, his terminology is inaccurate. Research by Singelmann (1978) shows that the economic development path of Western Europe regarding employment shifts does not generalize even to Canada and the United States (where labor moved into manufacturing and services concurrently), let alone to Japan (where labor moved into services *before* manufacturing). In Singapore, over 60 percent of the population was employed in services as far back as 1920 and over 70 percent of GDP (in constant prices) has originated in services since 1960, the first year for which reliable data are available (Seow 1980). The same shift of labor to services before manufacturing has been documented for West Africa (Bauer and Yamey 1951).

Bell's terminology contains two problematic implications: (1) that services are not themselves industries; and (2) that service sector vitality and growth are dependent, in a causal sense, on the dynamism of the manufacturing sector. The causal links between sectors are, in fact, much more complex than is reflected in Bell's term "post-industrial." European societies were not *only* extractive or agrarian societies prior to the eighteenth century; their service industries were also often quite important. For England, the Netherlands, and Portugal, for example, shipping and retail trade formed central portions of their economies.

The central role attributed by Bell to the Industrial Revolution and its impact on the manufacturing process is understandable. Cottage industries had existed for centuries, but the mechanization of the production process made it possible to produce tangible goods on a scale and in a variety not previously imagined. Because of the capital investment required, production facilities were centralized for economies of scale; consequently, labor moved from the home or decentralized sites to the production sites, and massive urbanization occurred. Innovations in manufactured goods transformed production processes, business practices, and personal lifestyles, as well as disrupting traditional power bases.

While the importance of the Industrial Revolution should not be underestimated, the transformation of the manufacturing process did not occur in a vacuum. Massive manufacturing development was only possible because of transformations that occurred in capital markets, making it possible to obtain funds from impersonal sources and to pool investment capital. Timely acquisition of raw materials and distribution of finished goods could not occur without major developments in infrastructure service industries such as transportation and communication. Of primary importance were the changes created by using the products of manufacturing, rather than the manufacturing process itself.

In reflecting on services, then, we must beware of accepting unthinkingly the natural implications of terms in common usage. Services are neither of lesser size or importance than the other sectors, nor do they have a parasitical dependence on manufacturing activity. Rather, services are industries that play a vital and dynamic role in any functioning economy, and that stimulate growth in other sectors.

DEFINING SERVICES

Up until this point, we have been focused primarily on what services are *not*. Indeed, one of the simplest and most common methods for defining services has relied on definition by exclusion; for example, services are often defined as all economic activities that are not agriculture, mining, or manufacturing.

As anyone who begins to read the literature on services is aware, much of that literature has focused on definitional issues. There is as yet no commonly accepted definition of services, nor is there agreement on which industries should be classified under services. Various research studies on the service sector reach different conclusions, in large part because of differing definitions of services. In order to develop an accurate and adequate definition of services, we must first understand the problems encountered in defining services so that they can be avoided.

Inadequate Definitions

Those who write about the service sector frequently comment that services are difficult to define because of the heterogeneous nature of the industries involved. How does one describe simultaneously air transportation and management consultation, restaurants and public defense? The purpose of a definition, though, is to uncover and delineate what it is that these diverse industries have in common. After all, growing cotton and raising chickens are quite different from each other, and yet we have no difficulty conceptualizing both industries as agricultural. Similarly, the textile and auto industries are quite different, and yet we agree that they are both manufacturing processes. Indeed, the number of diverse industry groups aggregated under manufacturing in the International Standard Industry Classification system is not that different from the number aggregated under services—28 for manufacturing and 33 for services (UN 1971).

Part of the confusion in the services' literature stems from the practice of "defining" services by listing industries instead of trying to articulate the essence of service activity that all such industries share. The first definition in Table 1.2 is a typical example of a "nondefinition" that provides no assistance in understanding the nature of services.

When attributes of services are given, they typically include intangibility, labor intensity, simultaneity of production and consumption, and perishability (see Table 1.2 for examples). With the exception of intangibility, many of the features attributed to service industries are in fact inaccurate generalizations on dimensions relevant to *all* economic activities. For example, the degree of labor intensity varies from industry to industry and from firm to firm in all three economic sectors. In many countries, farming and cottage industries (manufacturing) are labor-intensive; while in the United States, a significant proportion of service industries are capital-intensive, not labor-intensive.[5]

Simultaneity, also, is not necessarily a characteristic of service industries. One of the important trends in service trade, to be discussed in detail later, is the decoupling (separation) of production and consumption in the service sector. For example, computerized medical testing allows

TABLE 1.2
Examples of Inadequate
Definitions of Services

"*Service industry*. An industry that produces services rather than goods. The chief service industries are transportation; retail trade; insurance; . . . ."(Ammer and Ammer 1984, p. 421).

"[Services are] . . . consumer or producer goods which are mainly intangible and often consumed at the same time as they are produced. . . . Service industries are usually labour-intensive" (Bannock, Baxter, and Rees 1972, p. 372).

"Services. The component of the gross national product that measures the output of intangible items" (Greenwald 1973, p. 533).

"[Services] . . . are sometimes referred to as intangible *goods*; one of their characteristics being that in general they are 'consumed' at the point of production" (Pearce 1981, p. 390).

the tests to be conducted on a patient in one community while the physician making the diagnosis and prescribing treatment does so in a different community. The shift in banking from personal service to automated bank tellers, with an accompanying premium charged for live teller assistance, is another example. Economies of scale, increased efficiency for producers, and enhanced time and place utility for consumers are all benefits of the decoupling process.

A related characteristic often mentioned is the perishability of services because of assumed simultaneity of production and consumption. Table 1.3 illustrates the fact that differing degrees of perishability exist in all three economic sectors. In actuality, discussions of perishability in services are related to characteristics of the service *process* rather than those of the service *product*. When writers refer, for example, to empty seats on a plane that cannot be filled once the flight has begun, the actual issue being addressed is the idle production capacity that can result from a poor match between supply and demand.

We are left, then, with intangibility—the most common characteristic used to define services. While intangibility is an important trait, as a definition it is both inadequate and inaccurate. By defining services negatively (as "not tangible"), we are given no assistance in understanding what services *are*. Since many service industries do produce tangible results, limiting services to those industries with no tangible output is unnecessarily restrictive. Most professional services, for example, have some

TABLE 1.3
Perishability of Goods
and Services

	Product Characteristic		
Economic Sector	Perishable (less than 6 mos.)	Semi-durable (6 mos. to 3 yrs.)	Durable (more than 3 yrs.)
Extractive Sector	Fresh produce	Grains	Fossil fuels
Manufacturing Sector	Bread	High-tech equipment	Low-tech equipment
Service Sector	Cleaning Transportation Communication	Maintenance Professional services	Research Education Government

Adapted from S. Kuznets, *Commodity Flows and Capital Formation*, Vol. 1, (New York: National Bureau of Economic Research, 1938).

tangible documentation in writing of the service provided. In fact, one of the key marketing challenges for services is to provide a tangible representation ("facilitating good") of the service in order to ensure the customer's sense of having made a worthwhile purchase.

A Definitional Strategy

In order to construct a more adequate definition of service industries, we can use definitions of the other two economic sectors as models. *Extractive industries* can be defined as *the retrieval of raw materials from the physical environment so that they can be used as supplies for other economic activities*. Similarly, *manufacturing industries* can be defined as *the production of tangible goods from raw materials, which then serve as equipment and supplies for other economic activities*.

While customers buy a manufactured good for the utility, or service, which it can provide, that ultimate utility is only a potential inherent within the good itself—to be actualized when the service is performed. Even services, though, are not synonymous with the ultimate utility provided—that benefit being a matter of the effectiveness of the service delivery rather than the actual service product itself.[6] The key elements, then, in defining services are (1) the nature of the production output; (2) the unique inputs used; and (3) the purpose served by the production process.

Service Output

The distinguishing characteristic of service output is that it is primarily a process or activity—hence its essential intangibility. Manufactured goods, by contrast, are primarily objects and therefore always tangible. The classic definition by the Committee on Definitions of the American Marketing Association (1960) is helpful in making the activity/object distinction: "Services are activities, benefits, and satisfactions which are offered for sale or are provided in connection with the sale of goods" (p. 21). Hill's definition (1977) further clarifies the unique nature of service output:

> A service may be defined as a change in the condition of a person, or of a good belonging to some economic unit, which is brought about as the result of the activity of some other economic unit, with the prior agreement of the former person or economic unit (p. 318).

Thus, services are activities that produce changes in persons or the goods they possess, much as goods-producing activities bring about changes in raw materials.

Unique Service Inputs

In trying to identify the unique inputs used—we are aware already from the discussion above that the inputs will be persons or their possessions. A primary characteristic of service production is the complexity of the relationship that exists between the producer and the customer because of the involvement of the customer as a potential input. Contrary to popular belief, not all service operations involve direct, sustained interaction between producer and customer. If one of the competitive strategies service firms have been adopting in order to be more efficient has been to decouple (separate) producer activites from customer involvement, then we must account for varying types of interaction in our definition.

Rather than specifying a single type of producer-customer relationship as *the* production input, we can identify three general types[7]: (1) The producer may provide the service in isolation from the customer, as is the case in many repair operations and professional services. In such cases, the producer is acting as the customer's stand-in or agent. (2) The customer may self-serve, using equipment and/or procedures arranged and maintained by the producer (e.g., rental and leasing services). In these instances, the producer acts as supervisor and maintenance crew while the customer acts as "unpaid" employee. (3) The producer and the customer may produce the service in interaction with each other. The uniqueness of the labor input in services lies in the type of involvement that the customer has in the production process—whether through retaining the producer as a substitute, providing the labor directly, or assisting the producer in the service delivery.

Purpose of Service Production

In reflecting on the purpose served by the production process, a common denominator among all service industries is the provision of time, place, and form utility. In the most simple of economies, many service functions are performed within the extended family rather than by strangers in the market place. In a more complex society, the service sector facilitates a wide range of economic activities—bringing together borrowers and lenders/investors, disseminating information, and so forth.

Time, place, and form utility may be thought of as "intermediate utility" concerns, rather than "ultimate utility" concerns—i.e., they are an aspect of service production that cause or create the ultimate benefit experienced by the customer. For definitional purposes, such time, place, and form utility concerns may be combined with the multiple types of labor input to account for situations in which the producer either provides knowledge/information for the customer or makes it easier for the consumer to "self-serve."

Services Defined

In order to define services in a manner that both distinguishes them from extractive and manufacturing activities and identifies their essential characteristics in a parallel fashion, the following definition is proposed:

> **Services are economic activities that provide time, place, and form utility while bringing about a change in or for the recipient of the service.**
>
> **Services are produced by (1) the producer acting for the recipient; (2) the recipient providing part of the labor; and/or (3) the recipient and the producer creating the service in interaction.**

In the definition above, the centrality of time, place, and form utility is apparent. The change process involved is stated as "in or for" as changes occur not only to persons or their physical possessions. Rental services change neither the person nor a possession, but rather make it possible for the person to make use of physical goods without purchasing them—i.e., a change in accessibility created *for* the customer. The term "recipient" is used rather than "customer" as sometimes the two are not identical. For example, parents are the customers in purchasing educational services for their children, who are the recipients of the service—and who, it is hoped, are changed in a positive way by that service.

The focus on time, place, and form utility marks a departure from the traditional definition of services as intangibles. External support for such a shift in emphasis can be seen in the 1984 Canadian national study on services submitted to the General Agreement on Tariffs and Trade (GATT) that distinguishes among four types of services[8], one of which is entitled "embodied services." These services include films, books, and computer software—all of which package a service in a tangible good in order to provide time, place, and form utility for the customer. "Embodied services" have traditionally been placed in the manufacturing category of national accounts; however, computer software has fairly consistently been acknowledged as a service product despite its tangible form. The Canadian report is one of the first policy statements to acknowledge that "embodied services" are indeed services.

CLASSIFYING SERVICES

Those familiar with service sector literature will be aware that numerous classification systems have been proposed for the service sector, each focusing on different aspects of service delivery. Much of the work in services classification, unfortunately, has occurred independently of the actual classifications used by international agencies, such as the United Nations or the World Bank (see Appendix B), in collecting economic data from nations. Since the purpose of a classification system is to be able to increase both our understanding of economies and our ability to analyze and make comparisons among economies, systems that cannot be used for data collection are of only academic interest.

TABLE 1.4
Summary of Alternate
Classification Systems

Production-based Classification
Fisher-Clark (1935/1940)
- Primary (agriculture, mining)
- Secondary (manufacturing)
- Tertiary (residual)

Sabolo (1975)
- Primary (agriculture, stock raising, fisheries)
- Non-primary
- High use of capital and skills (transport, mining, manufacturing)
- Low use of capital and skills (trade)
- High use of skills, low use of capital (finance)

Fuchs (1968)
- Agriculture
- Industry (mining, manufacturing, transportation, utilities)
- Services (commerce, business, government)

Consumption-based Classification [service portion]
Singer (1981)
- Production services
- Collective consumption
- Individual consumption

Function-based Classification [service portion]
Foote and Hatt (1953)
- Tertiary (restaurants, hotels, repair and maintenance, laundry)
- Quarternary (transportation, communication, commerce, finance)
- Quinary (health, education, recreation)

Katouzian (1970)
- Complementary services (finance, transportation, commerce)
- New services (health, education, entertainment)
- Old services (domestic)

Browning and Singelmann (1975)
- Distributive services (transportation, communication, commerce)
- Producer services (finance, professional)
- Social services (health, education, defense)
- Personal services (domestic, hotels, restaurants, leisure)

U.S. Census Bureau (U.S. Dept. of Commerce, 1984)
- Transportation, communication, utilities
- Wholesale and retail trade
- Finance, insurance, and real estate
- Services (personal and business)

Classification Systems Proposed To Date

In order to help the reader understand and evaluate the various classification systems that have been proposed, the best known systems (see Table 1.4) will be critiqued briefly. While doing so, keep in mind the purpose of a useful industrial classification system—to categorize data in mutually exclusive classes according to principles that aid in understanding the economic activities reflected in the data. Since the system is to be data-based, it must comprise categories for which data can indeed be collected. In the service sector, the primary function of classifying service industries is to help us understand the economic trends that underlie the apparent heterogeneity of the industries.

Production-based Classification

The Fisher-Clark model is the most well-known of the theoretical classifications based on type of production. It can be used in data analysis by combining the categories traditionally used in data collection. Its failure to subdivide the service sector, however, masks the differences among the various types of service industries and makes possible only the most general analyses. Unfortunately, it is one of the most realistic systems at this time (and will be used throughout this volume) because most economic data are not reported in a sufficiently disaggregated manner to allow for more detailed subdivision.

Sabolo (1975), in his study of developing countries, has also taken a production-based approach focusing on the resources required. Such a system is of limited use in analyzing service sector data because it combines transportation services with mining and manufacturing, as does the United Nations in the summary tables presented in the *Statistical Yearbook*, thus obscuring the distinctions between the three sectors. While Sabolo himself criticized his classification system on the grounds that services cut across the three non-primary categories, a more serious problem is that the assumptions about capital requirements and skill level are no longer valid. Given the recent changes in the financial sector, one could no longer classify banking (particularly the move toward electronic funds transfer) as low in capital intensity!

The classification system used by Fuchs (1968) is essentially that used by the World Bank in its *Development Report*. Mining, construction, and utilities are classified with manufacturing in an "Industrial" category reflecting capital-intensive production methods. Such a classification system is both dated regarding the industries employing capital-intensive methods and does not help elucidate what is occurring in the service sector itself. Since many researchers use the aggregated World Bank tables without going back to the disaggregated data (if, indeed, they are available), the result is a continuing underestimation of the service sector and an inflation of the importance of the manufacturing sector.

Consumption-based Classification

Singer (1971), in studying Brazil, has proposed a services classification that focuses on type of consumption rather than on method of production. His categories distinguish among consumption by industries and institutes, consumption by the public, and consumption by individuals. Such a description is useful in alerting us to the multiple markets involved, but not in categorizing services for comparative purposes as the categories are not mutually exclusive. The same service activity—e.g., transportation—could fall simultaneously into all three categories if produced for all three markets.

Function-based Classification

The most common method of reclassifying services has been by the societal function of the service. Foote and Hatt (1953), for example, have suggested a tripartite division into those services that move domestic and quasi-domestic functions out of the household and into the marketplace, those services that facilitate the distribution and division of labor, and those services that change and improve the recipient. Conceptually, such a system has appeal because it potentially seeks to explain some of the dynamics underlying service sector development. The categories, however, are neither mutually exclusive nor clearly related to the form in which economic data are (or could be) gathered for analysis.

Katouzian (1970) made a similar proposal by dividing services into industries that are complementary to (and presumably dependent on) urbanization and manufacturing production, industries that provide services for mass consumption that were previously available only to the elite, and industries that are traditional and labor-intensive. The first two categories (as in Foote and Hatt's system) point out important trends in services, though we need to bear in mind that services are increasingly developing as complementary not only to manufacturing and urbanization but also to other services. Again, though, the categories proposed are neither mutually exclusive nor clearly related to the form in which economic data are (or could be) gathered for analysis.

Browning and Singelmann (1975) have focused more on the economic function of the service in their subdivision. Compared with the other classification systems reviewed, the Browning and Singelmann system has several major advantages: (1) separating services from extractive and manufacturing activities; (2) providing an appropriate level of detail regarding services; and (3) being adaptable to the format in which economic data are collected. Using this system, we can potentially capture the important trends addressed by others—the development of various forms of intermediate (producer) services, the contribution of services to enhancing quality of life, and the "marketization" of domestic services.

Three problems remain: First, Browning and Singelmann have aggregated the infrastructure services of transportation and communication with wholesale and retail trade, two general categories with historically different, though related, economic roles (see Chapter 2). In this volume, we will be separating the two categories whenever possible. Second, construction services and utilities have been excluded from the service sector. As we shall see shortly, both industry groups are controversial; however, both belong most appropriately in the service sector. Third, they propose a theoretically reasonable and meaningful distinction between "social" and "personal" services that is impossible to make in practice for many developing countries, as the statistical data are reported only in the aggregate. The only portion of that distinction that can be made, and will be made in this volume, is between public administration and other social/personal services.

One other system bears mentioning—that used by the U.S. Census Bureau and reflected in the *U.S. Industrial Outlook*. Utilities are included appropriately with other infrastructure services, although construction is excluded. The major problem is the use of "services" as a subcategory label—implying that the preceding categories are *not* services.

Areas of Controversy

As would be expected from the discussion above, part of the confusion regarding the nature and role of the service sector stems from inconsistency in delineating the service sector. As Fuchs (1968) points out, even the same researchers change classification systems from study to study.

A 1983 report by the United Nations Conference on Trade and Development (UNCTAD) has an excellent summary of the key points of contention, namely, public administration, construction, and utilities. The controversies revolve around three issues: (1) the importance of intangibility as a defining characteristic of services; (2) the nature of the consumer (intermediate or final); and (3) the ownership of the means of production (public or private).

In this volume, the basis used for classification is the *function* of the industry, regardless of the consumer (a marketing issue) or the owner (an economic or political issue). The classification system used (see Table 1.5) is a modification of the Browning and Singelmann model, and reflects the categories reported by the World Bank *National Accounts* and set forth by UNCTAD (1983b).

Before turning to the controversial industries highlighted by UNCTAD, a comment is necessary about the treatment of rental income from the ownership of buildings. Some writers argue for the exclusion of rental income from national accounts on the basis either that no labor is

TABLE 1.5
Classification System
Used in This Volume

| Classification | Equivalents in Major Data Systems | |
	United Nations ISIC[a] Category	World Bank Category
Extractive Sector	1 & 2	1 & 2
Manufacturing Sector	3	3
Service Sector	4-9	4-11
Infrastructure	4, 5, 7	4, 5, 7
Trade Services	6	7
Business Services	8	8
Community Services[b]	9	9-11
[b]When data permit, Community Services are further subdivided:		
Public Administration	9 (partial)	9
Social/Personal Services	9 (partial)	10, 11

[a]*International Standard Industry Classification.*

Note: For category definitions see United Nations, Indexes to the International Standard Industrial Classification of All Economic Activities (New York: United Nations, 1971); World Bank, *World Tables,* 3rd ed. (Baltimore, MD: Johns Hopkins University Press, 1983).

involved or that the labor involved is not accounted for in the corresponding labor statistics. Rental of buildings is only one of the many forms of recycling durable goods in an increasingly mobile society—an increasingly important service function. Renting and leasing play an important role in providing time, place, and form utility to the consumer and making private ownership of all possible durable goods unnecessary. "Ownership of Buildings" revenue, therefore, is classified for this study in "Personal Services" along with other rental activities.

In order to evaluate the effect of including or excluding the industries that are controversial, Table 1.6 presents the statistical consequences of the various classifications. As can be seen, the system for classifying industries depends upon how narrowly or broadly one conceptualizes services. Below is a brief rationale for the inclusion in the service sector of each of the controversial industries.

TABLE 1.6
Services As Average Percentage of GDP under Alternate Classifications: 1980

Definition of "Services"	World	Developed Market Economics	Developing Economics
Narrow Definition (excludes public administration, construction, and utilities)	46.5%	48.6%	37.4%
Including public administration	55.3%	58.1%	43.5%
Including public administration and construction	61.7%	64.5%	49.7%
Including public administration, construction and utilities	64.0%	67.0%	51.0%

Adapted from UNCTAD, *Protectionism and Structural Adjustment: Production and Trade in Services, Policies and Their Underlying Factors Bearing upon International Services Transactions* (No. TD/B/941) (Geneva: UNCTAD, 1983b, p. 21, #4), based on the World Bank, *World Tables,* 2nd ed. (Baltimore, MD: Johns Hopkins University Press, 1980).

Public Administration

There continue to be critics who cite the arguments of Adam Smith that "social overhead" activities do not belong in the national accounts as they are "nonproductive" activities. Leaving aside the issue of public sector productivity for a later chapter, such critics have overlooked the very vital roles played by public services in any economy—e.g., enhancement of available labor inputs and the potential lowering of political risk.

The real issue we need to address regarding public sector activities is separating the function of a service from the ownership of the means of production. In some economies, activities such as transportation, communication, or banking, are privatized; while in others, they are run by the government. When, as is the case in Gershuny and Miles (1983) or in the GATT report from the European Communities (1984), services are categorized only as "market services" (i.e., private ownership), or "nonmarket services" (i.e., governmental or nonprofit ownership), it is impossible to assess the economic contributions of various types of industries.

The most useful categorization, then, is to classify government-run industries by *function*—as is generally done in the national accounts. What remains in "public administration" would be the functions necessary to administer a society—executive, defense, legislative, and judicial. Incidentally, critics who see the service sector as irrelevant, or even counterproductive, in the development process usually assume that the service sector in developing countries represents an overextended public sector. In actuality, as can be seen in Table 1.6, public administration only accounts for 6 percent of GDP on the average in developing economies.

Construction

Review of the first fourteen national studies[9] on services submitted to GATT shows that they all include construction and engineering in the service sector. The generally accepted reason for classifying construction as a service, given that a durable good (buildings, bridges) is produced, is the importance of the professional services provided by architects and engineers. Ideally, as UNCTAD (1983b)has suggested,construction could be disaggregated into a service component and a goods component; however, the present convention is to place construction under services.

Such a convention has a useful, pragmatic consequence. Given that only the professional services portion of the construction account represents services, the "nonservice" portion can be viewed as a stand-in, or "shadow price," for all the service activities presently reported in the manufacturing account—including both in-house service departments of manufacturing firms, and the service subsidiaries of diversified manufacturing parent corporations. The United States government has estimated, for example, that at least 30 percent of the labor force classified as manufacturing workers in the United States are actually service workers and that "about 25% of US gross national product was accounted for [in 1980] by services used as inputs by goods-producing industries—more than the total value added to GNP by the manufacturing sector" (*U.S. national study* 1984, p. 13). Keeping such data in mind, we can see from Table 1.6 that the inclusion of 6.4 percent average GDP from construction in the service sector is unlikely to result in an overestimation of actual service sector activity.

Utilities

Ironically, while utilities are frequently called "public services," they are often excluded from service sector statistics and placed, instead, with manufacturing. Indeed, the first fourteen national studies for GATT each classify utilities in manufacturing. The reasons given for placing utilities in with manufacturing are usually that they are capital-intensive and have a tangible output. Utilities *are* services, though, because their primary function is to provide time, place, and form utility for the user. Utilities are a classic example of the mechanization of a previously domestic/household service that was originally labor-intensive and is now capital-intensive. In any case, as can be seen from Table 1.6, the average GDP contribution from utilities is minimal; hence, classification differences will have little effect on overall analyses.

A NEW ECONOMIC MODEL

From the preceding discussion, it is clear that traditional economic models are replete with assumptions about the nature and interaction of the economic sectors. As will be elaborated in Chapter 2, very few societies have followed the linear developmental mode implied by terms such as "tertiary" and "post-industrial." Models implying a unidirectional flow of economic activity from extraction to manufacturing to services are overly simplistic and inaccurate. What we need is a more interactive model of the economic sectors providing a graphic representation of the interlinkages which exist.

Far from being derivative or parasitical, the service sector is a vital force in stimulating and facilitating economic growth. All economies are dependent on the development of appropriate public administration structures and financial markets in order for economic activity to take place (Hartwell 1973). Business (financial and professional) services and government services serve as prerequisites for industry development in the extractive and manufacturing sectors. Within the extractive sector of the United States, for example, at least 10 percent of the value-added in agriculture comes from activities such as veterinary and forest services, and at least 20 percent of the value-added in mining comes from professional services. In addition, of course, business and government services are provided to other service subsectors, as well as to the final consumer.

Flow of Services

Figure 1.1 shows the flow of services among the various portions of the economy. The variety of service activity, separate from trade in goods, is clearly visible. Infrastructure services, such as transportation and communications, are provided to all portions of the economy (including the final consumer) without being linked to the flow of traded goods. Social services, such as health care and education, enhance the quality of the labor force available to work in all economic sectors. Public administration plays a crucial role in developing and implementing "policies that reduce business uncertainty and regulatory obstacles and provide fiscal incentives; in so doing they can encourage investment" (Eckstein and Hagopian 1983, p. 64) in all sectors.

Once one moves beyond very basic subsistence living where households are entirely self-sufficient, service activities are what create quality of life. A variety of "personal" service industries have been created to move formerly domestic functions into the market economy—e.g., restaurants, lodging, house cleaning and maintenance, and child care. Even many of the shopping/errand chores are being streamlined by technological innovations that will allow one to shop from the home (videotext) instead of spending hours going from store to store. The net result of these services industries is to allow persons more and more choice about how they spend their time.

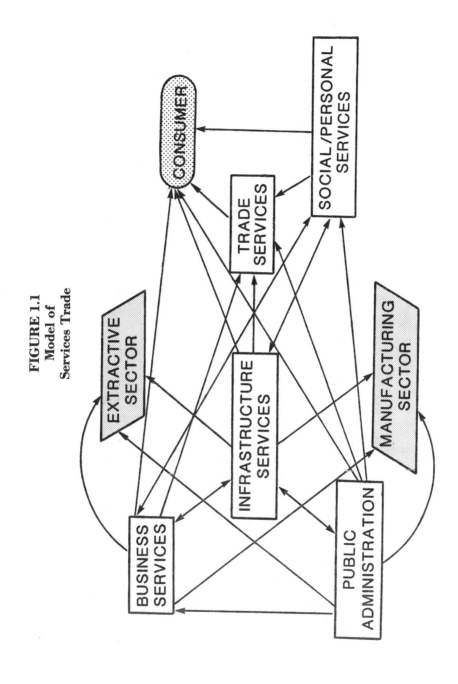

FIGURE 1.1
Model of
Services Trade

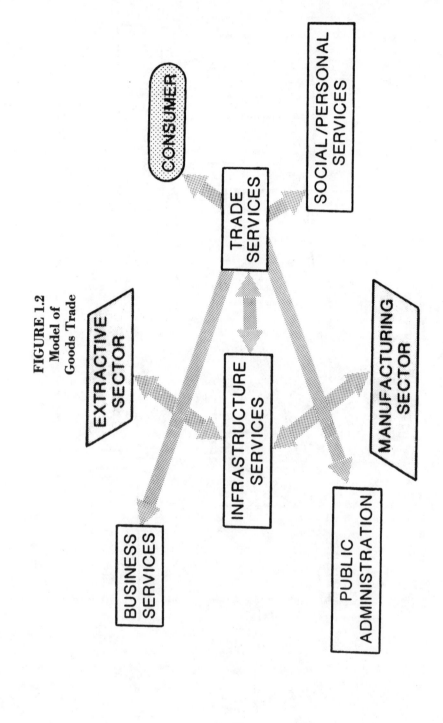

FIGURE 1.2
Model of
Goods Trade

CONSUMER

SOCIAL/PERSONAL SERVICES

TRADE SERVICES

EXTRACTIVE SECTOR

INFRASTRUCTURE SERVICES

MANUFACTURING SECTOR

BUSINESS SERVICES

PUBLIC ADMINISTRATION

Contrary to the popular belief that service industries are always dependent on the manufacturing sector, Figure 1.1 illustrates the fact that service industries provide products both to other service industries and directly to the final consumer. One of the fastest growing areas in the service sector is in services that distribute, or serve as market intermediaries for, other service industries, providing time, place, and form utility.

Flow of Goods

Turning to the flow of tangible goods, Figure 1.2 shows the vital role played by the infrastructure and trade services in the distribution of raw materials and finished goods. In a complex economy, infrastructure and trade services serve as intermediaries between the extractive and manufacturing sectors, and also between those sectors and both intermediate and final consumers. The service sector provides the basis for a global economy by making possible the timely distribution of goods to an increasing variety of markets both within domestic economies and concurrently in transnational markets.

The basic function of the manufacturing sector is to provide the equipment (assets) and supplies for the extractive industries, for other manufacturing processes, for commercial service producers, and for self-service. Consumers purchase durable goods not as ends in themselves, but in order to streamline or facilitate production of a service in a business or at home. Automobiles are purchased in order to provide one's own transportation services and thereby acquire time and place utility. Washing machines are purchased in order to provide one's own laundry services, stereo systems in order to provide one's own entertainment . . . and so forth.

Manufacturing activities have no meaning in isolation from the rest of the economy; they are not ends in themselves. The demand for manufactured goods—both in terms of type of good and their quantity—depends upon what is happening in the service sector. For example, the type of equipment purchased to duplicate materials will depend upon whether duplication is primarily a service produced *for* consumers (in which case that equipment must be able to sustain high-volume usage over prolonged periods of time) or *by* the consumer (in which case issues of maintenance and cost become more salient). Indeed, "the service sector purchased more than 80% of the $25 billion of computers, office equipment, and communications equipment shipped [in the United States] in 1982" (Kirkland 1985, p. 42).

Interactive Flow of Services and Goods

Combining the flow of services with the flow of goods (see Figure 1.3), we can see the relatively limited role played by the flow of extractive and manufactured goods and the major facilitating roles played by the various portions of the service sector. Rather than being peripheral or luxury economic activities, services lie at the heart of any functioning economy. "Weak infrastructure, one of the characteristics of developing countries, can seriously impair the growth and efficiency of activity by private entrepreneurs in agriculture, commerce, and manufacturing" (Willoughby 1983, p. 10).

There are a number of examples that could be cited to illustrate the essential interconnectedness of any economy. Agricultural operations depend upon being able to purchase manufactured equipment and have it repaired, to call on veterinary and other professional services, to obtain a range of insurance services, to trade in formal or informal commodities markets, and to use remote sensing devices to forecast crop yields and weather conditions.

Any manufacturing plant must have financial backing, utilities to operate, a political environment of reduced risk to remain open, a distribution system to receive raw materials and disseminate finished goods, and industries or individuals to purchase and use those goods. As manufacturing ventures expand into space, they will be made possible by space station infrastructure, including waste management, power sources, and food services.

Operations and maintenance services become more crucial as natural resources become scarcer, the costs of new ventures continue to rise, and the ventures themselves become more complex:

> A full spectrum of operations and maintenance services are used in any manufacturing or processing facility. Consulting activities, including studies, surveys and audits of systems, practices and procedures provide one basis for increasing the efficiency of operations and maintenance activities. A variety of systems and programs are available to control maintenance resources. Manpower training through either vocational centers or on-the-job programs provide an additional service.... In some cases, security services make up an important element in maintenance of a facility (Chittum 1985, p. 21).

The service sector is, in truth, the facilitative milieu in which other productive activities become possible. It is also, as we shall see, the crucial

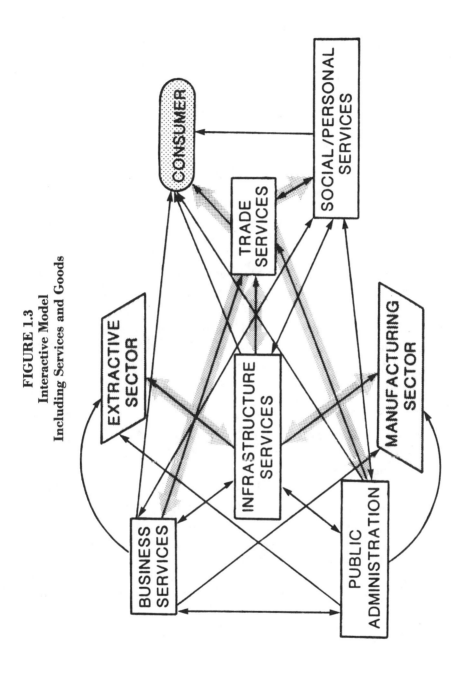

FIGURE 1.3
Interactive Model
Including Services and Goods

27

force for change toward a global economy. The development of new technology in research laboratories is changing the nature of work and leisure activities. The ability to move goods and services quickly and inexpensively is creating a global workplace where the nature of productive activities no longer depends upon either the raw materials or the consumer markets available at one location.

SUMMARY

In this chapter, the fallacies perpetuated by labeling the service sector as "tertiary," "residual," or "post-industrial" have been explored. Because of the inadequacy of prior definitions of services, major misconceptions about the perishability and intangibility of services have persisted. These misconceptions obscure the vital role played by services in domestic economies and international trade.

The defining characteristics of services have been listed as (1) the provision of time, place, and form utility; (2) the forms of producer-customer interaction; and (3) the fact that the utility for the customer resides in the activity performed. Five subdivisions of the service sector, which can be extracted from existing international data banks, have been proposed to clarify the role of services in an economy: Infrastructure Services (utilities, construction, transportation, communications, storage); Trade Services (wholesale, retail, hotels, restaurants); Business Services; Public Administration; and Social/Personal Services.

Finally, an interactive model of the economic sectors has been offered to help the reader visualize the actual role played by the service sector in any economy. The model helps highlight the fact that services are process industries that stimulate and facilitate growth in the other sectors, both domestically and internationally.

It is this interactive model that the reader should bear in mind throughout the rest of the book. These are the forward and backward linkages that make the service sector so central to economic planning. Services are the glue that holds any economy together, the industries that facilitate all economic transactions, and the driving force that stimulates the production of goods.

NOTES

1.   Gross Domestic Product (GDP) is defined as "the total final output of goods and services produced by an economy—that is, by residents and nonresidents, regardless of the allocation to domestic and foreign claims" (World Bank 1984, p. 275). Percentages and growth rates were calculated based on constant currency units, unless otherwise specified. When GDP figures are reported in US dollar figures, the conversion from domestic currency was made using the average exchange rate for the previous year.

2.   Kuznets' work on sectoral production and economic growth is noteworthy because of its focus on per capita GDP; however, his categorization of industries is inconsistent from study to study. In his major work, *Economic Growth of Nations*, he defines "industry" as including "mining, manufacturing, construction, electric power, gas, and water, transportation, storage, and communication" (p. 309)—thus incorporating industries from all three sectors.

3.   See Appendix A for a description of the various samples used in data analysis. Please note that the terminology used throughout this volume to refer to developmental categories is taken directly from the World Bank nomenclature and implies no judgment about the particular economy.

4.   Cited on page 37 in A.G.B. Fisher, "Production, Primary, Secondary, and Tertiary," *Economic Record* 15 (June 1939): 24–38.

5.   The relative capital intensity of service industries is addressed generally in the *US Study on Trade in Services* and more specifically in R.E. Kutscher and J.A. Mark, "The service-producing sector: Some common perceptions reviewed" (*Monthly Labor Review*, April 1983, 21–24). Having ranked 145 industry divisions on the basis of capital stock per employee, Kutscher and Mark found that "service industry divisions made up nearly one-half of the 30 divisions in the first two deciles of the ranking" (p. 23).

6.   Greenfield (1966) makes the distinction between manufactured goods, where the ultimate utility resides in an object, and services, where the ultimate utility resides in an activity; Hill (1977), however, points out that ultimate utility is separate from the product of a service industry.

7.   The idea of using multiple criteria for service production inputs came from the definitions proposed in W.J. Regan, "The Service Revolution," *Journal of Marketing* 27 (March 1963): 57–62; and in R. C. Judd, "The Case For Redefining Services," *Journal of Marketing* 28 (January 1964): 58–59. Regan's definition is as follows:

> ... [services] represent either intangibles yielding satisfactions directly (insurance), tangibles yielding satisfactions directly (transportation, housing), or intangibles yielding satisfaction jointly when purchased either with commodities or other services (credit, delivery) (p. 57).

Judd has provided a similar multiple framework in distinguishing among Rented Goods Services (the use of good without transfer of ownership), Owned Goods Services (the repairing or customization of a good), and Non-Goods Services ("experiential possession"). The actual service product may be associated with a tangible or an intangible form.

8.   The Canadian national study indicates that these categorizations are "based on a GATT Secretariat study and comments from a Task Force consultant" (1984, p. 11).

9.   The first fourteen reports submitted to GATT on trade in services were:

Canada	January 1984
United States	January 1984
The Netherlands	June 1984
United Kingdom	June 1984
Sweden	September 1984
European Communities	October 1984
Finland	October 1984
Japan	October 1984
Denmark	November 1984
Federal Republic of Germany	November 1984
Norway	November 1984
Switzerland	November 1984
Italy	December 1984
Belgium	May 1985

PART ONE
EXPLODING THE MYTHS

As we have seen in Chapter 1, part of the confusion regarding the service sector is rooted in definitional inconsistencies and inaccurate terminology. The confusion has deeper roots, though, and the next section explores in detail the economic myths that exist regarding the service sector.

In Chapter 2, we review assumptions about economic history and development from a critical perspective, in the context of economic data from 81 countries at four different levels of economic development. In Chapter 3, we examine issues regarding productivity in services, reassessing assumptions that the service sector is the nonproductive sector. Finally, in Chapter 4, we address in turn the arguments put forth in industrial policy debates for "reindustrialization"—or allocating resources to manufacturing rather than services.

2

REEXAMINING
ECONOMIC DEVELOPMENT

... prerequisites of the industrial revolution include ...
not only an agricultural revolution, but a number of service
revolutions—a commercial revolution, a financial revolution, a transport revolution, and, finally, a revolution in
government (Hartwell 1973, p. 363).

... many services play a far more important role in the
development process than is indicated by their direct contribution to gross domestic product (GDP). Due to interlinkages with other activities several services ... can
dramatically affect the overall development performance of
countries (UNCTAD 1984a, p. 4, #15).

We are accustomed to thinking of economic development only in
relation to "lesser developed" economies—i.e., those with lower per
capita Gross Domestic Product (GDP). Is that in fact accurate? Since
"economic development" is commonly used to refer to major structural
changes within an economy that makes growth possible, are not most
economies "developing" as they adapt in structural ways to changes in
technology—e.g., telecommunications and its implications for global
markets? Certainly "developed" or "industrialized" economies are not
stagnant but continue to change and mature.

Similarly, debates about the service sector seldom question the set of
basic assumptions that have developed over time about the role of services in developing economies. The recent report by the United Nations
Conference on Trade and Development (UNCTAD), released in August
1984, was one of the first to articulate and question such assumptions.

UNCTAD notes that conventional wisdom has assumed that service sector growth will occur automatically, without policy planning, primarily due to increases in per capita income. One implication of such thinking is that services are luxuries, rather than necessities, in the process of economic development. Since service industries are central to the development process, if they are *not* part of national planning, the entire process of economic development is adversely affected. We need, therefore, to rethink our perceptions of economic history and our understanding of world economies in order to include the service sector.

If we focus our attention beyond the self-sufficient household to economic exchange among groups and communities or societies, we are of necessity describing service activities. It is the service sector that provides the medium and support for such exchange. Retailers, and then wholesalers, appear as brokers to match consumers with producers who have a surplus of commodities originally produced only for domestic consumption. Transportation, communications, and storage firms appear to distribute the products; and capital markets develop to finance such exchanges.

ECONOMIC HISTORY REVISITED

Our assumptions about economic development have been so strongly colored by relatively recent assumptions about the importance of the manufacturing sector that it is difficult to maintain an accurate perspective on the world's economic history. It is not uncommon for historians to skip blithely from the Agricultural Revolution of the Neolithic Age (approximately 5000 B.C.) to the Industrial Revolution 6,500 years later as though very little of economic consequence had occurred in the interim. Some do acknowledge a Commercial Revolution, powered by service trade, as a precursor to the Industrial Revolution, but the idea of a Commercial Revolution is not nearly as widespread as that of the Industrial Revolution.

Services in Pre-Industrial Development

Upon reflection, we can see that the development of any society is directly linked to that of its service sector—"In the beginning were services...." The earliest formation of societies depended upon the establishment of common customs, codes, and rituals, overseen by religious and political leaders. Within the early clan or tribal group, specialists developed in the healing arts, the teaching of oral and cultural traditions, the structuring of recreation or leisure time activity, and the governance of the group. As clans began to interact, middlemen (distributive and producer service providers) facilitated the trading of goods and services—agricultural products, handicrafts, and knowledge ("soft technology").

The role of trade—a service sector industry—in economic development is so pervasive and integral that it has become invisible. One easily forgets that by the Bronze Age (around 3000 B.C.) international trade was well established. Greek colonization, Roman conquests, and Arab expansion all were made possible through international trade. Without wholesale and retail trade, early economies could not have grown and thrived.

Trade sprang initially from an uneven distribution of natural resources such as crops and metals. By the Late Bronze Age (1400-1200 B.C.), specialty crafts had emerged; for example, the Canaanites were famous for their purple dye, while the Greeks had an active trade in pottery. As Greek colonization began around the Mediterranean, trade also developed to meet consumer/colonist demands for familiar luxury products—e.g., oil, wine, and crafted goods.

Until the twelfth century A.D., merchants served primarily as brokers between the producer family units and the consumer markets. Social status in both Europe and Asia was still dictated by land holdings, with merchants having lower social standing. Businesses frequently ended with the death of the family head, and economic continuity was maintained by the landed aristocracy.

By the middle of the twelfth century, German and Italian merchant families had developed sufficient financial resources and commercial contacts to begin controlling and coordinating productive output in Europe. Merchants would purchase the necessary equipment (for example, looms for weaving cloth) and place that equipment in workers' homes—giving rise to cottage industries that were based on contracted labor. Types and quantity of goods to be produced were dictated by the merchants rather than by the worker-families. Thus there arose, at the instigation of the service sector, the first wave of "mass-market" production before the Industrial Revolution itself commences.

> ... it is not machines that cause industrial productivity, but the need
> for intensified productivity that induces the employment of
> machinery.... the whole gigantic transformation of human life

brought about by industrialism derived and continues to derive from
the need to reduce the price of goods and services to make them competitive in the largest possible market (Pipes 1970, p. 46).

As a complement to commercial trade, the role of financial markets
has been central in economic development. Financial institutions function as intermediaries between those with surplus capital and those who
need additional capital, bringing them together in a timely fashion. In addition to providing credit reserves, financial institutions monetize
economic activities and encourage excess production for the market
rather than simply production for self-sufficiency.

Historically, the availability of large pools of capital was restricted
because of various religious strictures against usury; and financial backing of commercial enterprises had been limited primarily to investment.
Commercial lending finally gained popular support in the seventeenth
century, with the Bank of Amsterdam, for example, having a wide international clientele.

The availability of commercial capital had several consequences. Merchants were able to borrow funds to expand their equipment inventory to
be lent to cottage industry workers, and thus consolidate further their control of production. Dependable financing was a major factor that allowed
the Dutch, French, and British to gradually supercede the Portugese and
Spanish in controlling international trade. The Industrial Revolution, when
it came, was only possible because of the avialability of capital markets.

Changes in transportation occurred hand in hand with the growth of
commercial trade and financial markets. The most notable impact, prior to
the introduction of power-driven machinery in the Industrial Revolution,
came from the shipbuilding industry. The great trade routes across the
Middle East had been opened by the Arabs who served as brokers between
Europe and Asia. When the Portugese were able to sail around Cape Horn
to India, they bypassed the Arabs and undersold the Venetians, thereby
cornering a large portion of international trade. Not to be outdone, the
Spanish attempted to sail west to India, thereby discovering the Americas.
Improvements in shipping were, in large part, responsible for increased
trade, which in turn fueled advances and economies in shipbuilding.

A final service industry to play a crucial role prior to the Industrial
Revolution was the government. One of the most important functions of
government through the ages has been to provide political stability so
that domestic and international trade could flourish—to the benefit of national coffers. Despite abuses of centralized power, the Roman Empire,

for example, was renowned for exporting administrative expertise to its conquered territories. The British domestic market, thanks to the Roman Empire, was developed as a result of the growth of central government and the abolition of local customs tariffs. In the eighteenth century, the dominance exerted in international trade by the British, French, and Dutch can be attributed in large part to the diplomatic and military support provided by their respective governments.

The functioning of the British economy just before the Industrial Revolution is an excellent illustration of the facilitative role played by the commercial revolution which preceded it:

> The effect of the commercial revolution . . . was thus to bring a special kind of maturity to the English pre-industrial economy. The merchants trading overseas had learned to operate confidently in an impersonal, international economy, where the scale of operations was large and far-flung, and where both the risks and rewards were potentially high. To reduce the uncertainties of these operations, they had created in the City of London an information system, an institutional structure and a business ethic which together provided a strategic base for expansion of national and international markets during the period of accelerating industrialization (Deane 1979, p. 71).

Services and the Industrial Revolution

The Industrial Revolution was a complex and lengthy process, stretching over several centuries. In the popular mind, it is associated almost exclusively with the development of power-driven machinery and the rise of the modern factory. Several key changes in the service sector, however, served to stimulate and sustain the Industrial Revolution. In the area of utilities, delivering new sources of power—first coal, then steam—changed the type of technology that was possible in much the same way in which first electricity and then nuclear and solar energy continue to revolutionize the ways in which we live. The necessary technological innovations sprang from professional research activities, grounded in improved educational systems. The transportation improvements made possible through technological innovations facilitated the timely movement of both raw materials and finished goods. Finally, innovations in financial institutions made possible the mobilization of necessary capital.

By the nineteenth century, the Industrial Revolution had changed both domestic economies and international trade in a number of ways. It brought the possibility of cost efficiencies in both production and distribution, vastly expanded the types of equipment available for service delivery, and began to shorten the time frame within which trade was conducted. With the potential for mass production of products, new consumer markets were needed, fueling both international trade and conquest.

Most important, though, the Industrial Revolution completed the changes in workers' lives begun during the development of cottage industries. We saw that merchants, rather than family heads, had begun to assume control of the production process in the twelfth century, although production continued to take place primarily in the home. With the need to establish centralized production facilities in order to accommodate mechanized production, there came a split between home and workplace. Not only did more and more people go outside their homes to work, but more and more family members moved to the cities where the factories were located.

Increased urbanization brought with it the need for urban service infrastructure development both to make it possible for so many persons to live in a limited space and to replace functions which had been provided within extended family networks in more rural communities. Because of this fundamental change, the changes brought about by the factory system made an indelible impression; and the manufacturing process itself came to be seen as *the* driving force in economic and social change.

Services in the Colonies

Several aspects of the service sector typically developed differently in countries with a long colonial heritage as compared with countries without that kind of heritage. While certain service industries—most notably those related to transportation and trade—did become developed, the nature of their development was frequently distorted due to control of crucial market segments by foreign-owned companies.

In most colonized countries, key service industries—e.g., professional services, financing—were either supplied by the colonial power and therefore not developed locally, or were developed in a structure that was particularly suited to the trade interests of the foreign country. During the fifteenth and sixteenth centuries, for example, transportation networks in Africa, South America, and Asia sprang up to move raw materials to ports for shipping to the colonial power, rather than to meet the needs of the domestic market. Simultaneously, coastal cities developed in the colonies as the trading ports for the colonial powers, beginning the core-periphery (urban/rural) split that has been featured in recent economic theories.

Similar observations can be made about financial markets. To the extent that a country was viewed as an extension of the colonial power, indigenous financial sectors were typically underdeveloped and unregulated. The colonial power was looked to for major capital markets.

Education is another area in which we see the direct influence of the colonizing process. In India, for example, the domestic university system was developed under the British to serve two major functions: to transmit British cultural values, and to provide a selection process for government service. Quality instruction for the development of highly trained professional and technical personnel was most usually imported—i.e., Indians went abroad for such instruction.

Seldom has the colonial legacy been one of nondistortion, and one of the challenges of national independence for all former colonies is to develop service sectors that are responsive to the needs of the country. Health and education services must become reoriented to mass markets. Transportation networks must be rethought to handle domestic as well as international needs, particularly the needs of households as distinguished from those of businesses. Communication networks need to be accessible and affordable for rural as well as urban dwellers. Financial markets need to become regulated and appropriate competition stimulated.

TRADITIONAL DETERMINANTS OF ECONOMIC DEVELOPMENT

Any economic theory must make assumptions about which factors have the most explanatory value. When traditional economic theorists, of whom Adam Smith was one of the most influential, developed their economic models for understanding what caused long-term growth in national income and wealth, they were understandably concerned with the role and effect of the manufacturing process which was revolutionizing both industrial production and lifestyles. Subsequent theorists have focused on different key variables that can be related, positively or negatively, to the service sector.

In order to understand the current beliefs about the role of services in development, we will examine two categories of theories[1]: (1) theories about production factors; and (2) theories about consumption or demand factors. In each instance, our task will be to evaluate the usefulness and validity of the theory for understanding the type of economic growth (or lack of growth) in any particular country.

Theories Based On Production Factors

When focusing on production factors, economic theorists frequently assumed that growth in the manufacturing sector precipitated change in the factors of production that were then linked to economic growth. The service sector was typically not mentioned, or mentioned as a passive recipient of changes originating elsewhere in the economy. Any positive role played by the service sector in economic growth was viewed as that of intermediary—a consequence of shifts in resource allocation that in turn led to economic growth.

Capital Formation

Adam Smith saw growth in capital formation and labor specialization as the most powerful explanatory variables of national economic growth. Since he linked both of these variables to the Industrial Revolution, he viewed the manufacturing process as particularly central to economic growth; indeed, his major thrust was to gain acceptance for manufacturing as a productive activity in a society where land ownership was still synonymous with productivity. Manufacturing, he held, was particularly important because it led to increased division of labor, increased rates of saving, and was focused on a demand less readily satiated.

Smith was accurate in assuming that the availability of capital for investment could facilitate or constrain economic development. Patrick (1966) has an excellent discussion of the proactive role of the financial sector in the development process. As we can see in Table 2.1, the percent of domestic investment in 1981 was positively correlated with the rate of GDP growth over the prior 10 years—that is, more rapid economic growth was associated with higher levels of domestic investment. Investment levels, though, were unrelated to the relative size of the manufacturing sector. For Industrial countries, a proportional increase in service sector GDP was associated with a decrease in investment as a percentage of GDP; but for Low-income countries, a proportional increase in service sector GDP was associated with an *increase* in percent of domestic investment. While investment levels are related to economic growth, the manufacturing sector is *not* the primary correlate of investment levels.

TABLE 2.1
Data on Domestic Investment
As a Percentage of GDP: 1981

Variable	Development Category			
	Low Income	Lower Middle	Upper Middle	Industrial
Average Percentage Investment	15.8%	24.3%	27.5%	21.3%
Correlation between Investment Percent and:				
Extractive % GDP	−.58*	−.37	.03	.46
Manufacturing % GDP	.19	.09	−.11	.19
Services % GDP	.63*	.28	.06	−.53*
Change in GDP (1970–81)	.69**	.44*	.61*	.66**

*p < .05
**p < .01

Data on domestic savings as a percentage of GDP are also relevant in light of Smith's assertion that development of the manufacturing sector would lead to an increase in savings rate. From Table 2.2, it is clear that savings increase as per capita GNP increases; however, percent of savings is correlated with manufacturing development only for the Lower-middle-income countries. Percent of savings is only related to overall economic growth for the Industrial countries.

Smith's oversight was his inability to envision technological progress and to understand manufacturing as a supporting actor, rather than the central player, in the economic drama. Manufacturing is not the only sector to benefit from technological innovations. Indeed, as we can see from data in Table 2.3, the majority of gross capital formation has been occurring in the service sector, confirming the results of an earlier study by the OECD (1974). While disaggregated fixed capital formation data are not available on a large number of countries, it does appear that one of the stages of economic development is a shift in emphasis from infrastructure fixed capital formation to fixed capital formation in business services.

Labor Allocation

Clark (1940) and Fisher (1935) are two of the best known theorists who focused on shifts in labor allocation. Their analysis was that, as

TABLE 2.2
Data on Domestic Saving
As a Percentage of GDP: 1981

Variable	Low Income	Lower Middle	Upper Middle	Industrial
		Development Category		
Average Percentage Saving	3.6%	15.3%	19.9%	21.1%
Correlation between Savings Percent and:				
Extractive % GDP	−.29	−.17	.31	.34
Manufacturing % GDP	.26	.42*	.19	.07
Services % GDP	.21	−.19	−.38	−.31
Change in GDP (1970–81)	.29	.19	.07	.63**

*p < .05
**p < .01

TABLE 2.3
Percentage of Gross
Capital Formation by
Economic Sector: 1981

Economic Sector	Low Income	Lower Middle	Upper Middle	Industrial
		Development Category		
Extractive Sector	19.1%	25.6%	15.1%	12.4%
Manufacturing Sector	23.0	22.4	16.4	19.9
Service Sector	58.0	52.0	72.4	67.7
Infrastructure	30.8	31.3	17.3	20.4
Trade	3.9	3.7	1.8	6.0
Business	18.3	13.2	11.1	32.1
Social/Personal	4.9	6.8	28.1	5.5

Calculated from data in the United Nations, *Yearbook of National Account Statistics: 1981* (New York: United Nations, 1983).

Note: For service subsectors, $\chi^2 = 48.4$, df = 9, p < .001.

TABLE 2.4
Correlations between
Percentage Employed in Each Sector:
1977 and 1981

	Development Category			
Correlation between:	Low Income	Lower Middle	Upper Middle	Industrial
1977				
Extractive & Manufacturing	-.56*	-.72***	-.54*	-.66**
Extractive & Services	-.89**	-.93***	-.71***	-.79***
Manufacturing & Services	.11	.42*	-.22	.05
1981				
Extractive & Manufacturing	-.84***	-.67***	-.49*	-.13
Extractive & Services	-.96***	-.96***	-.76***	-.74***
Manufacturing & Services	.66**	.44*	-.14	-.56*

*p < .05
**p < .01
***p < .001

societies advanced economically, workers would move from agriculture first into manufacturing and then into services. While their descriptions were accurate based on the data then available, the implications were not. They conceptualized labor shifts as occurring primarily in response to labor redundancy, instead of as a response to either development policies or enhanced opportunities in other sectors. What has occurred in many countries can more accurately be described as an attraction of labor to white-collar, people-related jobs in the service sector.

While historically the assumption has been that labor would move in the sequential pattern described by Fisher and Clark, Singelmann (1978) has pointed out that among the Industrial countries such a sequence has been true only of Western Europe. In Canada, Japan, and the United States, labor shifted out of the extractive sector into the service sector prior to or simultaneously with a shift into manufacturing.

At the present time, data in Table 2.4 indicate for the Industrial countries a strong relationship between lowered employment in the extractive sector and increased employment in services. The negative correlation between employment in manufacturing and employment in services indicates that employment growth occurs in one or the other, not both simultaneously.

For the developing countries, however, we see a different picture—in essence what Singelmann predicted would be the new employment trend. Labor has moved out of the extractive sector into both the manufacturing and service sectors. For the two lower groups, there is also a clear indication of synergy between the manufacturing and service sectors; employment increases in manufacturing are positively correlated with employment increases in services. None of the sectoral labor data are correlated with economic growth indicators, however. Structural shifts in labor force allocation do occur as per capita GNP rises, but the causal relationship is not clear.[2]

Comparative Advantage

Katouzian (1970) was one of the first to suggest that concepts of comparative advantage operate in the service sector much as they do in relation to trade in goods. He argued that England enjoyed a comparative advantage in shipping and finance that was largely responsible for its economic development. Similarly, certain countries have successfully exploited comparative advantage in tourism to fuel economic growth. Sapir and Lutz (1981) have provided us with detailed analyses of comparative advantage in transportation and insurance trade, demonstrating that national differences in human and physical capital do explain trade patterns in services.

One of the reasons why comparative advantage in services has not been explored further (in addition to data collection difficulties) is the widespread assumption that only "industrialized" countries have any substantial service sector activity. The comparison of sectoral percentages in employment and GDP in Figure 2.1 helps underscore why the traditional focus on labor inputs has obscured the importance of the service sector. At the lower levels of per capita GNP, extractive employment is clearly dominant even though the service sector produces the largest percentage of GDP at all levels of per capita GNP. Figure 2.1 also shows that the percentage of GDP originating in the service sector is greater than that of the labor force employed in services for all three developing country groups—disproving the common assumption that the service sector serves primarily to absorb exess labor rather than to be economically productive in its own right.

Theories Based On Consumption Factors

Economic growth is typically measured using as criteria changes in final production (GDP) or in standards of living. Unfortunately, most economic development theories have focused on the factors of production

FIGURE 2.1
Sectoral Percentages for
Employment and GDP: 1981

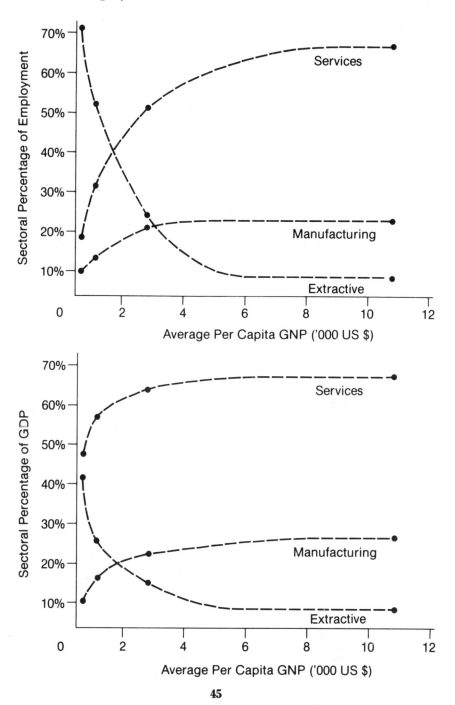

(such as labor) as both the causative and the outcome variables. Not only has the focus been incorrect, but vital variables related to the causative role of market conditions have been overlooked in the process.

The theories that we will address next have focused on the link between demand characteristics of consumer markets and GDP changes. The one drawback shared by each of the theories is a virtually exclusive focus on the ultimate consumer, ignoring the rapidly growing markets of intermediate (industrial/producer) consumers.

Per Capita Income

Kuznets (1971) developed the idea that service sector growth was linked to rise in per capita income.[3] The casual relationship—i.e., which comes first, service sector development leading to increased per capita income or increased disposable income which can be spent on services—is not clear. Certainly, recent trends indicate that, as disposable income rises, it is spent increasingly on services (Shelp 1981).

The data in Table 2.5 indicate that the higher the proportion of GDP from the extractive sector, the lower per capita GNP. Only for the Lower-middle-income group in 1977 and the Upper-middle-income group in 1981 was per capita GNP higher the larger the service sector. Generally speaking, there is little evidence that rising per capita income is causally related to economic sector development. Kuznets (1971) suggested that the relationship is more complex—rise in per capita GNP may be associated with an increase in demand for some services (transportation, communication, financial) but unrelated to increases in others. A more recent study (Kravis et al. 1982) found that as income increases, the prices of services also increase rather than the quantity purchased.

If we look instead at the average annual growth of per capita GNP for the prior ten years, we see relationships between growth rate and sectoral output only for the Low-income and the Industrial countries (see Table 2.6). Per capita increases in Low-income countries are associated with a decrease in production from the extractive sector and a proportional increase in the service sector. For Industrial countries, per capita increases in GNP are associated most recently with increase in GDP service sector.

Urbanization

Singlemann (1978) hypothesized that as nations urbanize, the service sector would expand. Our data indicate that this relationship is only true

TABLE 2.5
Data on Per Capita
Gross National Product
1977 and 1981

Variable	Development Category			
	Low Income	Lower Middle	Upper Middle	Industrial
1977				
Average Per Capita GNP				
(US $)	$198	$619	$1,641	$6,479
Correlation between				
Per Capita GNP and:				
Extractive % GDP	-.25	-.61**	-.54*	-.53*
Manufacturing % GDP	-.09	.44*	.22	.40
Services % GDP	.33	.49*	.38	.03
1981				
Average Per Capita GNP				
(US $)	$284	$916	$2,809	$10,684
Correlation between				
Per Capita GNP and:				
Extractive % GDP	-.41	-.16	-.42	-.48*
Manufacturing % GDP	.24	.30	-.19	-.01
Services % GDP	.38	-.09	.48*	.33

*p < .05

TABLE 2.6
Data on Average Annual
Change in Per Capita Gross
National Product: 1977 and 1981

Variable	Development Category			
	Low Income	Lower Middle	Upper Middle	Industrial
1977				
Change in Per Capita				
GNP (US $)	1.2%	2.9%	3.7%	3.7%
Correlation between				
Change in Per Capita				
GNP and:				
Extractive % GDP	–.58**	.11	–.24	.02
Manufacturing % GDP	–.06	–.18	.43	.36
Services % GDP	.69**	–.05	–.05	–.55*
1981				
Change in Per Capita				
GNP (US $)	1.1%	4.7%	4.0%	3.2%
Correlation between				
Change in Per Capita				
GNP and:				
Extractive % GDP	–.82***	–.08	–.30	–.19
Manufacturing % GDP	.40	–.16	–.30	–.19
Services % GDP	.80***	.23	.19	.55*

*p < .05
**p < .01
***p < .001

for the Upper-middle-income countries (see Table 2.7). Urbanization is related to increases in per capita GNP for each of the developing country groups, but not to growth rates. There is no necessary relationship between the expansion of the service sector and overall GDP growth for the developing countries, though a *decrease* in GDP growth is correlated with increased urbanization for the Industrial countries. Such a finding is suggestive of other research indicating that urbanization can have negative consequences if the urban centers are less than one million in population (Mera 1984).

Export-led Growth

If we wish to tie service sector activity and economic growth to market demand factors, the clearest link is through international trade. As the global economy becomes increasingly interdependent, trade is more and more the engine of growth—whether through being able to compete effectively in established markets, or through identifying and developing untapped markets. Most of the literature on export-led growth focuses on the export of goods to final consumer markets. Work remains to be done on the exporting of services to meet the rapidly growing demand generated by industries and service producers.

Trade in services has been largely overlooked because of a common assumption that, once again, only "industrialized" economies engage in international trade in services. In actuality, international trade in services is conducted by nations at all levels of economic development. From the data in Table 2.8, we can see that service exports remain a relatively constant percentage of total exports across all four country groups. While the Low-income countries export a somewhat lower percentage of services, the difference is not statistically significant.

DETERMINANTS OF ECONOMIC ACTIVITY

Economies are extremely complex, and the factors at work—not all of which are quantifiable—are varied. The preceding discussion has focused on what is not true of economies; now we will turn to the difficult task of trying to understand what *is* happening—particularly with regard to services. The variables to be considered include quality-of-life indicators (literacy,

TABLE 2.7
Data on Percentage of
Population in Urban Areas:
1977 and 1981

	Development Category			
Variable	*Low Income*	*Lower Middle*	*Upper Middle*	*Industrial*
1977				
% Urban	20.5%	35.6%	55.9%	73.5%
Correlation between				
% Urban and:				
Extractive % GDP	−.05	−.52*	−.50*	−.33
Manufacturing % GDP	.09	.58*	.11	.09
Services % GDP	.00	.25	.42	.25
1981				
% Urban	21.1%	38.8%	61.9%	75.3%
Correlation between				
% Urban and:				
Extractive % GDP	−.08	−.09	−.61*	−.50*
Manufacturing % GDP	.35	.30	−.08	−.03
Services % GDP	−.12	−.17	.54*	.37

*p < .05
**p < .01
***p < .001

TABLE 2.8
Services Exports as a
Percentage of Total
Exports: 1977 and 1981

Services as:	Development Category				
	Low Income	Lower Middle	Upper Middle	Industrial	Average
% 1977 Exports	13.6%	12.5%	20.8%	20.2%	16.8%
% 1981 Exports	14.5	13.7	21.4	18.3	17.0
% 1977 Imports	16.3%	21.0%	19.2%	18.4%	18.7%
% 1981 Imports	16.2	20.1	19.7	18.1	18.5

Calculated from data in the *U.S. National Study on Trade in Services* (No. 455-773-20145) (Washington, D.C.: U.S. Government, 1984).

life expectancy, per capita GNP), rate of urbanization, economic growth since 1970 (per capita and total GDP), financial indicators (inflation rate, domestic investment, domestic saving), sectoral percentages for GDP and employment, debt variables (external debt as a percent of GDP, debt payments as a percent of GDP), and trade variables (export and import figures for services and for merchandise).

Factor analysis was used in analyzing the data, rather than multiple regression, because several of the variables are correlated with each other and independence of variables is a prerequisite of multiple regression. The factors were named after the variable which loaded most positively on that factor. Only variables with factor loadings of .50 or higher were included (see Appendix C for exact factor loadings). "Lagging" of data was built in by using 1982 per capita GNP in categorizing the countries into four groups.

For readers not familiar with interpreting factor analyses, the factors listed in Tables 2.9 to 2.12 represent independent determinants of total economic activity. The loadings or weightings of variables on each factor are similar to correlations—varying between + 1.0 and − 1.0. Since the number of variables in each factor analysis should not exceed the number of cases (countries), the limited number of countries in the Industrial country group made it impossible to combine all data into one factor analysis. Therefore, 1977 and 1981 data for each group of countries were analyzed first to determine correlates of the domestic economy and then separately for correlates of international trade.

Domestic Economic Data

Tables 2.9 and 2.10 contain the domestic economy factors. Before describing the factors for each of the country groups, it is important to note that the extractive sector figures negatively in all categories of development. There is no evidence from these data that the extractive sector should be the primary focus of developmental efforts. In order to avoid unnecessary repetition, the negative role of extractive GDP and employment percentages will not be mentioned in each instance but should be borne in mind.

Low-income Countries

Contrary to traditional economic thought, we find that the GDP contribution of the service sector is clearly associated with both economic growth and fixed capital formation (investment) in the Low-income countries. Along with an increasing proportion of GDP from services comes a decrease in inflation and an increase in debt payments, or ability to service the country's debt. Here we see an indication that increased external debt can be positively associated with economic growth, particularly service sector growth.

As workers move out of the extractive sector, they move into both the manufacturing and service sectors, resulting in increased urbanization and longer life expectancy. Enhanced quality of life is associated with a larger proportion of domestic saving, or an increased ability to accumulate the capital necessary to finance economic growth.

The debt factor for this country group is interesting. We have already seen that external debt was associated with economic growth—and increased GDP from services. In 1977, the proportion of external debt acquired decreased as per capita income increased—presumably because more funds were available domestically for needed investment. By 1981, we find that the amount of external debt is *negatively* associated with the amount of GDP from manufacturing. While this may mean simply that the countries with a less productive manufacturing sector are the ones typically awarded external public financing, it may also be an indication that increased indebtedness does not necessarily result in enhanced productivity in either the extractive or the manufacturing sectors, though that is often the goal of external borrowing.

Lower-middle-income Countries

The Lower-middle-income countries, of all four groups, show the greatest benefit from manufacturing development; however, the quality of life benefits which were apparent in 1977 were no longer associated with percentage of GDP from manufacturing in 1981. Instead, employment in *services* was linked with manufacturing productivity in a synergistic relationship. By 1981, workers moving out of the extractive sector were moving primarily into service positions, rather than manufacturing ones, but the manufacturing sector was benefitting.

By 1981, domestic investment, or the ability to finance capital development, was associated with growth in GDP and per capita income. Quality of life indicators and external debt variables, while important, showed no direct relationship with the economic variables. Meanwhile, increasing percentages of GDP from services became associated with decreases in GDP from the extractive sector. The pivotal role of services as a support for manufacturing activities is more apparent for Lower-middle-income countries than for the other three groups, which are more clearly dependent primarily on services.

Upper-middle-income Countries

In 1977, the Upper-middle-income countries manifested the same manufacturing focus as the Lower-middle-income countries, but with inflationary effects and with little ability to finance economic development internally through domestic saving. By 1981, the leading determinants of economic activity were the quality of life variables that in turn were linked to service sector prominence. For the first time, we see evidence of service sector development *rather than* manufacturing development (with percentage GDP from manufacturing falling as that from services rises). The aggregate labor force shift is almost entirely from the extractive sector to the service sector.

In 1981, with the shift in focus from manufacturing to services, economic growth was related to increased domestic investment and lowered inflation. Although the Upper-middle-income countries are typically referred to as the NICs, or "Newly Industrializing Countries" (implying a primary focus on manufacturing-led growth), by 1981 percentage of GDP from manufacturing no longer played a positive role. Instead, the service sector had moved into a more prominent position.

TABLE 2.9
Factors for Domestic Economic Data: 1977

Development Category

Factor	Low Income	Lower Middle	Upper Middle	Industrial
1	**Growth** + Services % GDP + Domestic Investment % GDP + Change in Per Capita GNP + Change in GDP + Debt Payments % GDP − Extractive % GDP	**Manufacturing** + Manufacturing % GDP + Literacy Rate + Per Capita GNP + % Urbanization − Extractive % GDP	**Manufacturing** + Manufacturing % GDP + Manufacturing % Employed + Inflation Rate − Domestic Saving % GDP − Domestic Investment % GDP	**Personal Income** + Per Capita GNP + Services % Employed + Literacy Rate + Manufacturing % GDP + Extractive % Employed − Inflation Rate − Extractive % GDP
2	**Employment** + Services % Employed + Manufacturing % Employed + Inflation Rate − Extractive % Employed	**Employment** + Services % Employed + Manufacturing % Employed + Domestic Saving % GDP − Extractive % Employed	**Quality of Life** + Life Expectancy + Per Capita GNP + Literacy Rate + Services % GDP − Extractive % GDP	**Investment** + Domestic Investment % GDP + Domestic Saving % GDP + Change in GDP + Change in Per Capita GNP − % Urbanization
3	**Quality of Life** + Literacy Rate + Domestic Saving % GDP + Life Expectancy	**External Debt** + External Debt % GDP + Debt Payments % GDP	**Services** + Services % Employed % Urbanization + Services % GDP − Extractive % Employed − Extractive % GDP	**Services GDP** + Services % GDP + Literacy Rate − Manufacturing % GDP − Change in Per Capita GNP

4

External Debt
+ External Debt % GDP
− Per Capita GNP

Investment
+ Domestic Investment % GDP
− Inflation Rate

Growth
+ Change in GDP
+ Change in Per Capita GNP
− Inflation Rate

Quality of Life
+ Life Expectancy
− Manufacturing % Employed

5

Urbanization
+ % Urbanization

Growth
+ Change in GDP
+ Change in Per Capita GNP
− Life Expectancy

External Debt
+ External Debt % GDP
+ Debt Payments % GDP

6

Manufacturing
+ Manufacturing % GDP

Inflation
+ Inflation Rate
+ Services % GDP

55

TABLE 2.10
Factors for Domestic Economic Data: 1981

Development Category

Factor	Low Income	Lower Middle	Upper Middle	Industrial
1	**Growth** + Change in Per Capita GNP + Change in GDP + Domestic Investment % GDP + Services % GDP + Debt Payments % GDP − Inflation Rate − Extractive % GDP	**Services Employment** + Services % Employed + Manufacturing % GDP + Domestic Saving % GDP + Manufacturing % Employed − Extractive % Employed	**Quality of Life** + Life Expectancy + Literacy Rate + Per Capita GNP + Services % GDP − Extractive % GDP	**Personal Income** + Per Capita GNP + Literacy Rate + Services % Employed − Extractive % Employed − Inflation Rate − Extractive % GDP
2	**Employment** + Services % Employed + Manufacturing % Employed + % Urbanization + Life Expectancy − Extractive % Employed	**Growth** + Change in GDP + Change in Per Capita GNP + Domestic Investment % GDP	**Growth** + Change in Per Capita GNP + Change in GDP + Domestic Investment % GDP − Inflation Rate	**Investment** + Domestic Investment % GDP + Domestic Saving % GDP + Change in GDP + Extractive % GDP − % Urbanization
3	**Quality of Life** + Literacy Rate + Domestic Saving % GDP + Life Expectancy	**Quality of Life** + Literacy Rate + Life Expectancy + Per Capita GNP	**Services Employment** + Services % Employed − Extractive % Employed	**Services** + Services % GDP + Services % Employed − Manufacturing % Employed − Manufacturing % GDP

56

4	**External Debt** + External Debt % GDP − Manufacturing % GDP	**External Debt** + Debt Payments % GDP + External Debt % GDP	**External Debt** + Debt Payments % GDP + External Debt % GDP
5	**Personal Income** + Per Capita GNP	**Services GDP** + Services % GDP − Extractive % GDP	**Services GDP** + Services % GDP − Manufacturing % GDP
6	**Inflation** + Inflation Rate + Manufacturing % Employed		**Manufacturing Employment** + Manufacturing % Employed + Domestic Saving % GDP

Growth
+ Change in Per Capita GNP
+ Life Expectancy

Industrial Countries

For the country group with the highest per capita GNP, the sectoral proportions appear stablized at about 10% extractive, 23% manufacturing, and 67% services; and the factors found were quite stable over time. The primary determinant was rising employment in the service sector, associated with higher per capita income, lowered inflation, and higher educational levels. Concerns about the negative effects of labor shifts into the service sector appear unfounded.

By 1981, percentage of GDP from manufacturing played no positive role in explaining economic activity. Growth in GDP was closely associated with the proportion of domestic investment and saving—or the ability to finance capital formation from within the nation's economy— and with development outside the major urban areas. The service sector itself, from both a GDP and an employment perspective, played a positive role—in contrast to the "doom and gloom" forecasts of those who assume that an increased contribution from services coupled with a decreased contribution from manufacturing has to stifle economic growth.

International Economic Data

Tables 2.11 and 2.12 show the factors that emerged when data on service and merchandise (extractive and manufactured goods) exports and imports were added to the analyses. For these analyses, in order to keep the total number of variables to 17 (the smallest sample size), data on literacy rate, life expectancy, urbanization, and domestic investment rate were excluded.

Low-income Countries

Once again we encounter the unexpected result that trade variables, with service exports heading the list, are the leading variables in explaining economic activity in the Low-income countries. Trade expansion is closely linked to domestic saving, or the ability of a nation to meet its own needs for capital. Such data should help dispel any lingering doubts about the importance of international trade for these countries.

Even in the international context, the service sector remains an important ingredient of economic growth—being closely associated with increases in both GDP and in per capita income. Note that percentage of

GDP from the extractive sector is *negatively* associated with economic growth, while percentage of GDP from manufacturing showed no relationship. Service-led growth is clearly the strategy of choice for these countries.

With regard to employment patterns, workers are moving out of the extractive sector into both manufacturing and service positions. As the per capita income rises in these economies, both proportional saving and payments on indebtedness also increase. There is, however, an inverse relationship between indebtedness and percent GDP from manufacturing. Apparently, manufacturing development plays a positive role as long as it is not "indebted" manufacturing development.

Lower-middle-income Countries

The Lower-middle-income countries are a bit of an anomaly, being the only group for which international trade variables were not the primary determinant of economic activity in 1981. Instead, virtually the same variables that were prominent in the 1981 domestic analysis are weighted on the first factor—i.e., services employment and the percentage of GDP from manufacturing.

For these countries, services exports are not weighted with the other trade variables. Instead, a rising volume of services exports is directly associated with economic growth—to more rapid GDP growth and a more rapid rise in per capita GNP. Focus on services-exports-led growth is a strategy of choice for these countries.

Upper-middle-income Countries

As was true for the Low-income countries, the most important factor for the Upper-middle-income countries was international trade—the exporting and importing of both services and merchandise. The domestic service sector and its positive association with per capita GNP came next in importance.

The variables directly responsible for economic growth showed a shift between 1977 and 1981. In 1977, economic growth for these countries was associated with services exports—as was true in 1981 for the Lower-middle-income countries in 1981. By 1981, though, economic growth was occurring independent of external trade.

As with the domestic data, the external debt variables are unrelated to the other economic variables. Amount of debt incurred shows no

TABLE 2.11
Factors for International Economic Data: 1977

Development Category

Factor	Low Income	Lower Middle	Upper Middle	Industrial
1	**Trade** + Services Exports + Merchandise Exports + Services Imports + Merchandise Imports + Domestic Saving % GDP	**Trade** + Services Imports + Merchandise Imports + Merchandise Exports + Services Exports	**Trade** + Services Imports + Merchandise Exports + Merchandise Imports + Manufacturing % Employed	**Trade** + Merchandise Exports + Merchandise Imports + Services Imports + Services Exports
2	**Services GDP** + Services % GDP + Change in Per Capita GNP + Change in GDP + Debt Payments % GNP − Extractive % GDP	**GDP** + Manufacturing % GDP + Services % GDP + Per Capita GNP − Extractive % GDP	**Services** + Services % GDP + Services % Employed + Per Capita GNP − Extractive % Employed − Extractive % GDP	**Services Employment** + Services % Employed + Per Capita GNP − Extractive % Employed − Extractive % GDP − Inflation Rate
3	**Employment** + Services % Employed + Manufacturing % Employed + Inflation Rate − Extractive % Employed	**Employment** + Services % Employed + Manufacturing % Employed − Extractive % Employed	**Growth** + Change in Per Capita GNP + Change in GDP + Services Exports − Inflation Rate	**Growth** + Change in Per Capita GNP + Change in GDP + Domestic Saving % GDP

4   **Personal Income**
+ Per Capita GNP
+ Inflation Rate
− External Debt % GDP

Manufacturing
+ Manufacturing % GDP
− Debt Payments % GDP

5   **Growth**
+ Change in GDP
+ Change in Per Capita GNP

6   **Inflation**
+ Inflation Rate
− Domestic Saving % GDP

External Debt
+ Debt Payments % GDP
+ External Debt % GDP

Manufacturing
+ Manufacturing % GDP
+ Manufacturing % Employed
− Domestic Saving % GDP

External Debt
+ Debt Payments % GDP
+ External Debt % GDP

Manufacturing
+ Manufacturing % Employed
+ Manufacturing % GDP
− Services % GDP

TABLE 2.12
Factors for International Economic Data: 1981

Development Category

Factor	Low Income	Lower Middle	Upper Middle	Industrial
1	**Trade** + Services Exports + Merchandise Exports + Services Imports + Merchandise Imports + Domestic Saving % GDP	**Service Employment** + Services % Employed + Manufacturing % GDP + Domestic Saving % GDP + Per Capita GNP − Extractive % Employed	**Trade** + Merchandise Imports + Services Imports + Services Exports + Merchandise Exports + Domestic Saving % GDP	**Trade** + Merchandise Exports + Merchandise Imports + Services Exports + Services Imports
2	**Growth** + Change in Per Capita GNP + Change in GDP + Services % GDP − Inflation Rate − Extractive % GDP	**Trade** + Merchandise Exports + Services Imports + Merchandise Imports	**Personal Income** + Per Capita GNP + Services % Employed − Extractive % GDP − Extractive % Employed	**Personal Income** + Per Capita GNP + Services % Employed − Extractive % Employed − Inflation Rate − Extractive % GDP
3	**Employment** + Services % Employed + Manufacturing % Employed − Extractive % Employed	**Growth** + Change in Per Capita GNP + Change in GDP + Services Exports	**Growth** + Change in Per Capita GNP + Change in GDP − Inflation Rate	**Manufacturing** + Manufacturing % GNP + Manufacturing % Employed − Services % GDP − Services % Employed

4
Personal Income
+ Per Capita GNP
+ Debt Payments % GDP
+ Domestic Saving % GDP

External Debt
+ Debt Payments % GDP
+ External Debt % GDP

Growth
+ Change in GDP
+ Domestic Saving % GDP
+ Change in Per Capita GNP

5
External Debt
+ External Debt % GDP
– Manufacturing % GDP

Services GDP
+ Services % GDP
– Extractive % GDP

Manufacturing
+ Manufacturing % GDP
+ Domestic Saving % GDP
– Services % GDP

6
Inflation
+ Inflation Rate
+ Manufacturing % Employed
+ Per Capita GNP

Manufacturing Employment
+ Manufacturing % Employed

immediate positive economic effects. Finally, the Upper-middle-income group has a factor with a positive weighting from manufacturing GDP and employment and (for 1981) a negative weighting from services GDP—indicating that the synergism between manufacturing and services characteristic of the less developed countries no longer holds true in the Upper-middle-income countries.

Industrial Countries

Not unexpectedly, exports and imports of both services and merchandise are of primary importance in understanding the Industrial economies. While service sector employment was correlated with higher levels of per capita income, no clear positive role was apparent for changes in the proportion of GDP from services.

In contrast to the findings in the domestic economic data, the international data indicate a positive role played by the manufacturing sector, with manufacturing employment and GDP weighting positively while services GDP and employment weight negatively. This factor is much stronger in the 1981 data than in the 1977 data and suggests a competitive relationship between the two sectors regarding economic incentives and resource allocation.

Brief Sectoral Review

Several themes stand out in contrast to traditional views on economic development. International trade, including service trade, is important at all levels of development. Not only is exporting of services more important for developing countries than is commonly believed, but the consequences of importing services need to be of as much concern to policy makers as are those of importing merchandise. For the Lower-middle-income countries, in particular, service exports are strongly associated with economic growth.

The extractive sector is uniformly negatively associated with other economic variables. Clearly, it is not a sector propelling growth for any of the developmental levels—quite the opposite. These data should not be interpreted to mean that the extractive sector should be ignored; rather, it is not the sector of choice for additional resource allocation. If it is to play a more positive role in an economy, changes need to occur first in the supporting infrastructure industries.

The role of the manufacturing sector appears mixed. In no instance were increased proportions of GDP from manufacturing associated with economic growth. For Low-income countries, higher percentages of GDP from manufacturing were associated with lower external debt. For the developing countries in general, the relationship between manufacturing and services appears to some extent synergistic; while for the Industrial countries, there is a clear inverse relationship between the two sectors.

The role of the service sector is more prominent and central than is commonly believed. Factors related to services explained large portions of the variability in economic performance for all countries. Service GDP was associated with economic growth factors for the Low-income countries, and services exports were associated with economic growth factors for the Lower-middle- and Upper-middle-income countries. Service GDP, not manufacturing GDP, was associated with enhanced quality of life.

SUMMARY

What, then, do we know about the role of the service sector in economic development? We know that service industries historically have been at the heart of all economic growth, stimulating and facilitating production for the market rather than simply for self-sufficiency. We know that the service sector is an important source of both employment and income for countries at all levels of development. We know that the linear stage theories of economic development are not true—that even in Western Europe service sector development preceded manufacturing development. And we know that international trade in services is more important for developing countries than is commonly believed.

What of the factors traditionally believed to be associated with economic growth? Levels of domestic investment are associated with economic growth for all country groups as long as only domestic economic data are considered. Once international trade data are considered, domestic investment remains related only for the lower two development groups. Savings become more important in explaining economic variability when international trade data are included, as it is strongly associated with trade volume for the developing countries. Investment and savings are important, but by themselves are not sufficient to explain economic activity.

The data analyzed show that labor allocation by sector was important at all levels of development, with percentage of the population employed in *services* being the strongest positive indicator. International trade variables explained the most variability in economic activity. There was a clear link between trade and growth of the domestic economy only for the Lower-middle-income countries—and the link was with service exports. These data confirm findings of a positive association between manufacturing GDP and service sector employment (Galenson 1963), but only for the Lower-middle-income countries.

Turning to consumption factors, per capita GNP figured prominently for all country groups, but was not directly correlated with economic growth. For Industrial and Lower-middle-income groups, it was positively associated with employment in services and negatively associated with employment in manufacturing. Urbanization was only relevant in the context of the domestic economy where it was associated with increased employment in services and manufacturing for Low-income countries, but with slower growth in GDP for the Industrial countries.

The strongest explanatory variables of economic activity were the trade variables. Volume of exports and imports for both merchandise and services played a prominent role. Development strategies need to be linked to stimulating exports in both merchandise and services. Increasing imports appear to play a positive role in helping the economy expand, although they are not directly linked to economic growth variables.

In conclusion, then, economic development strategies need to be rethought to place more emphasis on service sector development. Recent efforts to direct more resources into the extractive sector appear ill considered unless attention is also given concurrently to service sector infrastructure. "... those who see agricultural development as the key to overall development might be running against the course of history" (ILO 1983a, p. 1).

Holding manufacturing up as the key to economic development also appears shortsighted. While all sectors of an economy are important, service development is crucial. Indeed, resource allocation to the manufacturing sector is premature unless physical infrastructure, financial, social, and political services are already well developed.

NOTES

1. No attempt has been made to review every existing theory regarding economic development; such an attempt would be presumptuous in the space available. Rather, theories have been included which are frequently referred

to in discussions about the role of services in economic development. Theories of economic development which focus more on political factors than economic inputs/outputs are discussed briefly in Chapter 7.

2. Bauer and Yamey (1951) make the additional point that actual service sector contribution is further obscured by the fact that at different levels of economic development delivery of various services shifts back and forth from the informal to the formal economy.

3. While Kuznets provided the clearest statistical data regarding the relationship between service sector growth and per capita GNP, albeit for developed countries, other theorists have also addressed this point. Fisher (1952) and Clark (1940), for example, felt that services exhibited a relatively higher income elasticity of demand, though Fuchs (1968) later took issue with the notion of income elasticity differences among sectors. Bell (1973), too, stated that increased income would lead to an increased demand for services (and hence service sector growth).

3

SERVICES AND PRODUCTIVITY

Conventional theory . . . stresses the inherent low productivity of the services sector. Recent analyses have, however, called this whole theory into question. Efficiency . . . depends to an ever-increasing extent upon the interlinkages which are established among the different productive activities and not only on the productive conditions in the activities themselves (UNCTAD 1984a, p. 2).

It appears that the substantial increase in employment that took place [in Canada] over the 1950-79 period in the service sector relative to goods actually enhanced the average level or productivity in the economy. This is in contrast to the popular view that the growth of the service sector in fact reduced the overall level of productivity (*Canadian national study* . . . 1984, p. 15).

The conventional view of services as inherently unproductive, or at least not as productive as manufacturing, is widespread and often stated as fact with little or no documentation. For example, in a leading article on U.S. employment, the *New York Times* reported that the shift toward more service jobs would erode productivity and impede economic growth, overlooking the fact that the major employment growth has been in high-paying, high-skill jobs.[1] Historically, this belief came from the views held by the Physiocrats that only agricultural output was "productive" (Higgs 1952). In traditional agrarian societies, status was directly linked to ownership of land and natural resources.

Adam Smith made an important contribution to modifying traditional views by arguing that manufacturing activities, not just agricultural activities, were productive. At the same time, however, Smith solidified the view, which has persisted into the present, that all "intangible" activities are unproductive[2].

> The labour of some of the most respectable orders in the society is ... unproductive of any value, and does not fix or realize itself in any permanent subject, or vendible commodity, which endures after that labour is past, and for which an equal quantity of labour could afterwards be procured (1904, p. 314).

Thus, as status symbols shifted to include ownership of the means of (industrial) production, the idea of owning something visible and tangible was retained.

Subsequent nineteenth-century economists—e.g., Malthus and Mill—reinforced Smith's identification of "productive" with "tangible." Malthus made a distinction between "productive labor" (which had a tangible product) and "personal services"

> ... which however highly useful and important some of it may be, and however much it may conduce *indirectly* to the production and security of material wealth, does not realise itself of any object which can be valued and transferred without the presence of the person performing such a service, and cannot therefore be made to enter into an estimate of national wealth (1951, p. 35).

Mill (1936) classified as productive only those economic activities which could be accumulated as "wealth." While he did include "human-capital" investment (i.e., health and education services) as productive, other service industries were categorized as "mere services" and dismissed as unimportant.

The distinction made between "tangible" as productive and "intangible" as nonproductive has become institutionalized in Western accounting practices. When one purchases a tangible good (such as office equipment), one acquires an asset whose useful life can then be depreciated over time. When one purchases a service, however, one incurs an expense and the utility of that service product is assumed to be time-limited. Kuznets (1971), expanding on Mill's categorization of some services as human-capital investment, has been one of the few to argue that intangible assets exist with regard to the service sector:

> ... effects of structural change on conditions of work give rise to required inputs ... [such as] education and research and

development ... which are not included under capital formation in the conventional economic accounts ... [but] are required by the changing production system for augmenting its output, paralleling in a way the requirement for material capital (p. 76).

Contemporary concerns about service sector productivity typically take the form voiced in the following quote from a recent writer: ''. . . if everyone is in the service economy, who is going to be in the producing economy making the money to pay for the services? Must something more concrete, somewhere down the line, stand behind the services, assuring that they are at least vaguely redeemable in the production of a good?'' (Alter 1982, p. 35). We can see that analyzing the productivity of the service sector is colored by a nagging sense that all ''productive'' activities must have a tangible end result.

In addition to the concerns about tangibility, there are basic assessment problems related to how productivity is defined and to what extent measures of productivity derived from tangible goods are applicable to intangible services. A major issue not usually addressed is the assumptions that underlie productivity models. ''. . . the traditional concept of productivity isolates the productive process from the social setting. . . . it implicitly assumes closed system characteristics. . . . A distinguishing feature of the service sector is the difficulty, and in many cases, impossibility of considering the production process as a closed system'' (OECD 1977, p. 116).

Once we have introduced some of the definitional issues, we will be looking first at macroeconomic measures of sectoral productivity—both of efficiency and effectiveness. Then we will turn to the external influences on the service production process and the questions these raise regarding the most appropriate methods of measuring productivity.

DEFINING PRODUCTIVITY

What does it mean to be ''productive'' in the service sector? This question is less trivial than it appears. Productivity has traditionally been defined as output per worker, or more generally as maximizing output while minimizing inputs. Applying such a definition to the service sector raises several issues: Can quantitative measures alone reflect accurately an intangible product? How is quality of output accounted for? Is the minimal use of inputs, whether labor or capital, always a goal?

In manufacturing, reliance on objective quantitative measures to reflect quality of production poses no real problem as output measures include only the number of goods produced that are of acceptable quality. In other words, if 100 pieces are produced, only 92 of which are acceptable in quality, then only 92 pieces are recorded as net output—provided, of course, that appropriate quality control is maintained. If quality control is maintained and production quality remains high, productivity increases are reflected. Poor quality, if detected, leads to a rejection of the good and a decrease in recorded productivity.

In service delivery, however, the issue of product quality is more complex. Services are frequently paid for in advance of production so that poor quality products automatically become part of the aggregate total. In addition, many service customers are paying, in part, for a certain quality of interaction with the service provider. "... the danger is that productivity can be increased at the cost of an organization's effectiveness—especially when inter-firm comparisons often regard a firm as necessarily more efficient than a competitor, if its productivity is higher. Yet the less efficient firm may be the more effective in meeting its goals" (Blois 1984, p. 55). If quality interaction is maintained, quantitative measures of output may be *lower* than if quality interaction is sacrificed for efficiency. For example, a bank teller who rapidly handles ten customers in as many minutes while irritating them by being brusque may be quantitatively more efficient than a teller who handles only two customers in a ten-minute period but who does so courteously and attentively. Qualitatively, however, that brusque teller is less effective, as will be clear from lowered customer satisfaction and less repeat business.

Qualitative issues are directly related to concerns about the effectiveness of services, which at the macroeconomic level is related to meeting national goals. If the service sector *does* function to absorb excess labor, for example, is that necessarily bad? Assuming for the moment that such absorption lowers the absolute efficiency of the service industries involved (rather than stimulating new industry growth), which is more costly to a society—slightly diminished efficiency in the service sector, or the drain of supporting unemployed workers? In fact, increasing the labor intensity of selected service industries can *increase* the perceived effectiveness of service delivery as customers could be given more individual attention.

A variety of researchers (e.g., Heaton 1977) have drawn attention to the problems inherent in a definition of productivity that attends only to the efficient use of easily quantifiable resources and neglects measures of the quality of the resulting product. In service industries, we must be concerned not only with the efficiency of resource allocation, but also with the effectiveness of service delivery (i.e., achieving the goals of service provision). A more appropriate definition for productivity in services could be stated as *maximizing output of acceptable quality, while minimizing the total costs of the production process*. Such a definition includes both objective/quantitative and subjective/qualitative concerns, while including a range of cost considerations.

THE EFFICIENCY OF THE SERVICE SECTOR

In the analyses below, two different types of input measures are used. Labor inputs include such measures as numbers of workers employed in each sector. Capital inputs include such measures as constant dollars spent on fixed capital formation.

Output data are for Gross Domestic Product (GDP) as defined in the United Nations standards for national accounts, rather than for Gross National Product (GNP), and thus the data calculations are relatively uniform across nations. GDP more accurately reflects economic activity in the context of a global marketplace since it "measures the total final output of goods and services produced by an economy—that is, by residents and non-residents, regardless of the allocation to domestic and foreign claims"(World Bank 1983b, p. 105).All GDP data are in constant dollars, unless otherwise stated, in order to control for the effects of inflation.

Static Efficiency Measures

Economic productivity in the three sectors is most commonly measured by analyzing the ratio of output to input for a given point in time—a static measure of efficiency. Below are analyses of GDP output by sector for each of the four country groups, first per labor input and then per capital input.

Output per Labor Input

Looking first at the relationship between labor and GDP, Table 3.1 shows ratios of percentage GDP from services to percentage of the working population employed in the service sector. Ratios of 1.0 indicate that

TABLE 3.1
Ratio of Percentage GDP
to Percentage Employment by
Economic Sector: 1977 and 1981

Economic Sector	Development Category			
	Low Income	Lower Middle	Upper Middle	Industrial
Extractive Sector				
1977	.71	.66	.67	.61
1981	.58	.51	.62	.84
Manufacturing Sector				
1977	.81	1.02	.93	.82
1981	.98	1.11	.96	1.09
Service Sector				
1977	1.72	1.40	1.18	1.19
1981	2.74	1.73	1.19	.99

Calculated from data in the International Labour Office, *Yearbook of Labour Statistics* (Geneva: ILO, 1983); World Bank, *World Tables*, 3rd ed. (Baltimore, MD: Johns Hopkins University Press, 1983).

a given proportion of the work force is producing an equivalent percentage of GDP. Ratios of greater than 1.0 indicate that that same proportion of the work force is responsible for greater percentage of GDP (i.e., higher productivity), while ratios less than 1.0 indicate a responsibility for a lesser percentage of GDP (i.e., lower productivity).

From these data, it is apparent that only in the Industrial countries might there be reason to believe that productivity is lowered in the service sector, and then only for 1981. The productivity ratios for the manufacturing sector do not support the commonly stated notion that the manufacturing sector is *de facto* the most productive sector; rather, they support earlier findings that while the productivity of the service sector declines with rising per capita GNP, it remains higher than the productivity of the other two sectors (Chenery and Syraquin 1975).

For developing countries, especially those with the lowest per capita income, the service sector is clearly more productive than the other two sectors—confirming findings in earlier research on developing countries (Blades, Johnston, and Marczewski 1974). Bear in mind that, by the nature of the ratio used, the service sector is more productive *relative to other sectors* in the economy. Given the labor concentration in the extractive sector, every worker who moves out of the extractive sector is most productive if working in the service sector.

Output per Capital Input

What about the productivity of capital inputs? Again, we look at the ratios of percentage GDP in 1981 to the percentage of gross fixed capital formation in 1980 for each sector (see Table 3.2). Such data are not available for many countries; therefore, these data are only suggestive. First note that the majority of capital formation is occurring in the service sector—in direct contradiction to beliefs that service industries are always labor-, not capital-, intensive. There is a difference in emphasis, though, by level of economic development. The developing countries emphasize capital formation in infrastructure industries, while more industrialized countries emphasize capital formation in business (financial) service industries.

From the data in Table 3.2, it is clear that service industries in the 14 countries surveyed, though on the whole not as "productive" as the other sectors, are making better use of capital resources than is commonly believed. Although comparable data are not readily available for other countries, some data from Sweden underscore the efficient use being made of capital invested in service industries (see Table 3.3). In Sweden, most service industries have higher returns on total capital and on equity than is true for the goods-producing sectors. Capital stock per employee varies widely by type of industry, being particularly high for the insurance industry.

TABLE 3.2
Ratio of Percentage GDP (1981)
to Percentage Fixed Capital Formation (1980)
for Selected Countries

	Development Category			
Economic Sector	Low Income (n = 1)	Lower Middle (n = 4)	Upper Middle (n = 3)	Industrial (n = 6)
Extractive Sector	9.61	2.95	5.16	3.25
Manufacturing Sector	3.84	4.22	3.97	4.93
Service Sector	7.81	4.22	1.67	1.61

Note the small sample size; these data should be interpreted with caution.

Calculated from data in the United Nations, *Yearbook of National Account Statistics: 1981* (New York: U.N., 1983); World Bank, *World Tables*, 3rd ed. (Baltimore, MD: Johns Hopkins University Press, 1983).

TABLE 3.3
Swedish Data on Selected
Measures of Capital Input Productivity
(Private Sector): 1981

Industry	Return on Total Capital (%)	Return on Equity (%)	Capital Stock Per Employee (SEK 1000)
Extractive/Manufacturing	7.0	6.7	377
Services			
Construction	8.0	30.3	58
Commerce	8.2	18.7	107
Transport	6.2	4.9	421
Banking	11.0	28.5	188
Insurance	6.0	10.9	1,607
Professional services	7.0	22.7	114
Other services	15.9	50.4	51

From the *Swedish National Study on Trade in Services* (Stockholm: Swedish Government, 1984).

Dynamic Efficiency Measures

In analyzing the productivity of economic sectors, a more revealing and relevant analysis is the change in productivity over time. Such analyses can control for shifts in resource availability (such as population changes) and initial inequities in resource distribution—for example, portions of the service sector have historically been labor-intensive. For the analyses below, the average annual change rate (i.e., the compound growth rate) in GDP over time is compared with the average annual change rates for labor and capital inputs, giving a measure of marginal productivity.

Change in Output per Labor Input

Table 3.4 shows the ratio of average annual change rate in GDP to the average annual change in employment. Here it is apparent that as workers move into the service sector they in turn produce a proportionally higher percentage of GDP. Even for the older Industrial countries where, historically, there have been a disproportionate number of persons

TABLE 3.4
Ratio of Average Annual
Growth Rates for GDP and Employment
By Economic Sector: 1977-81

Economic Sector	Development Category			
	Lower Income	Lower Middle	Upper Middle	Industrial
Extractive Sector	1.52	1.04	.65	3.41
Manufacturing Sector	.58	.61	1.17	1.54
Service Sector	2.71	7.39	2.31	9.28

Calculated from data in the International Labour Office, *Yearbook of Labour Statistics* (Geneva: ILO, 1983); World Bank, *World Tables*, 3rd ed. (Baltimore, MD: Johns Hopkins University Press, 1983).

working in services, allocating labor resources to services continues to be a productive allocation of resources.

Change in Output per Capital Input

What happens if we perform the same calculations for fixed capital formation? In Table 3.5, we can see suggestive results from 14 countries. In this small sample, increased capital investment in the extractive sector does not result in higher GDP returns for the developing countries. Fixed capital formation is most productive in manufacturing only for the Industrial countries. The productivity of capital assets is least productive in the service sector only for the Upper-middle-income countries.

THE EFFECTIVENESS OF
THE SERVICE SECTOR

Productive effectiveness in the service sector is seldom discussed as such; however, it is an extremely relevant issue when evaluating alternative strategies for resource allocation. What are the consequences of developing various portions of the service sector? What role can or should the service sector play in meeting national development and economic growth objectives?

While effectiveness in delivering particular services is difficult to measure, there are ways to estimate the effectiveness of the service subsectors within an economy. Below are suggestions of the type of

TABLE 3.5
Ratio of Average Annual
Growth Rates for GDP and
Capital Formation
(Selected Countries): 1977-81

	Development Category			
Economic Sector	Lower Income (n = 1)	Lower Middle (n = 4)	Upper Middle (n = 3)	Industrial (n = 6)
Extractive Sector	9.88	14.19	6.71	5.17
Manufacturing Sector	4.05	7.97	5.19	7.64
Service Sector	5.05	12.16	3.68	6.83

Note the small sample size; these data should be interpreted with caution.

Calculated from data in the United Nations, *Yearbook of National Account Statistics: 1981* (New York: U.N., 1983); World Bank. *World Tables*, 3rd ed. (Baltimore, MD: Johns Hopkins University Press, 1983).

analyses that could address the issue of effective service delivery for infrastructure, trade, and business services, followed by a discussion of the particular issues in public administration.

Infrastructure Services Effectiveness

M. Israel, president of the Pacific Telecommunications Council, "views the creation of a telecommunications infrastructure as a necessary prerequisite for the development of other sectors of a country."[3] Causational studies need to be undertaken comparing countries at different levels of development regarding the relationship between capital investments in communications and transportation infrastructure and economic growth. Unfortunately, sufficiently disaggregated data for such analyses are difficult to find for developing countries.

World data indicate that telephones per capita is an excellent estimate of economic progress. In order to evaluate the effectiveness of any infrastructure industry, though, outcomes must be related to a nation's development goals. Number of phones in use may be a less appropriate measure than, for example, dispersion of phones throughout rural areas. Similar issues arise in relation to other measures of infrastructure support. Energy source usage statistics are available, but they must be related to national goals. Below is an example of what happens when ultimate goals are not kept firmly in mind as the yardstick against which to assess effectiveness:

Complaints from passengers wishing to use the Bagnall to
Greenfields bus service that "the drivers were speeding past queues
of up to 30 people with a smile and a wave of the hand" have been
met by a statement pointing out that "it is impossible for the drivers
to keep their timetable if they have to stop for passengers."[4]

Trade Services Effectiveness

While domestic and international trade volume data are available in the
aggregate, industry-specific data need to be reviewed to determine if the mix
of products and services being exported and imported is optimal. Domestic
wholesale and retail trade flows need to be disaggregated to determine how
readily accessible items are to the customer. Type of trade service (mail-
order, supermarket, sole proprietor establishment) needs to be examined.

Trade services associated with tourism are typically closely
monitored. In light of suggestions that tourism has the most positive
economic effects if domestic and international tourism are integrated, the
mixture of types of trade needs to be analyzed. Assumptions about
multiplier effects from tourism need to be reexamined to include intangible costs and benefits.

Business Services Effectiveness

Analysis of investment patterns in financial and business service industries are particularly important for developing countries in light of the
data indicating that higher per capita GNP is associated with more
capital investment in such services. Professional licensing requirements,
money available for research and development, and immigration laws
need to be reviewed to determine how attractive an economy is to profes-
sionals whose skills are needed.

In addition, data on business services need to be correlated with
development goals regarding access to such services. For example,
Nigeria has been successful in developing rural branch banking, though
there is a need for further governmental incentives for commercial banks
to ensure sufficient competition in rural services (Umoh 1984).

Public Administration Productivity:
A Special Case

Particular concern is usually expressed about the productivity of the
public sector, often thought of as "non-market" services. Some writers

(e.g., Bacon and Eltis 1978) have argued that Britain's economic problems could be attributed to shifts in labor force allocation from the private sector to the public sector, resulting in decreased productivity. Many writers who assume that the service sector is nonproductive do so because they equate the service sector with the public sector. In actuality, the public sector is typically less than a third of the service sector—no more than 20% of total GDP.

When productivity in the public sector is decried, what is never mentioned is the shift in output measurement between the public and the private sectors. In the private sector, output is valued at fair market value—i.e., including value added to input resources. In the public sector, however, output is valued at total input costs without any additional figure (e.g., fair market equivalent) for value added. Since labor is only one of the various inputs, traditional static productivity ratios will always show a ratio of less than 1.0. What we have, then, is a measurement problem, not a productivity problem.

In examining Pacific Basin sample data on the productivity ratios for both the static and dynamic measures in public administration (see Table 3.6), the traditional reasons for concern are immediately apparent. For the static measures, most of the ratios for the four country groups are well below 1.0. However, the dynamic measures show quite a different story. Here *all* of the ratios are above 1.0—i.e., marginal productivity increases for each additional public administration worker are substantial, particularly in the developing countries.

The public sector as a whole, then, is more productive in an absolute sense than is commonly thought, and fair market equivalents would need

TABLE 3.6
Productivity in Public Administration
(Pacific Basin Sample): 1971-81

Productivity Measure	Pacific Basin Sample			
	Low Income	Lower Middle	Upper Middle	Industrial
Percentage:				
GDP/Employment	.4	1.4	.7	.3
Ratio of Average Change Rate:				
GDP/Employment	1.2	1.5	6.3	1.3

Calculated from data in the Economic and Social Committee for Asia and the Pacific, *Statistical Yearbook for Asia and the Pacific: 1981* (New York: United Nations, 1983); United Nations, *Yearbook of National Account Statistics: 1981* (New York: United Nations, 1983).

to be used to estimate exactly how productive. The question of relative productivity, though, is another matter. The recent trends toward "privatizing" public services—i.e., contracting them out to private firms—suggests that productivity in the private sector is greater than that in the public sector. Governments seem to be realizing that their own resources should be allocated selectively to those public administration functions which *must* be carried out by government in order to ensure economic stability, rather than to those functions which private enterprises can handle just as well (or better).

EXTERNALITIES AND SERVICE PRODUCTION

One of the features of service operations is that they are open systems and as such are heavily influenced by a variety of external factors. The three economic sectors have been differentiated based on the factors that can limit productivity: "... the primary sector ... is limited by *natural growth* factors, the secondary by *mechanical* factors, and the tertiary by relatively unaided *human skill*" (Wolfe 1955, p. 406). To this list, we could add that service productivity is limited by the manner in which the customer participates in the service delivery.

Producer-Customer Relationship

Interpreting productivity measures appropriately, especially at the microeconomic level, hinges on understanding the complexities of the relationship between customer and service producer. In Chapter 1, services were defined as dependent upon one of three types of relationships: (1) the producer acting for the customer; (2) the customer providing a portion of the labor (self-service); or (3) the customer and the producer providing the service jointly (coproduction).

Services Delivered by Producer Only

When the producer acts as the customer's agent, service delivery is very similar to that of the manufacturing process. Efficiency of production is tied to availability of needed resources, effective scheduling of work flow, and other related issues. Increases in productivity can be measured directly as increases in numbers of service transactions conducted.

Self-Service by Customer

When the customer is used as a primary labor input without interaction with the producer, recorded industry productivity will be affected in two ways. First, labor costs for the self-service industry are, from a certain perspective, understated as the customer becomes an unpaid part of the work force. On the other hand, the price of the service is reduced accordingly compared with "full service" by the producer: thus, the customer is paid indirectly.

Second, customers typically enter a service delivery system as "naive" employees. Unless they have used the system successfully before or are accompanied by a knowledgeable person who provides "on-the-job" orientation, they are usually unaware of the structure of service production and what constitutes appropriate behavior on their part. A poorly prepared customer will adversely affect efficient service production and thus decrease the rate at which new sales can take place.

Coproduction by Producer and Customer

Recently, researchers have become aware that consumers in "high-contact" service delivery systems—i.e., those in which there is a necessary interaction between the consumer and the producer (Chase 1978)—must be trained or "socialized" to perform their role appropriately (P. Mills 1984). Inappropriate consumer behavior—e.g., failure to bring needed documents, insistence on inappropriately customized service, nonresponsiveness to questions, poor implementation of professional recommendations—significantly increases the time required to provide service, increases consumer and producer frustration, and decreases consumer satisfaction.

> In services . . . the consumer frequently plays an important role in production. Sometimes, as in the barber's chair, the role is essentially passive. . . . But in the supermarket and laundromat the consumer actually works, and in the doctor's office the quality of the medical history the patient gives may influence significantly the productivity of the doctor. Productivity in banking is affected by whether the clerk or the customer makes out the deposit slip—and whether it is made out correctly or not. . . . Productivity in education . . . is determined largely by what the student contributes, and . . . the performance of a string quartet can be affected by the audience's response (Fuchs 1968, pp. 194–195).

Once again, the skill level and cooperation of the customer become important. In addition, in order for services to be effective, they must be perceived as such by clients; hence, the subjective assessment of the quality of service that is received in return for the price paid by the public or the individual client is central to the issue of productivity. No matter how much the quantitative measures of productivity (i.e., efficiency) increase, criticisms will continue to be made unless clients feel that they are getting what they are paying for. In coproduction settings, then, productivity is affected not only by the skill with which customers perform their jobs, but also by the quality of the producer-customer interaction. Effective service delivery often necessitates a *decrease* in the total number of service transactions and an increase in the interaction time with each customer.

Capacity Management

One of the peculiarities of managing service operations effectively is the need to maintain optimal customer participation when customers are directly involved with the service delivery system. If too few customers patronize the service firm at any given time, production capacity stands idle and the firm's revenues are lowered. In some service industries, there may also be a negative impact on service delivery for psychological reasons. For example, if a concert is held in a large auditorium with only a very small audience, customers may question their own judgment in coming while performers may give a less than optimal performance. Of course, there are some service settings such as restaurants where, from the customer's perspective, the lack of crowding due to underutilized capacity constitutes a pleasant bonus.

At the other extreme, the presence of too many customers, while generating short-term revenues, may ruin long-term service prospects if quality of service delivery suffers. Customers may avoid overcrowded restaurants, for example, which are excessively noisy and where service is slow. One component of service pricing is the opportunity cost of waiting. Tourist attractions which are overcrowded may lose their popularity. Again, though, there are certain service settings where large numbers of customers are a distinct advantage. Rock concerts are an example where the more crowded the setting, the better the service is often perceived to be—and the enthusiasm of the crowd can have a positive motivating effect on the performers.

In order to maintain both revenue efficiency and delivery effectiveness, strategies for matching supply and demand need to be carefully thought through (Sasser 1976). In order to increase revenue flows within a given production capacity without sacrificing quality of service, demand for services can be altered in a variety of ways. The most common methods are to shift demand timing through pricing and through reservation systems. A wide range of services have adopted off-peak pricing to encourage the use of facilities during times when capacity is under-utilized. For example, transportation systems offer lower fares, utilities charge lower rates, and movie theaters may have special daytime prices.

Reservation systems are widespread throughout the transportation and hospitality industries, as well as in professional and personal services. While they can be effective in smoothing demand, there is the problem of production capacity standing idle because customers do not keep their reservations. Some firms attempt to ensure customer arrival, or at least partial revenue compensation, by charging a fee for broken appointments. Others offer the option of "standy-by" or "walk-in" appointments, often at a reduced rate, in order to have a ready pool of alternate customers to draw on if reservations are broken.

Two other approaches to altering demand focus instead on creating demand which can be met using excess production capacity. One such approach is to create nonpeak demand for alternate products. For example, schools have begun renting out their facilities for conferences or community events when school is not in session. Resorts may provide employee training programs during the off-season. Of course, care must be taken that the original service to be delivered does not suffer through abuse of the facilities or spillover into the production time of the original service.

Another approach is to offer complementary services which the customer may purchase while waiting for the initial service. Restaurants have added cocktail lounges. Theaters have added food and beverage stands. Airlines have instituted in-flight purchasing (either on board or by mail-order with a catalog provided for browsing) and rental in-flight computer games. Again, care must be taken to be sure that production capacity is not diverted away from the delivery of the primary service. For example, airlines would not want customers to feel that general service levels were lowered because the crew on an international flight were preoccupied with selling duty-free items.

On the supply side, there are several strategies which can be adopted in order to be able to increase production capacity when needed at minimal cost. Making use of part-time employees during busy periods is the most common; however, caution should be exercised as those temporary employees must produce the service and may not be motivated to maintain quality. Permanent part-time employees who are well-trained and well-motivated (and well-compensated) are usually a better alternative. Employees may be cross-trained so that they can move out of low-demand (or low priority) positions and into high-demand positions when needed. Often necessary but seldom-used equipment can be shared with other service producers, as is being done with medical equipment and airport facilities. Finally, the self-service portion of service delivery can be increased so that more customers can be served.

Maintaining Acceptable Quality

Most services are skill-intensive, meaning either technical skills or interpersonal skills. The quality of the service delivered depends in large part on how motivated the staff are to produce the service efficiently and effectively. Since we have defined productivity as maximizing output *of acceptable quality*, we must be in a position to assure such quality.

Quality control in services is essentially a personnel function. While adequate supervision plays a part, the most important component is the attitude of the service producer. A variety of strategies are available. Career planning, annual reviews of progress made, and training for career enhancement can all be powerful motivators. Production is also enhanced when employees are able to affect the structure of their jobs and make suggestions to increase efficiency.

In high contact, or coproduction, settings several specific issues arise. Quality of service can be markedly enhanced if the employees are able to understand accurately the experience of the customer. For example, employees may be rotated through the "customer service" function so that they hear the complaints voiced by customers (Tansik 1984), or employees may be assigned to go through the service delivery process as anonymous customers.

Another important issue in maintaining quality service delivery is to rotate personnel in "high contact" positions away from customer interaction periodically, whether through providing a variety of daily tasks or through temporary assignment to a "low contact" position. Employees in high contact positions "burn out" quickly if alternatives are not provided. America West has done this creatively by rotating all its service representatives through baggage handling periodically.

SUMMARY

In order to reflect both efficiency and effectiveness concerns, productivity has been defined as maximizing output of acceptable quality, while minimizing the total costs of the production process. Productivity in the service sector is higher than traditionally believed, and is more productive than the economy as a whole if one considers changes in marginal productivity. With the increasing emphasis on fixed capital formation in services, further increases in service productivity can be expected along with increased demand (and hence better resource utilization) for manufactured goods. In fact, for the United States, the Office of the U.S. Trade Representative has estimated that at least 25 percent of the demand for exported U.S.-manufactured goods come from service industries (*US national study* 1984).

Effectiveness of service delivery is often overlooked in favor of quantitative efficiency measures. The quality of services delivered and their relevance to national development goals, though, are crucial issues which need more attention. In addition, service delivery is affected by a variety of externalities, including the extent of interaction between producer and customer, the need to match productive capacity with consumer demand in high-contact services, and the difficulties inherent in maintaining quality of service delivery.

Ongoing problems in measuring service sector productivity include how best to reflect qualitative, or effectiveness, aspects of service delivery in our measures of productivity, how to capture more accurately the output of the public sector, and how best to change perceptions regarding the importance and productivity of the service sector as a whole.

NOTES

1. See "America's Astounding Job Machine," *New York Times* (June 17, 1984), pp. 1; 25; "Myth of the Vanishing Middle Class," *Business Week* (July 9, 1984), pp. 83; 86.

2. J.B. Say was one of the few nineteenth-century economists to question Smith's position by asserting that all economic activities which satisfy human needs are productive:

> ... the industry of the physician, however, as well as that of the
> public functionary, the advocate or the judge, which are of ... the

same class, satisfies wants of so essential a nature, that without those professions no society could exist (1964, p. 120).

A. Marshall carried the debate into the twentieth century. While unwilling to classify services as wealth-producing, he was also unwilling to state that services were unproductive as the consequences would be to say:

> ... that a singer in an opera is unproductive, that the printer of the tickets of admission to the opera is productive; while the usher who shows people to their places is unproductive, unless he happens to sell programmes, and then he is productive (1961, p. 67).

3. See M. Gawdun, "Pacific Telecommunications Conference '85: Staff Report," *Telecommunications* (March 1985), pp. 90–92.

4. Quoted from a newspaper in the Midlands of England in P. Ryan, "Get Rid of the People, and the System Runs Fine," *Smithsonian* (August 1977), p. 140.

4

SERVICES AND
INDUSTRIAL POLICY

> Industrialization could not have occurred, or would have occurred more slowly, had there not been an expansion of social overhead services like transport and education, and of intermediate services like retail and wholesale trade, which were necessary as productive activities became more specialised, more localised and more roundabout (Hartwell 1973, p. 366).

> The U.S., indeed the entire industrial world, is profoundly changing the way it uses men and materials, capital and manufacturing processes. We are undergoing what economists call a structural change. . . . It is precisely through the shrinking of old industries—learning to make more with less—that new industries became possible and with them a broadening of the horizons of life for most people (Cook 1982a, pp. 161; 163).

The United States and other "industrial" economies continue to lament the "erosion" of their manufacturing sectors.[1] Rallying cries for "reindustrialization" pepper the presses in both the United States and Europe. Why is the United States in particular so insistent on attributing its own growth to being primarily a "manufacturing economy"? The United States has never had more than 36 percent of its population employed in the manufacturing sector nor had more than 34 percent of GDP resulting from manufacturing—and that in 1943 at the height of World War II production.

In order to understand and reevaluate the issues raised in industrial policy debates, we must first understand what is meant by "deindustrialization" and "reindustrialization". Deindustrialization is the term that has been coined to refer to the *absolute* decrease in manufacturing contribution to Gross Domestic Product, although in many cases it is also used to refer to *relative* decreases in percentage of GDP from the manufacturing sector. In the debates over industrial policy, reindustrialization usually refers to the priority allocation of an economy's resources to the manufacturing sector or to the creation of incentives to stimulate manufacturing sector growth in preference to other sectors.

Is a decrease in manufacturing's contribution to the total economy a cause for concern? Does an economy lose vitality if it becomes less dependent on, or driven by, the production of tangible goods? Are there perhaps parallels here to the cries of alarm that rang out when agriculture ceased to be the dominant sector in most economies? Are we witnessing a steady undermining of industrial strength or, as Cook (1982a) suggests, the inevitable next step in industrial restructuring?

REEXAMINING THE
MANUFACTURING SECTOR

The rapid growth of the Pacific Basin countries—especially the Asian Newly Industrializing Countries (NICs)—is most usually attributed to their dynamic manufacturing sectors. One would assume from the descriptions given that manufacturing was the dominant sector in each economy. As a matter of fact, each of these economies derives over half its GDP from service industries (Riddle and Sours 1985). The recent tendency of several of the dynamic Pacific Basin countries to move away from an emphasis on heavy manufacturing industries has gone all but unnoticed. In the recession of the early 1980s, Singapore decided that its manufacturing focus had made it too vulnerable to recessionary forces and began to reposition itself as a financial center for the Pacific region (Leung 1983). Even Indonesia has backed off from heavy manufacturing products ("Indonesia aborts . . ." 1983).

Has there actually been a decline in the relative size of the manufacturing sector? From Table 4.1, we can see that the answer depends upon which base year is used for comparison. Using 1965 as the base year to compare with 1981, GDP from manufacturing remained constant for the Low-income countries, increased for Lower-middle-income and Upper-middle-income countries, and decreased for Industrial countries.[2] Using

TABLE 4.1
Trends in Sectoral GDP
Percentages: 1965-81

| Percent GDP from: | Development Category | | | |
	Low Income	Lower Middle	Upper Middle	Industrial
Extractive Sector				
1965	50.2%	36.3%	21.8%	9.5%
1973	43.5	31.4	17.4	8.0
1981	41.8	26.7	14.8	7.4
Manufacturing Sector				
1965	10.2%	14.6%	18.3%	38.3%
1973	12.5	18.4	21.4	25.8
1981	10.2	16.0	21.9	26.6
Service Sector				
1965	39.6%	49.1%	59.9%	52.2%
1973	44.0	49.5	60.8	65.0
1981	48.0	57.4	63.8	65.8

Calculated from data in the World Bank, *World Tables*, 3rd ed. (Baltimore, MD: Johns Hopkins University Press, 1983).

1973 as the comparison year, GDP for Low-income and Lower-middle-income countries decreased while both Upper-middle-income and Industrial countries showed a slight increase.

What about changes in the absolute size of the manufacturing sector? The sectoral growth rates in Table 4.2 demonstrate that between 1970 and 1981 the manufacturing sector registered positive growth gains in all four country groups. The issue, then, is not deindustrialization, but a reluctance to accept manufacturing as constituting no more than approximately 25 percent of an economy. The role of the manufacturing sector as a supplier of equipment and supplies, dependent upon external demand, is consistent with manufacturing comprising a relatively modest portion of any economy.

The issue is further clouded by the fact that some economists have been using deindustrialization to refer to a decline in the number of new jobs in manufacturing rather than to a decline in manufacturing GDP. Employment growth rates in manufacturing for Industrial countries have indeed been close to zero or negative since the late 1970s, exactly what one would expect with the integration of technological innovations into manufacturing processes. The implications should not be overlooked, however. "The economic rationale of the emphasis on manufactured

TABLE 4.2
Average Annual GDP Growth
Rate by Economic Sector:
1970-81

Average GDP Growth in:	Development Category			
	Low Income	Lower Middle	Upper Middle	Industrial
Extractive Sector	2.4%	3.9%	2.5%	3.6%
Manufacturing Sector	2.9	7.8	6.0	4.7
Service Sector	2.2	3.9	5.6	2.9

Calculated from data in the World Bank, *World Tables*, 3rd ed. (Baltimore, MD: Johns Hopkins University Press, 1983).

goods exports lies in their potential for providing employment opportunities and foreign exchange earnings at low capital cost'' (Hasan 1982, p. 27). If increased resource allocation to the manufacturing sector does not generate a proportional increase in new jobs, then such a development strategy demands rethinking.

All of the ''stage'' theorists posit manufacturing focus as an essential step in economic development.[3] If manufacturing is indeed essential to development, we should see significant correlations between the percentage GDP due to manufacturing and measures of economic growth—e.g., annual change in GDP and per capita GNP. Such correlations are present in the data only for the Industrial countries; further, for those same Industrial countries, increases in per capita GNP were also correlated with the percentage of GDP from services. The evidence indicates that while manufacturing may be a dynamic portion of an economy, it is not *the* engine of growth.

If we examine only the developing countries exhibiting extraordinarily high or low growth rates (Extreme Cases sample), we can get a clearer indication of the relationship between the manufacturing sector and overall economic growth (see Table 4.3). Again no exclusive role is apparent for manufacturing. While the manufacturing sector exhibited the highest average growth rate for the High Growth countries, it was also the most variable sector so that the difference between the samples was not statistically significant. Only the growth rate for the service sector was significantly different between the two groups and correlated with overall economic growth. The service sector, then, is at least as important as the manufacturing sector in any growing economy. It would be more accurate

TABLE 4.3
Average Annual GDP Growth
Rate by Economic Sector
(Extreme Case Sample): 1965-82

Variable	Low Growth	High Growth	SD	t-test
	Extreme Case Sample			
Average GDP Growth in:				
Extractive Sector	1.90%	3.74%	.99	1.86
Manufacturing Sector	2.10	9.55	3.63	2.05
Service Sector	2.26	7.93	1.55	3.63***
Total Economy	2.20	6.82	1.24	3.74***
Correlation between Growth Rates:				
Manufacturing & Services	.64	.57		
Manufacturing & Total Economy	.63	.84		
Services & Total Economy	.95**	.91*		

*p < .05
**p < .02
***p < .01

to say that economic growth is a synergistic process, rather than manufacturing-dependent.

Manufacturing can and does play a dynamic role in an economy, often exhibiting above-average growth and an efficient use of capital and human production inputs. Manufacturing, though, is also very vulnerable to economic recession and to any decrease in demand for equipment and supplies in other portions of the economy. Further, there is little evidence that, as a sector, manufacturing can play a direct role in job creation, especially as the sector becomes increasingly technologically intensive. Industrial policies linked only to the manufacturing sector are short-sighted and unnecessarily limited.

SOURCES OF MANUFACTURING BIAS

Since the United States views itself and is viewed by many others as an economic role model, its assumptions about manufacturing-led growth have major consequences in influencing the economic policies not only of developing countries but also of the major lending institutions. In positing manufacturing-led development as the model, the United States has, in essence, been urging its own wartime economic model on others as the ideal. Why has such a bias toward manufacturing-led growth developed?

Historical Scarcity of Manufactured Goods

One reason for the existing manufacturing bias is the role played by the manufacturing sector historically in relation to national standards of living. Prior to the twentieth century, production and distribution costs for manufactured products were expensive and a luxury of the affluent. The strength of a nation's domestic manufacturing sector was directly responsible for the standard of living possible for the majority of citizens.

Over the past 30 years, however, competition in world markets has increased, and the cost of imports has fallen dramatically since World War II. The average consumer in many countries can now select from an array of international products, and no single national economy needs to supply the full array of manufactured goods in order to maintain the standard of living desired by citizens.

Reporting of Economic Data

Another reason why an industrial bias has developed is the manner in which economic data are recorded and discussed. Data from both the agricultural and manufacturing sectors are reported in the aggregate; in other words, we talk about "manufacturing" rather than "cars" and "televisions." Data from the service sector, however, are reported industry by industry—i.e., banking, transportation, and so on. Each service industry group appears relatively minor by itself; it is only in the aggregate that the dynamism of the sector becomes apparent. We can see illustrated in Table 4.4 the differences in perception created by reporting macroeconomic data in the disaggregated fashion or by sector totals, using data from a popular text on U.S. economic history. As the figures are reported, it would appear that services had varied between 10 percent of total GNP in 1930 and 13 percent of the total in 1970, rather than between 60 percent and 68 percent. Table 4.5 illustrates the same distortion in international economic data, using selected countries at each level of development.

While disaggregation in macroeconomic reporting conceals the dynamism of the service sector, lack of industry detail in other settings can imply a lack of importance. In the *1985 U.S. Industrial Outlook*, 44

TABLE 4.4
Percentage of Gross National
Product by Industry
Sector (U.S.A.): 1930-70

Industry	1930	1940	1950	1960	1970
As Reported:					
Agriculture	8%	8%	7%	4%	3%
Mining	2	2	2	1	1
Construction	4	3	5	5	5
Manufacturing	24	27	31	30	28
Trade	16	18	18	16	15
Finance	14	10	9	11	11
Transport	11	10	8	9	8
Services	13	11	10	11	13
Government	7	11	10	13	16
Aggregated:					
Extractive Sector	10%	10%	9%	5%	4%
Manufacturing Sector	24	27	31	30	28
Service Sector	65	63	60	65	68

Adapted from A.W. Niemi, Jr. *U.S. Economic History: A Survey of the Major Issues* (Chicago: Rand McNally, 1975), p. 15.

chapters (65 percent) were devoted to the manufacturing industries that comprise 25 percent of the economy and 20 chapters (29 percent) addressed the service industries that comprise 70 percent of the economy (the remaining 5 percent addressed extractive sector industries). Frequently, the service sector is not even mentioned—as for example in many of the OECD country studies, and in a 1985 book on the Pacific Basin where the chapter on Singapore addressed only the extractive (2 percent of GDP) and manufacturing (28 percent of GDP) sectors as though they comprised the entire economy.

In assessing the vitality of an economy, both national governments and international monetary agencies report a variety of economic indicators. Such indicators are uniformly linked to goods production and seldom reflect service sector activity appropriately. The industrial production index (IPI), used in the United States, measures production from mining, manufacturing, and utilities in order to predict business cycles. Other economic indicators used by the United States are listed in Table 4.6. As can be seen, service sector activity is directly represented only for

TABLE 4.5
Percentage Gross Domestic Product
by Industry Sector
(Selected Countries): 1981

Industry	Low Income: India	Lower Middle: Thailand	Upper Middle: Brazil	Industrial: Japan
Disaggregated:				
Agriculture	37%	25%	10%	3%
Mining	1	1	1	0
Manufacturing	16	21	28	35
Construction	5	5	6	7
Utilities	2	2	3	2
Transport/communication	7	6	7	6
Trade	12	16	17	14
Finance	3	6	7	14
Services	9	13	14	15
Government	8	4	7	4
Aggregated:				
Extractive Sector	38%	26%	11%	3%
Manufacturing Sector	16	21	28	35
Service Sector	46	53	61	62

Calculated from data in the World Bank, *World Tables*, 3rd ed. (Balitmore, MD: Johns Hopkins University Press, 1983).

construction and retail trade. Much of the dynamism of the service sector simply is not captured by the measures used. In addition, the measures that aggregate data from manufacturing and services often conceal important trends. In the early 1980s, rising unemployment figures in the United States caused considerable concern. Few analysts recognized that unemployment was increasing in the manufacturing sector but decreasing in the service sector. Indicators reported by *The Economist* for OECD countries are similarly manufacturing oriented—e.g., manufacturing inventory levels, new plant and equipment.

Service sector contribution is also masked by accounting conventions designed for manufacturing operations. Manufactured goods are recorded as assets acquired, while services are recorded as expenses incurred. The *Swedish National Study on Trade in Services* (1984) has an excellent commentary on the misinterpretations which can result from the methods of accounting for service investment:

TABLE 4.6
Statistical Indicators
Reported by the U.S.
Department of Commerce

Indicator	Includes Data Specific To:		
	Manufacturing	*Services*	*Both*
Leading Indicators:			
Average hourly workweek, production	X		
Average weekly initial claims, state unemployment insurance			X
Index of net business formation			X
New orders, durable goods industries			X
Contracts & orders, plant & equipment			X
Index of new building permits, private		X	
Change in book value, inventories			X
Index of industrial materials prices	X		
Index of stock prices, 500 common stocks			*
Corporate profits after taxes (quarterly)			X
Index: price to unit labor	X		
Change in consumer installment debt		X	
Roughly Coincidental Indicators:			
GNP in current dollars			X
GNP in 1958 dollars			X
Index of industrial production	X		
Personal income			X
Manufacturing and trade sales			*
Sales of retail stores		X	
Employees in nonagricultural jobs			X
Unemployment rate, total			X
Lagging Indicators:			
Unemployment rate, over 15 weeks			X
Expenditures, new plant & equipment			X
Book value, inventories			X
Index: labor cost per output	X		
Commercial loans outstanding			X
Bank rates: short-term business loans			X

* Service industries underrepresented.

Adapted from J.E. Hanke and A.G. Reitsch, *Business Forecasting* (Newton, MA: Allyn and Bacon, 1981), p. 171.

... companies tend to put money into activities like R & D, marketing, education and organisation, which are not classified as investments but as production costs. So when companies extend their service activities and take on investments in "human capital" the investment expenditures fall according to the official statistics. A survey done by the National Industrial Board shows that these kind of investments are of about the same magnitude as the "conventional" investments and that the so called *immaterial investments will continue to increase* (p. 13).

When economists grow alarmed about decreasing investment levels, what may in fact be occurring is a shift in importance from investment in capital goods to investment in "capital" services.

In traditional Western economic analyses, labor intensity, lack of raw materials, inbred management, and marginal capitalization are typically viewed as competitive weaknesses. Ironically, in the Asian Newly Industrializing Countries (NICs), these very aspects of Asian firms are the characteristics that have allowed the service aspects (particularly the marketing function) to remain paramount. The very lack of traditional assets used to evaluate U.S. firms has given the Asian firms a high degree of flexibility in their operational styles, allowing them to get into and out of markets more rapidly than their heavily-leveraged counterparts in the United States. Such flexibility is particularly important if product life cycles are inherently growing shorter.[4]

U.S. Economic History

Having achieved an enviable domestic per capita income and control of major world markets, it is not surprising that the United States has been viewed by many Western-educated national leaders as the source for guidance in the economic development process. As the British hold on Asia loosened after World War II, the United States stepped in as champion and regional role model. Few considered the possibility that the United States had achieved its position of economic leadership more from the fortuitous consequences of having survived two major world wars without being invaded than from having developed an economic strategy that could initiate and sustain competitive advantage.

We may argue, in fact, that manufacturing development in the United States has had both positive and negative consequences. Since natural resources were abundant, early economic development in the United States was relatively rapid. After winning independence from

England, the U.S. balance of trade improved markedly. Volume of trade with England and the West Indies was substantially unaffected by the political separation, plus U.S. exporters were able to set their own prices unrestricted by mercantilist policies. Although most manufactured goods were imported until the mid-nineteenth century, a positive balance of payments was maintained through exporting an agricultural surplus and performing shipping services for other nations (Peterson and Gray 1969). The United States benefitted, for example, from the Napoleonic Wars between England and France by having very competitive shipping prices. Since neither country allowed shipments directly from the other, U.S. shippers did a brisk business in reexporting goods between the two.

By 1860, the momentum of the Industrial Revolution was making itself felt, however, and the nature of the U. S. economy began to undergo radical changes. Rapid westward expansion combined with the new technology available to funnel major resources into railroad construction. The capital required for development of the railroads led to two major new developments in the U.S. economy—the concept of ownership separate from management, and the centralization of money and investment markets. Both of these trends—the diversification of ownership and the concentration of financial power—laid the groundwork for the rise of the large manufacturing concerns (Porter 1973). Simultaneously, the development of the transportation and communications infrastructure allowed businesses to think and plan in terms of national, and ultimately international, markets.

Initially, the size of U.S. firms was tied to the wealth of an individual or small group of partners, much as it had been earlier in Europe. Firms were family enterprises that often closed permanently with the death of the owner. Competitive market entry was easy, while failure was not uncommon and carried with it no special stigma. The owner/manager retained control over when or how to do business; firms could be closed temporarily during harsh financial times and then reopened.

With the availability of large pools of capital, prestige became attached to the amount of fixed assets a business owned. Of course, large fixed assets usually require equally large liabilities and imply huge start-up and shut-down costs. No longer could owners afford the luxury of adapting production to external business conditions; instead, they needed to continue production/sales even if at a loss. Decisions affecting workers became dictated by the debt structure of the corporation rather than by the more humane considerations characteristic of small family firms, which were more dependent upon community goodwill.

The rise of large corporations in the United States has been the center of political controversy for the past century (Porter 1973). While the increases in productivity and standard of living made possible by the introduction of new technology were viewed positively, there continues to be considerable criticism of the changes in national values that occurred. Although the United States, in practice, never achieved equal opportunity for all, immigrants from countries where poverty was greater and social class stratification more rigid certainly viewed the United States as offering more opportunities for the hard-working individual. But, as power and the means of production became more concentrated in the hands of a few, the ideals of being one's own boss and equal opportunity for all could no longer be convincingly maintained.

A second consequence of corporate development, and potentially more damaging, was the rise in impersonal and ultimately adversarial relationships between managers and workers. The initial step in this process came from the separation of ownership and management (Berle and Means 1968). As the labor force expanded at any one business, personal relationships between owners and workers became more difficult to maintain. Owners became less responsive to worker concerns regarding working conditions, and workers felt less and less commitment to a "joint venture." As professional (and often temporary) managers took the place of owner/managers, the estrangement grew at a more rapid rate. Labor unions became vital in order to protect workers' interests.

The present reindustrialization debate in the United States, then, reflects the economic history outlined above. Having industrialized at a high social cost and having established an adversarial management-labor environment, conscious reorientation toward services is difficult. Labor unions fear job losses and therefore resist change. In the less confrontational environment of Western Europe, greater strides have been made toward management-labor cooperation in restructuring employment. U.S. labor unions and politicians still cling to a vision of the United States as the industrial (i.e., manufacturing) heartland of the world. "Although in these environmentalist times the very label 'smokestack industry' has become pejorative, it is still difficult to visualize the landscape of an economically powerful U.S. somehow devoid of smokestacks or their modern equivalent" (Wojnilower 1985, p. 16).

The debate overlooks a number of economic realities regarding the U.S. economy, not the least of which is the decline in the ability of service exports to offset the massive deficit generated in the merchandise trade account. Too much attention has been paid to subsidizing and contributing to the inefficiencies of manufacturing industries, such as steel and automotive, which are no longer competitive in world markets. As Etzioni (1980) has pointed out, the United States sorely needs to shore up its infrastructure and human capital foundations. If resource allocation is to be debated, let us include services in the debate.

REEVALUATING "REINDUSTRIALIZATION" ARGUMENTS

One of the implicit assumptions in the reindustrialization arguments is that "developed" economic structures remain static over time rather than undergoing a process of continual change. In actuality, economies are continually evolving and changing in response to a variety of factors—e.g., technological advances, demographic shifts, changing consumer expectations. When static measures of sectoral percentage are used, fears in the United States about loss of manufacturing prowess are understandable, as manufacturing has declined as a percentage of GDP. When sectoral growth rates (a dynamic measure) are used, we see that U.S. manufacturing production increased during the 1970s "by an amount equal to or larger than that of any major nation except Japan and Italy" (Schultze 1983, p. 7).

In order to appreciate the fervor with which proponents of "reindustrialization" argue their positions, we need to understand the rationale underlying the positions taken. While economic analysis indicates proposed "reindustrialization" plans are overly simplistic, the issues raised are too important to overlook. Until the realities of service-led growth are understood and fears laid to rest, subsidies and protection of inefficient, out-dated manufacturing industries will continue. As we examine the arguments put forth to defend concern about "deindustrialization," let us not forget the ease with which tangible goods are counted up and pointed to as evidence of productivity while invisible services are taken for granted and overlooked.

Multiplier Effects

In 1984, when the U.S. economy had been service-dependent for at least 25 years, Hewlett-Packard President John Young stated: "A strong manufacturing sector is central to this country's [U.S.'s] ability to compete. We shouldn't point to our surplus in services and convince ourselves that probably everything is going to be all right. Manufacturing is the base that creates many of those services" ("Manufacturing is in flower" 1984, p. 52). Implicit in his comment was the assumption that only manufacturing enterprises have the ability to create multiplier effects throughout an economy.

Western economists have accused the service sector of superseding the manufacturing sector and thereby undermining the vitality of developed economies. It is true that for the Industrial countries percentage GDP in services and percentage GDP in manufacturing are negatively correlated—i.e., as the service sector continues to increase, the percentage of GDP from manufacturing decreases. Such an inverse relationship is not true, though, for the developing countries. For developing countries, the growth of both manufacturing and services occurs concomitantly; further, it is the more rapid growth of the service sector that makes the difference between the High Growth countries and the Low Growth countries.

Looking at another growth indicator—change in per capita GNP—manufacturing GDP is only associated with rising per capita GNP for the Lower-middle-income countries. For the other three country groups, rising per capita GNP is associated with increased *service sector* GDP. In fact, GDP from services is most strongly associated with positive growth in GDP and per capita GNP for the Low-income countries.[5]

Viewing services as unable to generate economic ripple effects overlooks the performance of service industries during times of economic recession. The evidence indicates that many service industries appear "recession resistant"; if affected, they tend to be affected later in the recessionary period and less seriously than manufacturing industries (Minter 1982; Urquhart 1981).

There are a variety of ways in which the ripple effects of service sector growth can be demonstrated. The vast majority of new jobs created in the United States and Europe since the late 1970s have been in the service sector. Using McDonald's as an example, the new jobs it has created have in turn provided "jobs for thousands engaged in farming, meat processing, packaging, equipment manufacturing, and distribution" (Kirkland 1985, p. 42). Those jobs created in the manufacturing sector have been primarily in service functions (Kirkland 1985). In developing countries, when labor moves out of the extractive sector, it moves into both manufacturing and service industries. As we shall discuss in more detail in Chapter 10, it is service sector employment which is correlated with enhanced quality of life.

The U.S. government has estimated that at least 25 percent of goods exports are purchased by international service firms. Detailed data are not readily available for a wide range of countries, but preliminary analysis shows that a large portion of domestic purchases of goods also originates with service firms. Data from Australia are presented in Table 4.7 by way of illustration, showing that 72.6 percent of all manufactured products in 1974-75 were purchased by service sector firms, while 16.7 percent were supplied to other manufacturers and 9.5 percent sold directly to the final consumer.

Another way of illustrating the importance of the service sector as a purchaser of manufactured goods is to look at gross capital formation in the service sector. We have already seen in Chapter 3 that the majority of fixed capital formation has been taking place in the service industries. Recent data from the People's Republic of China are interesting as that country's economic policies (e.g., the Great Leap Forward and the Four Modernizations) have been focused on manufacturing rather than on service sector development. While the growth rate in the manufacturing sector is greater than that of the service sector overall, we can see from Table 4.8 that the fastest rates of capital formation growth have been in service industries—utilities and transportation.

TABLE 4.7
Percentage of Purchasers of
Goods and Services By Economic
Sector (Australia): 1974-75

			Sold By:			
	Extractive Firms		Manufacturing Firms [a]		Services Firms [b]	
Purchased By:	Agriculture	Mining		Transport	Wholesale	Retail
Extractive Firms	3.7%	5.6%	1.2%	1.8%	3.5%	1.2%
Manufacturing Firms	26.3	33.2	16.7	8.0	27.7	1.0
Services Firms	66.0	51.0	72.6	58.3	48.6	6.9
Final Consumer	4.0	10.2	9.5	31.9	20.2	90.9

[a] Utilities are included in manufacturing figures in original source.
[b] Data presented in original source only for these three service subsectors.

Calculated from data in R.A. Layton, "Trade Flows in Australia, 1974-75: An Assessment of Structural Change," *Journal of Macromarketing* 4 (1984): 62-73, Table 5.

TABLE 4.8
Changes in Gross Fixed Capital
Formation by Economic Sector
(People's Republic of China): 1952-79

Economic Sector	Amount (bill Yuan)		Percentage		Average Annual Growth Rate
	1952	1979	1952	1979	
Extractive Sector	¥ .58	¥ 5.79	13.4%	11.6%	8.9%
Manufacturing Sector	1.69	25.69	38.8	51.4	10.6
Service Sector	2.08	18.51	47.8	37.0	8.4
Utilities	.16	2.99	3.8	6.0	11.4
Construction	.09	1.15	2.0	2.2	9.9
Transport/communication	.76	6.41	17.5	12.8	8.2
Commerce	.12	2.06	2.8	4.1	11.1
Science/health	.33	3.35	7.7	6.7	8.9
Other	.62	2.56	14.1	5.1	5.4
Total Economy	¥ 4.36	¥ 44.99			9.5%

Calculated from data in G.C. Chow, *The Chinese Economy* (New York: Harper and Row, 1985), p. 237.

National Self-Sufficiency and Self-Image

As part of the reindustrialization debate, there are a set of related arguments having to do with the need for self-sufficiency and control over one's domestic economy. The United States has been particularly outspoken about the need for national self-sufficiency for defense reasons; however, the United States occupies a relatively unique position. The continental United States occupies a large land mass isolated on two sides by oceans, and has only two neighboring countries with which to maintain borders. The outlying states of Alaska and Hawaii, coupled with U.S. military installations in the Republic of Korea, northern Europe, the Caribbean, and the Mediterranean, allow the United States the possibility of "forward" national defense without endangering the bulk of the country itself.

The United States has not had a war waged inside its borders for over 100 years. One might argue that U.S. concern with national defense issues is more a matter of maintaining an image of preeminence as a world power and the "guardian of the free world" than actual necessity. As William Claybaugh, partner in Space Fund I, commented: "If the Russians have a lunar base in the early nineties and we [U.S.] can't begin to think of doing that until ten years later, you're talking about national phyche, a nation's understanding of itself and its role in the world" (Osborne 1985, p. 45). While traditional military ideology presumes the need for a manufacturing-based self-sufficient economy, absolute self-sufficiency is unnecessary, assuming that strong ties have been built and maintained with allies.

For most nations, self-sufficiency is unrealistic, if not impossible. Many of the new nations, particularly in Africa, were created based on political considerations rather than economic concerns. National boundaries appear haphazard and cut at random across ethnic and cultural groupings. Abundant natural resources to support the economy are the exception rather than the rule.

In the continental United States population density is relatively low, natural resources are abundant (though diminishing), and virtually all of the land is habitable. By contrast, Japan has a population half that of the United States on a land mass less than one-twentieth the size of the United States, only 16 percent of which is habitable. Resource self-sufficiency for Japan is totally unrealistic.

Japan is another illustration of the effect of national self-image on industrial policy. Until recently, the Japanese viewed themselves as relatively poorly endowed in resources and accumulated wealth; hence the wide range of restrictions on imports of capital and goods into the Japanese market. Attachment to "industrial strength" as embodied in key heavy industries allowed a number of lower value-added manufacturing industries to survive past their point of maximum contribution to the economy. Japan is now in the process of moving all such enterprises off-shore and readjusting to services as its coming competitive edge.[6]

SUMMARY

The current furor over reindustrialization has been aptly called "a solution in search of a problem" (Schultze 1983). Concerns over manufacturing erosion stem from a combination of inaccurate economic analysis and an inability to accept the need for continuous economic restructuring in growing economies. For Industrial nations, the result is an unfortunate expenditure of political energy on the wrong issues.

For developing nations, "reindustrialization" advocates can have particularly disastrous consequences. Overemphasis on manufacturing sector development neglects the vital facilitating role played by the service sector. Increased manufacturing production is irrelevant if the products cannot be distributed for sale. More important, overemphasis on the manufacturing sector ignores the clear relationship between sector growth and growth in the whole economy for developing economies.

Those who see manufacturing as *the* economic sector need to be very clear that comparative advantage does not stem from the manufacturing sector for all economies. In an increasingly interdependent global economy, all sectors play their part. Of them all, it is the service sector, not the manufacturing sector, which is indispensable.

NOTES

1. Note that by convention "industry" refers to manufacturing; however, services are also industries.

2. See Appendix A for a definition of the four country samples referred to.

3. While Clark (1940) and Bell (1973) are both explicit in their descriptions of manufacturing as the second stage in development, such a role for the manufacturing sector is also implied in Rostow (1971).

4. For a more detailed exposition of these concepts, see D.I. Riddle and M.H. Sours, "Service industries as growth leaders in the Pacific Basin: The role of managerial assumptions" (Paper presented at the Pan-Pacific Conference: A Business, Economic and Technological Exchange, Honolulu, March 1984).

5. A study of Gibralter's economy has confirmed the positive ripple effects from the service sector by demonstrating that the income multiplier effects for services—particularly communications and finance—are stronger than those for the manufacturing sector (Fletcher and Snee 1982).

6. In the Japanese economic literature, the term "softnomics" is being used to refer to service-oriented economic policies. See, for example, JETRO, *Softnomics: The Service-Oriented Economy of Japan* (Tokyo: JETRO, 1984).

PART TWO
SERVICES IN GLOBAL MARKETS

Assumptions about service delivery have blinded many analysts to the global trends which are occurring in the service sector. Most of the major multinationals either have services as their major focus or have diversified into services to decrease their vulnerability to recessionary trends. Multinationals from the developing countries are increasingly active in services, particularly consulting and hospitality services. The service sector is becoming both more globalized and more specialized.

Along with the joys of potential economies of scale and wider markets have come the sorrows of trying to cope with cultural differences in attitudes toward service sector development and service delivery to the customer. In attempting to adapt worldwide, a variety of strategies are emerging. In Chapter 5, we analyze international services trade and the measurement problems which exist. In Chapter 6, we develop the concept of the service purchase bundle as a model for delivering services effectively, for understanding the kinds of competitive changes now occurring domestically and internationally in services, and for describing the kinds of ongoing changes which we can anticipate in the service sector. Finally, in Chapter 7, we review the role of culture in expectations regarding services and in service sector development.

5

PERSPECTIVES ON THE INTERNATIONAL SERVICE SECTOR

Services are traded in response to intermediate rather than to final demand. Viewed in this fashion, services can be seen as providing an essential link among economic agents, both domestically and internationally, that enables the interdependent functioning of domestic and world markets (Sapir and Lutz 1981, p. 23).

New, sophisticated services are changing the way all industries do business and contributing to the transformation of the world economy. . . . Two trends in particular have brought services more to the forefront of economic concern. . . . Today, a growing number of sophisticated manufactured imports require continued service input to keep them in operation; this input in many cases is not available in the importing markets. . . . Second, as economies become more information based . . . knowledge, skills, and information have become increasingly valuable and saleable (*U.S. national study* 1984, p. 9).

Ever since the early 1970s, international trade has been growing rapidly and becoming an increasingly important aspect of national economies. While global Gross Domestic Product has expanded at an average annual compound growth rate of 14.2 percent, both trade in merchandise and trade in services worldwide have had annual growth rates of approximately 20 percent; and foreign direct investment has grown at an annual rate of 23 percent (UNCTAD 1983b). Virtually every country now engages in service trade, including those with the lowest per capita GNP.

107

In fact, a number of developing countries—e.g., Singapore, Egypt, Israel—have a substantial dependence on trade in services.

Unfortunately, trade in services is invisible in more than the sense of being intangible. A nation's "trade balance" traditionally refers to the balance in that nation's current account reported by the International Monetary Fund (IMF) for merchandise (extractive and manufactured goods), rather than to the overall balance for merchandise and services. Summaries of economic statistics (e.g., U.N. *Yearbook of International Trade Statistics*, government publications) often contain detailed information on numerous categories of merchandise trade but little or no disaggregated information on services trade, if indeed services trade ("invisibles") is mentioned at all. Typically, export and import figures are given for commodities and manufactured goods with no indication that other forms of trade also exist.

If information on services *is* presented, the unwary may miss it altogether. *The Economist*, for example, presents summary statistics in each issue, one column of which (labeled "Current Account Balance") does include service transactions. The first column, however, is titled "Trade Balance" and refers only to the merchandise account, although no footnote so indicates. In its annual publication, *The World in Figures*, a ranking of countries by volume of services trade is presented and so identified; however, it follows tables on "world trade" which reflect only merchandise trade.

All too frequently, the data on services trade are reported as net balances (exports/credits minus imports/debits) rather than separately as exports and imports, masking the volume of trade that is occurring. If *The Economist* reports Switzerland as having a trade balance (i.e., merchandise portion of current account) of −$3.6 billion and a current account balance of +$3.5 billion, it is a matter of simple arithmetic to calculate that the services or invisibles portion of the current account must have shown a $7.1 billion surplus. What is not clear is whether Switzerland's $7.1 billion surplus was a result of services trade flows in the billions or trillions.

The traditional categories used to report services trade—shipment, other transport, travel and tourism, other private services—are far too few to capture the complexities of present international services trade, particularly the newer services related to communications technology.[1]

> Many analysts find that several business services (services performed which complement management or operations of a business . . .)

escape the balance of payments accounts entirely. These omitted services include advertising, kinds of insurance, and probably most of the new computer and communications services. Consequently, many analysts believe that the balance of payments, as currently compiled, underestimates the volume of U.S. services trade by as much as 50 percent (Kelley 1985, p. 6).

Missing, too, are any data on direction of trade—i.e., which services are being traded between which countries.

Unfortunately, the data problems that plague national GDP accounts are multiplied in the national current trade accounts. Some of these problems are discussed below; others are more technical and the interested reader is referred to Krommenacker (1984), the UNCTAD report on protectionism (1983), and the various national studies on trade in services that have been undertaken for the GATT.

THE COMPOSITION OF TRADE IN SERVICES

Once one recognizes that services play a substantial role in international trade, the natural questions are, "Which ones? Exported by whom?" The answers to those questions are more difficult to determine than one might suppose. National current accounts are neither comparable nor satisfactorily disaggregated. Based on the data available, however, we can trace some suggestive trends.

Services Exporters and Importers

When we ask who the major players are in services trade, the answer depends upon the manner in which the question is interpreted. From the perspective of sheer volume, the single country which exports the most services is the United States with approximately 12 percent of the world market in 1980. The European Economic Community as a whole, though, was responsible for 47 percent of the world market in 1980. The industrialized market economies by 1981 accounted for 73 percent of all world exports in services and 70 percent of the imports (see Table 5.1). While the industrialized countries dominate international services trade, they also trade mainly with each other.

If we look at services exports as a percentage of GDP—i.e., how dependent an economy is on services exports—the picture shifts. The

TABLE 5.1.
International Trade
in Services: 1981

| Variable | Low Income | Development Category | | |
		Lower Middle	Upper Middle	Industrial
% Total Exports	2%	5%	20%	73%
% Total Imports	3%	8%	19%	70%
Major Exporters (volume)	China India	Egypt Philippines Thailand	Mexico Singapore Jordan	U.S.A. U.K. France
Major Importers (volume)	China India	Indonesia Nigeria Thailand	Mexico S. Africa Yugoslavia	Germany Japan U.S.A.
Major Exporters (as % GDP)	Haiti (6%) Sri Lanka (6%)	Jamaica (15%) Tunisia (13%) Egypt (10%)	Singapore (65%) Jordan (31%) Panama (29%)	Austria (13%) Norway (13%) Belgium (12%)

Calculated from data in the *U.S. National Study on Trade in Services* (455–773–20145). (Washington, D.C.: U.S. Government Printing Office, 1984).

U.S. services exports are only 1.4 percent of GDP, while exports from several of the developing countries—e.g., Singapore, Jordan, Panama—are a substantial portion of each economy. While the Industrial countries may dominate the market, services trade is particularly important to developing economies.

It is also helpful to look at service exports as a percentage of total volume of trade. As we have already seen in Chapter 2 (Table 2.8), the proportion of services in international trade has remained relatively constant for each country group between 1977 and 1981. Table 5.2 shows that the growth rates for services exports in the four country groups are also, statistically speaking, the same across the country groups. Certainly, one could not infer that services were of less interest to developing countries than to industrialized economies. The smaller services trade volumes in developing countries, compared with Industrial countries, are due to having smaller total trade volumes.

Internationally Traded Services

Total trade figures in services are informative, but they leave unanswered the question of what precisely is being traded. We can get a

TABLE 5.2
International Trade Statistics:
1977 and 1981
(millions of US$)

	Development Category			
Variable	*Low Income*	*Lower Middle*	*Upper Middle*	*Industrial*
Average Volume in 1977:				
Services Exports	$150	$278	$1,258	$8,662
Services Imports	200	546	1,328	8,670
Merchandise Exports	807	1,950	4,791	37,562
Merchandise Imports	881	2,029	5,608	38,500
Average Volume in 1981:				
Services Exports	$259	$523	$2,766	$14,513
Services Imports	347	962	3,009	14,460
Merchandise Exports	1,018	3,303	10,216	64,897
Merchandise Imports	1,652	3,715	11,752	65,726
Growth Rates for:				
Services Exports	4.0%	4.3%	5.1%	3.6%
Services Imports	4.7	3.8	4.9	3.6
Merchandise Exports	3.5%	3.6%	4.9%	4.4%
Merchandise Imports	4.7	4.2	4.7	3.7

Calculated from data in the *U.S. National Study on Trade in Services* (455-773-20145). (Washington, D.C.: U.S. Government Printing Office, 1984).

general picture of the composition of trade in services by looking at the major categories in the current accounts for selected countries among the top 25 services exporters (see Table 5.3).

From the breakdown of services exports statistics, we can learn several things. The largest category (and most rapidly growing) is that of "other private services"—consulting, telecommunications, computer services, leasing. No details are given in the IMF accounts so country materials must be examined. The Republic of Korea's substantial exports in this category, for example, are in part from its world leadership in construction/engineering services—having successfully exported the skill it developed during reconstruction after the Korean War to the Middle East when major construction projects began there.

TABLE 5.3
Major Categories of Services Exports
(Selected Countries): 1980

	Categories Used In Balance of Payments Statistics				
Country	*Shipment*	*Other Transport & Passengers*	*Travel & Tourism*	*Other Private Services*	*Total*
Industrial Countries					
United States	9%	35%	27%	29%	100%
United Kingdom	16	30	19	35	100
France	4	32	25	39	100
Germany	16	19	19	46	100
Japan	38	31	4	27	100
Upper-middle-income Countries					
Singapore	9	34	24	33	100
Republic of Korea	20	20	8	52	100
Yugoslavia	10	23	36	31	100
Greece	2	23	44	31	100
Average	14%	28%	23%	36%	

Calculated from data in the *U.S. National Study on Trade in Services* (455-773-20145). (Washington, D.C.: U.S. Government Printing Office, 1984).

"Shipment" is the smallest category of traded services on average—which is interesting in light of popular perceptions of international services trade as tied to the physical exporting of manufactured goods and commodities. Services associated with the distribution of goods typically constitute less than 20 percent of domestic economies or of international service trade, although this percentage may be higher for developing economies (Frank 1981).

PROBLEMS IN MEASURING SERVICES TRADE

Trade in services is difficult to measure because in most instances there is no clear activity at the border to determine that international service transaction has occurred. When exports and imports of services are totalled worldwide, they should be approximately equal, or show a zero balance. Studies have shown that, by 1983, trade in services was under-reported by as much as $100 billion; that is, approximately $100 billion

TABLE 5.4
Global Service Account Balance
Discrepancies By Category:1970-80
(billions of US$)

Category	1970	1975	1980	Change Rate
Shipment & Transport	-$5.1	$15.8	$32.6	-20.4%
Travel	.8	.7	- 1.7	-20.0
Investment	-2.0	-1.0	-11.6	-19.2
Other services	-1.3	-4.0	-16.8	-29.2
Discrepancy Total	-$7.6	-$20.1	-$62.7	

Calculated from data presented in E. Veil, "The World Current Account Discrepancy" (*OECD Occasional Studies*, June 1982), pp. 46-63.

more was reported as imports than was reported as exports—a variance of approximately 30 percent. Table 5.4 shows the increase over time in discrepancies in the various account balances. Shipment and other transportation services have the largest gap between reported exports and imports, but the magnitude of increase in the discrepancy is greatest for the catchall category of "other services."

Veil (1982) has concluded, after a thorough analysis of alternate explanations, that the discrepancies are due to an underreporting of exports rather than timing differences or an underreporting of imports. In some of the national current accounts, the exports may be underreported by as much as 40 percent! Clearly, trade in services is of a much larger volume than is commonly thought, and caution should be exercised in any trade analysis based on the current accounts.

In order to illustrate the implications for international trade negotiations, Table 5.5 presents data on the same service transactions from the accounts of Japan and the United States. We can see immediately that data inconsistencies can result in miscommunications around common trade objectives. Japan would be entering trade negotiations assuming a debit in services trade almost twice as large as that perceived by the United States.

Defining Services Trade

To further complicate matters, there is a lack of agreement regarding what constitutes trade in services, related to questions raised earlier about how to define services. Service products are not simply shipped

TABLE 5.5
Japan/U.S. Bilateral
Services Trade Data: 1980
(millions of US$)

Current Account Category	Japanese Data	U.S. Data	Discrepancy (Japanese-U.S.)	Ratio[a]
Exports to U.S.:				
Shipment & Transport	$4,145	$2,112	$2,033	1.96
Travel	264	185	79	1.43
Investment	3,332	940	2,392	3.54
Other Services	1,885	64	1,821	29.45
Government	1,034	2,871	-1,837	.36
Total Exports	$10,660	$6,172	$4,488	1.73
Imports from U.S.:				
Shipment & Transport	-$5,725	-$1,809	-$3,916	3.16
Travel	-1,787	-774	-1,013	2.31
Investment	-2,931	-4,266	1,335	.69
Other Services	-3,532	-978	-2,554	3.61
Government	-61	-223	162	.28
Total Imports	-$14,036	-$8,050	-$5,986	1.74
Services Trade Balance	-$ 3,376	-$1,878	-$1,498	1.80

[a]Ratios were calculated by dividing the U.S. data into the Japanese data. Identical data would yield a ratio of 1.0.

Adapted from data presented in G.J. Cloney, II, *A Review of Problems Relating to Trade Policy: Use of Balance of Payments Data Describing Trade in Services* (Background paper prepared for the International Chamber of Commerce Commission on Obstacles to Trade in Services, Paris , 1982).

across national borders as is the case with merchandise. In some instances, service production is linked to the comsumer's presence; in others, the service is delivered through communication channels not normally monitored for trade (telephone conversations, postal services).

In defining international trade in services, there are two major issues. The first has to do with how one determines that an international—as opposed to a domestic—transaction has taken place. Since either the producer, the consumer, or the service itself can move, the issue is more complex than it might appear at first glance. The second issue is that of defining which of the international transactions are service transactions.

Determining International Trade in Services

There are two major approaches in the literature on services to defining what constitutes international trade in services: "location" and "ownership." Under the "location" concept (curently used by IMF), international trade occurs only if the two parties involved reside in different countries. Corporations and affiliates are assumed to be residents of the country in which they are operating. Thus, consulting services purchased in Indonesia by a German corporation doing business there would be viewed as a domestic transaction; only the repatriated profit would be considered an international transaction—and would be credited to "investment income" for Germany, with Indonesia debited accordingly. If that same German firm "purchased" its consulting services from its corporate headquarters in Munich, then the entire transaction (not just the profit) would be recorded as an *international* trade, credited to Germany and debited to Indonesia.

Under the "ownership" concept, all activities of foreign-owned firms would be attributed to the country of the owner(s), with the percentages necessary to establish foreign ownership varying by up to 50 percent according to country guidelines. For that same German firm, all service purchases made locally in Indonesia would be considered international trade, while services obtained from Munich would be considered a domestic transaction. In this instance, local purchases would be credited to Indonesia and debited to Germany, while all purchases from Munich would appear only in the national accounts of Germany and not in any balance-of-payments statistics.

Clearly, the conceptual issues are complex. One could argue that the "location" concept is most relevant in defining domestic economic activity. Indeed, such is the rationale for the current definition of Gross Domestic Product as including all economic activity within a nation regardless of the nationality of producers and consumers. The purpose of GDP data is to provide a sense of the intensity of economic activity within a particular country; the national background of the players is irrelevant.

Regarding international trade statistics, however, the issue is to track and describe the flow of funds around the world. The "ownership" concept does so most accurately. When consulting services are purchased in Indonesia, they are purchased (ultimately) with Deutsche Marks—a flow of currency from Germany to Indonesia. When consulting services are purchased from Germany by the German affiliate, there is no ultimate flow of currency outside the country (though it may have been routed through Indonesia).

Determining Service Components of Trade

Another major issue in tracking international transactions is how they are categorized. Virtually every country reporting to the IMF categorizes services sold or bought on the basis of the primary function of the parent firm involved. Borg-Warner, for example, has diversified into armored car transport and retail inventory financing in order to reduce its vulnerability to recessions. Since it is categorized as a manufacturing firm, all of its international transactions—whether manufacturing or services— fall into the merchandise account.

The practical reasons for such accounting practices are clear. To divide all of a corporation's business transactions into service and nonservice activities would require infinitely more paperwork in a context where firms already resist the reporting requirements. Several serious distortions exist, though, given the present accounting methods. Manufacturing diversification into services is increasingly common; thus, to the extent that firms trading in services are controlled by manufacturing parent companies, trade in services is understated. In addition, well over half of the activities of many manufacturing firms are in actuality service activities—marketing, accounting, management, research and development. If these services are traded within a corporate framework but recorded as merchandise trade, trade in services will again be understated.

Forms of Services Transactions

Depending upon how "international services" are defined, virtually any service can become a traded service. Conventions vary widely, however, in what is meant when we talk about trade in services. We can define trade in services based on an exporting model derived from merchandise as referring only to the flow of private service transactions across borders, or we can also add services purchased by consumers who cross borders, by government officials, and by foreign-owned affiliates. Each addition changes the proportion of world trade attributed to the service sector, as we can see in Table 5.6.

Across-the-border Transactions[2]

The most conservative definition of service trade is typically described as that of a producer resident in the country of production and a

TABLE 5.6
Services as a Percentage
of International Trade Based
on Various Definitions: 1980

Definition	World	Industrial Countries	Developing Countries
Across-the-border	10.9%	12.1%	8.6%
Plus Travel	15.1	16.5	10.2
Plus Government	16.4	17.9	11.9
Plus Affiliates	25.8	28.8	16.6

Calculated from figures presented in UNCTAD Secretariat, *Protectionism and Structural Adjustment* (TD/B/941). (Geneva: UNCTAD, 1983b), Table 13.

consumer who resides in a different country, with the service itself crossing the border. Included here would be activities such as freight and passenger transportation, motion picture rental, insurance and reinsurance, communications, and a variety of professional services. Of course, in the case of passenger transport, the consumer physically moves across borders; however, the move is part of the service rather than a precondition to purchasing the service.

The model for this conservative definition is clearly the export of goods, and the underlying concept is that volume of trade can be measured at the border. Services comprised about 8 percent of total trade in 1980 under such a definition.

Travel of Consumer to Producer

In a number of international service transactions, the producer remains in the home country while the consumer (tourist, business person, student, trainee) travels to make the service purchase. The service itself does not cross borders. Since direct contact between consumer and producer is necessary to deliver the service and the producer either elects or must remain in the home country, the consumer must go to the producer. Often, the service is provided simultaneously for the domestic and foreign market by the domestic producer. Tourism is one of the most common examples of such a service transaction, as are the education and training of foreign nationals. Addition of these services—sometimes referred to as "non-traded services"—raises the percentage of services to 15 percent of world trade.

Government as Exporter/Importer

If the expenditures of travelers abroad are to be included in services trade, then it is logical that we also include expenditures by diplomatic and military personnel stationed outside their home countries—which would bring the total percentage to 16 percent of world trade. One problem in categorizing government purchases in services is that these purchases also include the acquisition or sale of military equipment and supplies; however, such sales frequently entail the provision of a service such as training.

Affiliates of Producer

In other instances, direct contact with the consumer is needed or desired but the consumer is either not able or not motivated to leave the domestic environment. Or the consumer may be traveling, in which case both the consumer and the producer are outside their respective home countries. In order to make the sale, the producer must move to the host country, perhaps through an affiliate structure of branches or subsidiaries. Examples include hotels, restaurants, and commercial banks.

Figures on income from foreign affiliates are traditionally reported in the balance of payment accounts as investment income, or "factor services" (i.e., income from a production factor), because capital ownership is involved. The IMF makes no distinction between investment in manufacturing ventures or investment in service operations. Data from the United States suggest that only one-third of foreign direct investment is in service operations; if so, then the contribution from affiliates needs to be lowered appropriately, bringing the total services exports to approximately 15 to 19 percent of world trade—the percentage estimated in Chapter 2 (see Table 2.8).

Implications For Trade Negotiations

Trade among and between countries is generally industry-specific or at least takes place with reference to particular industries. This brings us to another problem regarding trade statistics for services. The statistics maintained by the International Monetary Fund are gathered for the purpose of accounting for payment balances among nations. The data are not collected or reported by industry and hence are not useful in understanding and negotiating industry-specific issues. In Table 5.7, we can see an

TABLE 5.7
Categorization of Insurance
Transactions in the Balance
of Payments Current Account

Service Category	Credit (+)	Debit (–)
Shipment & Transport	Export of merchandise insurance (net premiums)	Claim payments on merchandise insurance exports
Travel	Personal insurance purchased by visitors	Claim payments on personal insurance to visitors
Investment	Earnings of overseas branches & subsidiaries Interest on balances held with nonresident reinsurers	Net interest accruing to nonresidents on life policies with resident insurance companies
Other Services	Exports of nonmerchandise insurance (net premiums) Services provided by resident brokers and adjusters Management services provided to overseas subsidiaries or unrelated firms	Claim payments on nonmerchandise insurance Services provided by nonresident agents, brokers, and adjusters Management services provided by subsidiary or unrelated firms

From G.M. Dickinson, "International Insurance Transactions and the Balance of Payments" (in *Essays in the Economic Theory of Risk and Insurance*, Geneva: Association Internationale Pour L'Etude de L'Economie de L'Assurance, 1978).

example of the difficulties in trying to determine trade volume in a specific industry.

Efforts to negotiate trade in services have understandably been structured along trade guidelines developed for manufactured goods. In many instances, this approach of generalizing from established codes to services has worked well. Multilateral negotiations on barriers to trade in the GATT have historically not been extended to matters of "investment." In the service sector, the distinction between trade and investment is not as useful or as clear-cut as it is for manufactured goods. Since many services require direct contact between consumer and producer, establishment of affiliates—i.e., "investment"—in local markets is a necessity. For affiliates, discrimination in terms of trade is apparent primarily if the local conditions *within* the host country market are examined for preferential treatment to domestic firms, rather than through an examination of trading conditions *between* the two countries.

CHANGES IN SERVICE SECTOR STRUCTURE

One of the major reasons for the large gap between theoretical assumptions about the service sector, particularly in international trade, and actual practices in services is the rapid change that has been occurring since the early 1970s. Assumptions about the amount and kind of contact needed between producers and consumers of services were based on technological limitations that have since disappeared. Current immigration policies, for example, assume that the physical presence of a service provider is necessary, overlooking the large volume of services that can be conducted across borders via telecommunications.

Just as changes have occurred in the manner in which services are to be delivered, so too is the very structure of the service sector changing. While the majority of service firms are still small entrepreneurial enterprises, service multinationals are on the rise. *Fortune* began its annual listing of the largest U.S. service corporations ("The Service 500") in 1983, most of which have international components—e.g., Hospital Corporation of America, Dun and Bradstreet, Holiday Inns, Citicorp, American Express, CIGNA. Table 5.8 gives some comparisons between the largest U.S. industrial/manufacturing firms and the largest U.S. service corporations, showing that U.S. service corporations compare favorably with their manufacturing counterparts in size and profitability. As a matter of fact, the top service corporation has over twice the asset holdings of the top three manufacturing corporations.

Formerly disparate industries are integrating to form a recognizable whole. The concept of "financial industries," to encompass banking, securities brokerage, real estate, and insurance, developed in the 1970s and matured in the early 1980s. In the communications sector, telephone, telegraph, postal, broadcasting, computer, and media services have become integrated under the rubric "telecommunications" and are now being referred to by some as the "information transmission industry."

It is impossible to predict the varieties of new services that will develop other than to say that they will be numerous and most of them cannot now be imagined. Who would have imagined in the 1960s that computers could become so small and inexpensive that, theoretically,

TABLE 5.8
Comparative Data on the
Largest U.S. Service and
Manufacturing Corporations: 1984

Variable	Service Corporation		Manufacturing Corporation	
	Name	Amount (mill US$)	Name	Amount (mill US$)
Assets	Citicorp	$150,586	Exxon	$63,278
	BankAmerica	117,680	GM	52,115
	Fed. Natl. Mortgage	88,359	E.I. du Pont	42,808
Revenues	Sears Roebuck	$38,828	Exxon	$90,854
	Phibro-Salomon	28,911	GM	83,889
	K Mart	21,096	Mobil	56,047
Net Income	Metropolitan	$5,468	IBM	$6,582
	Prudential	4,898	Exxon	5,528
	Aetna Life	2,671	GM	4,517
Earnings Per Share (growth: 1974-84)	Pulte Homes	69%	AM International	66%
	Zayre	54	Hasbro Bradley	66
	Wal-Mart Stores	42	Teledyne	53
Average Return To Investors (1974-84)	Pulte Homes	71%	Advanced Micro	71%
	Humana	58	Prime Computer	66
	Southwest Airlines	54	Hasbro Bradley	64

From "The Fortune 500," *Fortune* (April 29, 1985), pp. 265-316; and "The Fortune Service 500," *Fortune* (June 10, 1985), pp. 175-204.

workers could have their own? Who would have predicted that checking accounts, which in 1984 were still not common in some developing countries, would be replaced by an all purpose debit card good virtually worldwide?

Rather than trying to forecast the rise or decline of particular services, let us look instead at the kinds of forces that result in structural and product changes within the service sector. If we can understand these and begin to note their occurence, we will be in a position to anticipate new shifts that are likely to occur.

The Effect of Information Technology

The Information Revolution has been widely discussed and analyzed—in fact, some writers and speakers substitute "Information

Society" for "Service Society," reflecting the intimate connections that are being forged between high technology, the "information economy," and the service sector (see Figure 5.1). In actuality, what has occurred is a change in the way in which we are able to process information—a change that affects every aspect of the way in which business is conducted.

The relatively low cost and "user friendliness" (ease of use by less skilled workers) of microcomputers has meant that they are proliferating at a rapid rate. From both a cost and use perspective, microcomputer technology is much more accessible to developing economies than was the massive and expensive mainframe computer technology that preceded it. We can anticipate a "leapfrogging" effect, with developing economies able to move directly from paper-based to microcomputer-based management and service delivery. Solar-powered and battery-powered computer equipment will circumvent the previous limitations of undependable power supplies.

Information processing, utilization, and manipulation is a large part of service activities; thus, we would expect the impact on the service sector to be substantial. The most obvious effect has been the increase in capital intensity of service industries. In the United States, information technology may soon revolutionize such traditional areas as income tax reporting by allowing the government to calculate the initial tax returns for taxpayers to approve or amend.[3]

The implications are numerous. In addition to the plethora of new services made possible through technological innovation, the structure of the work environment itself is changing. Firms can offer services directly in a market with no local physical presence through the use of Service 800, which provides the firm with a local phone number and then redirects those calls automatically anywhere in the world.[4] Physical proximity is no longer necessary for joint tasks; in fact, electronic mail and computer bulletin boards can make it easier to keep in touch with colleagues than trying to find someone by wandering around an office. The newer "voice mail" makes it possible to further personalize messages left.

Work can be accomplished at home or off-site on microcomputers and then be transmitted worldwide via phone modems or communication satellites. Countries like Jamaica with large English-speaking populations have positioned themselves to provide "offshore" support staff functions for U.S. multinationals via telecommunication links (Power 1983). Communities and countries can recruit a variety of global service operations, such as credit card verification, to meet employment and development goals.[5]

FIGURE 5.1.
The Interrelationships of the Services, High Technology and Information Sectors in the Private Sector Economy of the United States

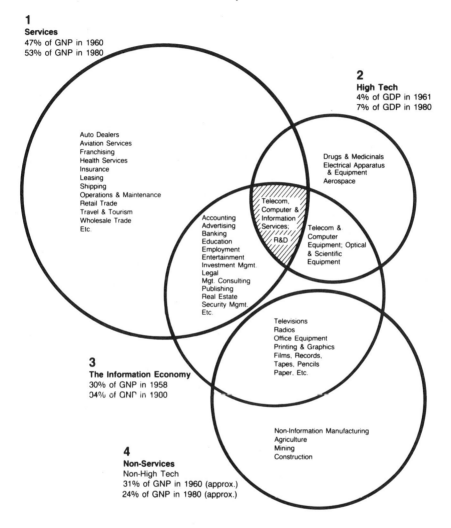

1. Bureau of Economic Affairs, U.S. Department of Commerce.

2. "U.S. loss of comparative advantage in technology: facts and their implication for economic potential in national security." Working draft by Michael Boretsky, U.S. Department of Commerce.

3. According to Michael R. Rubin in a study at press at Princeton University.

4. GDP figures cited in footnote (2) have been subtracted from Bureau of Economic Affairs figures for GNP in the Non-Services sector thus yielding approximations only.

Source: U.S. Department of Commerce, International Trade Administration, Office of Service Industries. Reproduced by permission.

123

With increased transmission effectiveness and lowered costs, teleconferencing is making it possible to reach real-time decisions with input from all concerned. Video transmission allows such decision-making to be based on nonverbal as well as verbal communication, and facilitates personal relationships among firm members who have never met face-to-face. As office systems are automated, many repetitive tasks can be centralized for an entire corporation while still being instantly accessible to branch offices. Financial consolidation of cost centers worldwide can occur virtually instantaneously. All of the above mean potential economies of scale in service management and marketing activities.

One of the effects of automating offices is that the power structures are being affected. Managers are able to perform tasks for themselves that formerly were handled by support staff. It is often faster and more informative for a manager to perform a variety of "what if?" analyses at the computer terminal than to ask staff to generate such reports. Now that individual computers can be connected in a network system, centralized data are readily available to all staff, and support staff are increasingly assigned to maintaining and updating bases rather than to traditional typing and filing tasks. No longer is access to particular information the prerogative of departmental heads; once it is entered in the system, information can be retrieved quickly by anyone tied into the network. Granted that information is power, that power is now spread more equitably across staffing lines.[6]

The implications for service workers are not necessarily positive. While many routine tasks can be computerized, the computer can also be used to monitor performance in an impersonal manner, creating added stress. With increased automation, attempts to influence labor-management negotiations through threatened strikes become less effective if large portions of the work load can simply be transferred electronically to other sites.

> Just as the Industrial Revolution led to task specialization and eliminated the sense of purpose and accomplishment long available to individual cottage workers, so too the new technology could repeat the errors of the past. The new technology can easily be transformed into an instrument of control and regulation that could offset the substantial gains of employee freedom and responsibility (M. Mills 1984, pp. 66–67).

Increased computerization has the positive consequence that workers can be geographically dispersed and still work together effectively. Since dispersal also means that employees and managers can work out of their homes, opportunities open up for many who are physically restricted—e.g., the physically handicapped, parents with small children at home.

The Formal Production of Domestic Services

In terms of lifestyle effects, the movement of domestic functions into the market economy—i.e., from informal to formal production—has had profound implications. Before the availability of appliances to streamline the production of domestic services, daily support activities were provided by outsiders only for the very affluent families. Typically such domestic workers were women who were paid subsistence wages and received few benefits. Paid vacations, 40-hour work weeks, health insurance, and disability or retirement benefits were provided only at the personal whim of the employer. Now franchises, such as Mini Maids of America Inc., have been created, providing adequate pay and benefits to workers as well as quality assurance to customers.[7]

Over the years, food services, laundry and dry cleaning services, and beautician services have become available outside the home for mass markets, providing families with choices between self-production and purchase. As women have entered the external labor force in growing numbers and the number of single parent families has increased, child care services have developed to fill the gap. In some instances, day care programs have been government-mandated and subsidized. In other instances, businesses have realized that worker productivity increased when parents were not worrying about their child's welfare; hence, the increase in business-sponsored child care centers.

As incomes have risen, families have needed or been willing to pay for services produced in the home provided production was dependable and reasonably priced. Catering services are nothing new; the new service activities are in the production and supervision of routine, rather than special, domestic functions. In the United States, for example, there are now firms whose staff will arrive in the morning to wake children, feed them breakfast, and get them off to school. Children can be met after school and taken to appointments for health care or instruction. Homes anywhere in the world can be furnished and maintained. Clothes and gifts can be selected.

Similarly, service firms have developed to handle many aspects of interpersonal relationships. The village matchmaker or solicitous relative is being replaced by computerized dating services not only in Western

European countries but also in developing countries such as People's Republic of China. Traditionally wifely functions of remembering birthdays and anniversaries and gift selection are being replaced for both women and men by specialty firms.

What has happened to the women who used to work only in the home and are now employed outside the home? The vast majority of them are employed in the service sector, though at significantly lower wages than their male counterparts (Springer and Riddle 1985). In the United States, the wage discrepancy is $.59 to every dollar earned by males; in Europe, the discrepancy is $.74 to the dollar. One of the common characteristics of women's positions in the service sector is "emotional labor"—performing the emotional support tasks for strangers, which they used to produce only for their families (Hochschild 1983).

Another issue to bear in mind is that once "domestic" work is produced in the marketplace, it is reckoned into the national accounts and recorded as productive labor. When the same tasks are performed only for the family, they are dismissed as unproductive and the woman is described as "not working." Estimates in the early 1970s indicated that a U.S. mother of three preschool children would merit a starting salary of $12,000, plus benefits, vacation time, and time-and-a-half for overtime, if all of her domestic tasks were valued at the going market rate. Some of the developing countries have recognized the economic importance of women's work and begun including its value in GDP (Blades, Johnston, and Marczewski 1974).

Privatizing Public Services

Cultures differ in the role played by the government in providing services for citizens, ranging from nearly total government monopoly in socialist economies to moderate government involvement in capitalist economies. Across the board, though, there has been a movement toward delegating traditionally public sector services to the private sector. In England and the Federal Republic of Germany, for example, private hospital management companies now operate selected health facilities under contract to the government. In Chile, Health Central has subcontracted the provision of health services to the indigent from the government on a capitation basis (using a health maintenance organization model).

Public services are a peculiar anomaly in the service sector in that they are on a "forced purchase" basis—i.e., we all pay for them whether or not we make use of them. These services can be thought of in two general categories: administrative services necessary to remain a nation, and social overhead services which provide the quality of life desired by the citizens. Administrative services continue, by and large, to be provided by a nation's government—e.g., legislative, judicial, defense services. There are some interesting exceptions, though, such as the subcontracting of prison, security, and surveillance functions.[8]

Social overhead services, on the other hand, have experienced increasing competition from the private sector. Just as private health management corporations now provide an increasing percentage of hospital care, so too private voluntary organizations (often called the "third sector") have been providing a larger proportion of charitable services. Education services, though typically offered free at the primary levels in the public sector, continue to have strong private sector competitors unless such are restricted by governmental regulation. Public health and nutrition services worldwide have competitors such as Weight Watchers International and Nutri/Systems Inc. Control Data, through computerized services, is successfully competing in a variety of programs for the socially disadvantaged.

Critics of public sector efficiency and responsiveness have been pushing successfully for the subcontracting of many social overhead services to private sector companies. In sanitation and waste disposal, for example, private subcontracting is increasing throughout North and South America. Other frequently subcontracted services include maintenance, street cleaning, claims processing, and abandoned car removal.[9] Critics have also been successful in precipitating the dissolution of major government monopolies—for example, American Telephone and Telegraph (U.S.) and Nippon Telegraph and Telephone (Japan)—making way for vigorous private sector competition.

The consequences of blending the public and private sectors are several. Governments can be viewed as large corporations that, as do private-sector corporations, create incentives to attract desired workers and "price" their services to reflect desired outcome. When government is unresponsive to consumer needs, it increases the likelihood of private sector competition. With judicious planning, government officials can focus their attention in the areas where their expertise is most needed, and encourage the private sector—directly or indirectly—to handle other needed services.

SUMMARY

As we examine issues of trade in services more closely, we have seen that there are numerous unresolved issues. At the very least, problems exist in obtaining appropriate and comparable data on services trade. More serious issues include the growing discrepancies in current accounts. If it is true that the service sector can play a dynamic role in the growth strategies of developing countries (see, for example, Baer and Samuelson 1981), then an accurate and comprehensive understanding of the present status of trade in services is essential.

Those currently involved in the ongoing work to measure services trade more accurately need to be sensitive to the ways in which the service sector has changed and will continue to change. Measuring professional services rendered based on work permits issued, for example, is inadequate when a growing volume of such services are delivered via telecommunication links rather than face-to-face. Traditional divisions between domestic and commercial, public and private, are less and less meaningful. Our conceptualizations of how services are delivered and by whom need to be open to continuing revision.

NOTES

1. The IMF (1977) definition of trade specifies that "the changes in economic relationships that the balance of payments registers stem primarily from dealings between two parties; these parties are usually a resident and a nonresident" (p. xv). The categories of services trade reported in the balance of payments are defined as follows:

> Shipping: freight; insurance; other distributive services for goods.
> Other transport: transportation of persons.
> Travel and tourism: goods and services bought by foreign travelers.

Other private services: nonmerchandise insurance; communications; advertising; brokerage; management; foreign periodicals; processing and repair; merchanting; professional and technical services.

2. Cloney (1981) has provided a very thoughtful discussion of types of services traded that parallels the categories discussed in this chapter. His primary distinction is between "across-the-border trade" and "establishment trade." In "across-the-border trade," he includes logistic services for international transport and supply, producer services for foreign production of goods and services, and other directly traded services. In "establishment trade," he includes services provided in the importing country by foreign-controlled producers (affiliates of producer) and services provided in the exporting country to visitors (travel of consumer to producer).

3. See J. Wilke and C.L. Harris, "At the IRS, A Backlog Today—A Revolution Tomorrow," *Business Week* (April 29, 1985), pp. 109; 112.

4. See "International Toll-Free Numbers Boost US Firms' Foreign Business," *Communication News* (August 1984), pp. 36–37.

5. See R. Smith, "Some Unlikely Places Benefit From the Boom in Financial Services," *Wall Street Journal* (March 31, 1983), pp. 11; 17.

6. See P. Nulty, "How Personal Computers Change Managers' Lives," *Fortune* (September 3, 1984), pp. 38–48.

7. See "Paying to Keep the Home Fires Burning," *Business Week* (March 12, 1984), pp. 84; 87.

8. See J.L. Mercer, "Growing Opportunities in Public Service Contracting," *Harvard Business Review* 62 (March-April 1983): 178; 186–187.

9. See I.D. Canton, "Learning to Love the Service Economy," *Harvard Business Review* 63 (May-June 1984): 89–97.

6

THE SERVICE PURCHASE BUNDLE

Obviously it would be helpful to do business in foreign cities without having to have a physical presence there. Enter an international version of the domestic 800 toll-free phone number. . . . Service 800 numbers are local telephone numbers in foreign cities. When prospects or clients dial the local number, the calls are automatically redirected by Service 800 into the subscriber's office in a neighboring country or on the other side of the world ("International toll-free numbers" 1984, p. 36).

As the technology of communication has grown increasingly sophisticated, the needs of traveling executives have evolved as well. . . . more hotels have begun taking an interest in finding how best to help traveling executives, supplying everything from extensive reference material to multiple computer terminals . . . [to] twenty-four-hour currency exchange, twenty-four-hour Telex facilities and language translation—either by employees or by outside services—in German, Italian, Spanish, French, and Japanese.[1]

As services are becoming more international and economies of scale are becoming increasingly possible, the actual content of services received by the customer is also changing. The changes are being fueled not only by technological innovations but also by particular sociological trends. Disposable income worldwide continues to rise as do expectations about standard of living. Consumers are more willing to pay for services that provide more than the basic necessities. Time-savings and convenience have become more highly valued.

The key to success lies, of course, in accurately assessing consumer needs and expectations. It goes without saying that different customers have differing needs that influence both their selection of services and their satisfaction with the service provided. In large part, those needs and expectations are formed by cultural values and mores. The successful service firm is one that is able to modify service delivery techniques, when appropriate, in order to match them to the needs of the customer.

The intangibility of services makes it difficult to articulate what it is that a customer wants from a service purchase. In this chapter and the next, we will be developing the concept of the "purchase bundle" as a model for analyzing services (see Figure 6.1). The "purchase bundle" has both intangible and tangible components, referred to as the implicit service components, the explicit service components, and the facilitating good(s).[2] This chapter is concerned with the purchase bundle itself, while Chapter 7 will explore the cultural dimensions of service delivery.

UNDERSTANDING THE IMPLICIT SERVICE COMPONENT

The implicit service component is the link between customer needs and the form in which those needs can be met. It is the "why" of service delivery, the rationale for organizing service delivery in a particular manner. For example, if a "fast food" chain wants to attract customers with a strong need for convenience, it would need to provide the implicit service component of "ready access" that can then be translated into the explicit form of providing a fast food outlet within a specified distance of the customer.

Identifying Customer Needs

Success in service delivery lies in identifying the relevant customer needs, so that the implicit component required can be matched with the appropriate explicit service component. For example, some bank customers may purchase money market accounts because of a need for savings security, while others may be interested in investment and growth.

Customer needs can be thought of as falling into categories resembling Maslow's (1954) hierarchy of needs. The notion of a literal

FIGURE 6.1
The Service Purchase Bundle

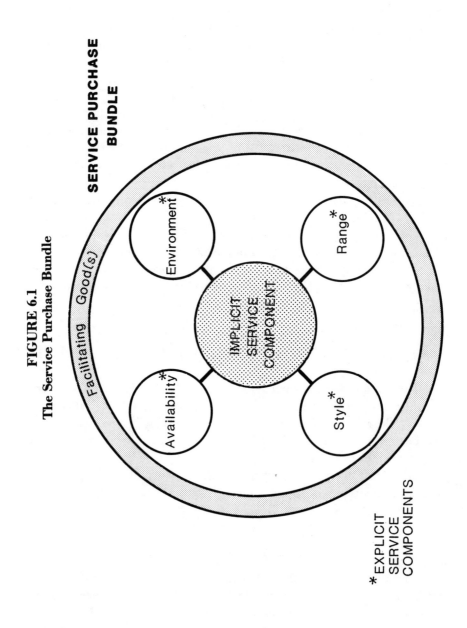

SERVICE PURCHASE
BUNDLE

Facilitating Good(s)

Environment*

Range*

IMPLICIT
SERVICE
COMPONENT

Availability*

Style*

* EXPLICIT
SERVICE
COMPONENTS

hierarchy—i.e., lower needs which must be met before higher ones emerge—has been questioned in the research literature and, in any case, is irrelevant to our conceptualization. What is more important is the fact that these categories of needs exist consistently across cultures and so are useful in conceptualizing international markets.

Comfort

Comfort encompasses the needs for a sense of physical well-being, sensual enjoyment, and freedom from worry. When this need is strong, customers are particularly sensitive to the physical surroundings within which services are delivered. They are also sensitive to maximizing personal convenience. Customers are often willing to pay a premium price in order to have relatively routine tasks handled for them.

Security

Security includes the need to feel physically safe and protected from the possibility of psychological or bodily harm. Also included is the need to feel that one has been treated fairly and is not at risk. Customers often want reassurance that they are receiving the authentic service or that the quality of service will guarantee being problem-free in the future.

Belonging

Belonging represents the need to feel accepted and cared about as part of a group. Customers with a strong belonging need respond well to being treated informally or as "part of the family." Visible evidence of group membership—uniforms, badges—is particularly important in helping meet this need.

Status

Status refers to the need to feel respected as a member of an elite and to be recognized as superior in some manner. While customers with strong belonging needs want to melt into a group, customers with strong status needs want special treatment. Customers respond well to more formal treatment and to any indication of clientele exclusivity.

Autonomy

Autonomy represents the need to feel in control of one's environment and to act on one's own relatively unrestricted. Customers with strong autonomy needs often elect service delivery with a large self-service or customization component.

Self-Actualization

Self-actualization refers to the need for continuing growth and change. Customers with strong self-actualization needs enjoy the opportunity to learn, grow, and contribute to the societal good. Such personal growth often comes through a significant portion of self-service activity.

Customer needs must be accurately identified for successful service delivery to take place. For example, home banking services in the United States have not been widely accepted as concerns about the security of one's account have not been adequately addressed.[3] Presently, there are at least four trends in consumer needs (Partel 1984) as consumers become more affluent which service firms should take into account: the need to leverage financial resources, the need to leverage personal time and effort, the need to plan for the future, and the need for flexibility. Successful service marketing would need to identify which of these needs was salient for the target customer group.

Customer Needs and the Implicit Service Component

The implicit service component is the link between identified consumer needs and the way in which the service is to be delivered. Superior Oil's philosophy about information processing services is a good illustration of such an approach:

> To be truly successful, the information center must be driven by end users' needs . . . our information center is more than a physical location staffed with experts waiting for clients to walk in for assistance; it is a class of service. We have the bulk of our experts working directly with clients in their offices. This approach enables users to more quickly develop insight into our overall operation and acquire a realistic understanding of how our various services can be used to improve their productivity and effectiveness.[4]

TABLE 6.1
Linking Customer Needs
with Implicit Service Components

Customer Need	Alternate Implicit Service Components
Comfort	Readily accessible location
	Luxurious surroundings
Security	Guaranteed availability
	Fair treatment
Belonging	Group membership
	Special codes, uniforms
Status	Member of an elite group
	Special recognition
Autonomy	Self-determination
	Individual attention
Self-Actualization	Altruistic results
	Knowledge enhancement

Each of the needs above can be expressed in a variety of ways as the implicit component of a service delivery system (see Table 6.1). In the fast food industry, convenience could also be translated into the implicit service component of immediate service without waiting, or accessibility during most hours of the day or evening.

The delivery of the implicit service component is subject to tremendous subjective interpretation on the part of the customer owing to both personal and culturally determined expectations. Physical convenience for one customer may mean traveling no further than one-third of a mile if many options are available nearby, while for another three miles may be sufficiently accessible if transportation is readily available and "fast food" outlets are relatively scarce. In one culture, security may stem from having everything taken care of for oneself—"you don't have to worry about a thing"—while in another it may mean being supplied with very detailed information so that one feels in control throughout the service delivery process—"you'll know exactly what's going on."

Customer Assessment of Services

Since implicit services are essentially under the customer's perceptual control, it is important to bear in mind that customers use different strategies to evaluate the level of service being offered for a given price (Sasser, Olsen, and Wyckoff 1978): (1) Some customers evaluate a *single attribute* related to their dominant need at the time. The service will be purchased only if that dominant need is met. (2) Other customers evaluate a single attribute, but are sensitive to *thresholds*, or minimal levels of service addressed to other customer needs. The service is purchased if the dominant need is met, as long as minimally acceptable levels are maintained on other service dimensions. (3) Finally, some customers calculate a subjective *weighted average* of all attributes. The service is purchased if, over all, implicit needs are met better than by another service firm.

The successful service marketer must be able to assess accurately how the firm's customers will be evaluating the service level/price combination. If belonging needs are key, for example, a customer will patronize a more expensive service firm that caters to those needs, rather than a less expensive firm which is extremely impersonal in its service delivery. If, on the other hand, the customer is not particularly sensitive to one need over another, price will play a much more dominant role.

CHANGES OCCURRING IN EXPLICIT SERVICE COMPONENTS

Explicit service components are characteristics of service delivery controlled by the service producer. They constitute how the service is to be offered, as well as which services will be made available. Because services themselves cannot be patented, retaining a competitive edge depends in large part upon a firm's ability to modify its implicit services as needed.

In order to understand and compare the manner in which different services are provided, the explicit services offered can be conceptualized in four categories: (1) *Availability* includes all factors bearing on how easy or difficult it is for the potential customer to gain access to the service. (2) *Environment* refers to the physical appearance of the service facility (including decor themes), the degree of formality with which customers are treated, and the degree of privacy granted to customers. (3) *Style* includes all aspects of the customer-provider interaction, such as how friendly and courteous the provider is, and how much interaction exists between provider and customer. (4) *Range* refers to the variety of services offered, as well as the manner in which they are organized and the degree of customization made available.

Changes in Availability

One of the major changes in the service sector has been in the area of availability of services, fueled by both consumer expectations and technological innovations. In most areas of service delivery, consumers have sufficient selection among service providers to make services a buyer's market. As a consequence, new services are constantly being created. Carson Pirie Scott & Co., for example, has created Corporate Level, a store-within-a-store where the professional woman can find a wide variety of services in one place—from clothes to photocopy services.[5]

Extended Hours

Increasingly, customers are becoming accustomed to 24-hour access to services, at least in modified forms. Food products can be purchased from a range of convenience stores (open 15 to 24 hours a day) in more and more communities. Computerized banking services allow customers to access their accounts at any time of day or night to pay bills or check account balances. If such immediacy in service access does not exist in a market, the most usual reason is that national labor policies forbid the working of late night shifts in nonemergency industries in an attempt to minimize the disruption of family life.

Financial services, in particular, are being transformed by extended access to markets. One of the benefits of the maturing of the telecommunications industry has been the ability to integrate world financial markets. Round-the-clock, real-time trading is now possible in stocks, commodities, and currencies, coupled with instantaneous electronic funds transfer.

Extended Locations

Assumptions about the physical location of services are changing. As corporations think more in terms of world markets, we are seeing changes like VISA machines being available (in hotels, airports, etc.) in a variety of countries, capable of dispensing travelers checks in local currency to customers regardless of the nationality of the bank through which they hold their VISA card. Planning ahead, at least one far-sighted Texas bank has already applied to open a branch office on the moon.

A variety of services are attempting to locate closer and closer to the customer. Western Savings in Arizona, for example, has set up offices in

Smitty's supermarkets—convenient for grocery shoppers and open seven days a week with low incremental overhead. U.S. Project Orbis (in China) and African Medical and Research Foundation (in Kenya) fly doctors in for needed services. Freestanding minor emergency centers typically have multiple sites throughout a community and offer service from 8 a.m. to midnight with no appointment needed at a savings of 40% over traditional hospital emergency rooms.[6] One enterprising service delivers home-cooked meals to customers disembarking from commuter trains, while auto repair services are appearing at airports so that cars can be worked on while customers are out of town.[7]

At the extreme in extended location are the service firms that deliver to the customer in the office or home. Home health care, for example, is a booming business and a great cost savings over hospitalization.[8] Similarly, some corporations are using home health care as a benefit to working parents—lessening absenteeism by providing care for sick children.

Extended Access to Information

Customer expectations are rising in terms of the amount of information they expect to have directly available. European restaurants have traditionally posted their menus outside the front door for customer inspection. Technological changes are making information readily available in new areas. Computerized clearinghouses can inform clients of the lowest available mortgage rates (plus qualify them for loans).[9] Judicial proceedings, which have been notoriously slow and fraught with barriers to information retrieval, now can link the court reporter's stenotype machine with a minicomputer which makes transcription and display on video monitors occur in a matter of moments.[10] Implications include a drastic reduction in the amount of time required to obtain transcripts of testimony (from an average of six months to same-day service) and enabling and hearing-impaired to participate in legal proceedings on an equal basis.

Videotext and teletext are on the rise in Japan, England, France, and the United States.[11] As the systems become more sophisticated and the prices drop, more and more people will be banking, shopping, and handling financial matters from their home. The Japanese plan to connect their entire nation via optical-fiber cables to integrate telephone, data, facsimile, and image communication in an Information Network Service (INS). In addition to the videotext services available through CAPTAIN

TABLE 6.2
Sample Categories of Services
Available in Japan Via CAPTAIN

Category	Daily	Weekly/Monthly	As Needed
		Frequency of Update	
News	General, economic, sports, weather		Earthquake information
Financial	Exchange rates Retail prices Telebanking	Corporate information	Advice; tips Tax guide Economic forecasts
Education		School entrance exam practice, information & reservations	Guide to school selection & loans
Medical			Health tips & treatments Guide to clinic & hospitals
Distribution	Retail prices Teleshopping	Bargain sale guide Entertainment/events	Product information Stores & locations
Transportation	Plane/train seats Hotel vacancies & reservations	Public transportation schedules	Ticket guide Overseas travel procedures
Entertainment	Sports results Concert & theater reservations	Guide to TV, radio Video software Fishing spots	Events guide Games, quizzes

Adapted from H. Taniike, "The CAPTAIN System and Its Services," *Japan Computer Quarterly* 61 (March 1985): 10–41, Table 12.

(see Table 6.2), INS will enable hospitals to monitor patients remotely through reflection-circuit services, and deaf customers to receive hard-copy messages via sketch phones.[12]

Changes in Environment

Service producers have long known that environment can be a powerful marketing tool. The hamburger available in a fast-food outlet can be sold for triple the price in a sit-down restaurant with mood music and elegant furnishings. Customers need to feel that they are getting what they pay for.

Using Environment to Manage Risk

The physical environment exerts a major influence on the customer's initial impression of the service operation. When customers are in the position of purchasing (or contracting to purchase) a service *before* that service is actually produced, such a purchase is perceived as relatively risky. The physical environment can be used effectively to reassure customers of high-quality, consistency, and dependable service.

In franchises, an unfortunate trend of individualizing establishment environments has been developing. What franchises are overlooking is the fact that customers often frequent franchises in foreign countries because they believe they know what to expect when entering the establishment and therefore trust the quality of service to be delivered. The varied environments serve to differentiate one franchise establishment from another, rather than the corporation from its competitors. The consequence is likely to be an undermining of one of the major marketing strengths—i.e., perceived consistent quality of service.

Specialized Facilities

Another trend that we see gaining momentum is the adapting of the physical environment to specific market segments. Making service facilities physically accessible to the differently abled (physically impaired) is only one of a variety of changes occurring. The establishment of "no smoking" areas in restaurants, buses, trains, and airplanes is another example. So, too, is the addition of exercise clubs to hotels in order to appeal to the fitness-conscious client.

As the number of businesswomen increases, hotel chains, such as Ramada Inn, are creating sections of the hotel geared to ensuring physical safety and freedom from harassment. Typically, a floor is designated for women clients, accessible only by special key. Service personnel on the floor are all female, and often a special lounge area is provided where women can eat together, watch television, or visit. Some praise the added ability of women to network effectively in such all-female settings, while others see the sex-segregation as cutting women off even more from the informal "old boy" networks of their male colleagues. Internationally, though, there is a definite market for such facilities among women from sex-segregated backgrounds.

Airlines have adopted a similar tactic by creating special membership clubs in major airports. For a fee, members of clubs, such as the Ambassadors Club (TWA) or Admirals Club (American Airlines), can enjoy more comfortable surroundings while they wait between flights. Amenities include refreshments, newspapers and magazines, financial news wire, conference rooms, and assistance with flight reservations.

Standardized Apparel

The work force also forms part of the physical environment. Standard apparel, such as uniforms, can be used to strengthen brand loyalty, decrease perceived customer risk, and build employee cohesiveness.

> Distinctive apparel makes the service stand out for the consumer. He or she can identify *with* it. This strategy will help to build patronage and customer loyalty. For example, the gold blazers worn by real estate agents in the Century 21 organisation enable this service to be positioned as a national 'brand.' A recent Burger King advertisement depicts an employee sitting next to a McDonald's worker. The identities of the two companies are communicated only by the distinctive uniforms worn by each representative (Solomon 1985, p. 70).

Appearance and Behavior of Clientele

One vital aspect of physical environment in high-contact services is the clientele themselves. Ramada has reflected an awareness of this point by an advertising campaign: "The difference between a good hotel and a fine hotel is determined by the guests." Dress codes in prestigious establishments are an attempt to ensure that the clientele will not detract from the setting. Private schools often maintain their image of status through adopting school uniforms. Club Med has taken a similar approach by providing standard dress for customers in order to ensure a sense of egalitarianism.

Public opinion appears to be swinging more in the direction of personal taste and heterogeneity and to be less accepting of apparently elitist standards used to discriminate on the basis of class or ethnicity. In order to ensure the necessary environment, service firms are moving away from apparent social class cues to the idea of teaching a client appropriate behavior; thus, all customers are welcome, but every effort is made to ensure that those customers will behave appropriately.

Changes in Style

Naisbitt in his book, *Megatrends,* talks about the movement toward "high tech-high touch." Efficiency in service operations typically increases as the amount of contact between producer and customer decreases; however, there is clearly a certain amount of personal contact that is necessary to ensure customer satisfaction. Service firms are handling the challenge of balancing operations efficiency with customer satisfaction in a variety of ways.

Specialization of Function

One of the most common tactics has been to spin-off a customer service function in order to provide interaction with customers at relatively little cost. For years, receptionists and secretaries have served such an interface function—instilling in customers a sense of special attention by remembering names and relevant information. Now we see a growing trend toward the use of paraprofessionals to extend such personalized attention. Paramedical or paralegal staff, whose salaries are quite modest, interact with the client, freeing the high-paid medical or legal professional to perform the needed service without having to take time to interact with the customer.

Self-service

Despite the general need for "high touch," a number of services are successfully increasing the portion of self-service in their product by offering self-service in competition with full-service firms. At times, such self-service behavior is induced through offering savings to the customer—for example, medical self-testing kits, which are cheaper than laboratory services. Services such as Comp-U-Card offer customers substantial discounts on a variety of consumer items; for an annual fee, customers can access the electronic catalog of over 60,000 products to comparison shop and place orders.

At times, the customer is offered no choice but to self-serve. For example, an increasing number of hotels are using billing cards. As the customer inserts the card to gain access to various services—drinks, food, video entertainment, computer usage—the card records the amount of the transaction. At the time of checkout, the card is "read" by the cashier and the customer charged accordingly. We can anticipate that hotels will start differentiating themselves based on the amount of human-contact service provided. In Hong Kong, rapid transit ticketing is all self-service, with automated scanners that record and verify length of trip.

Similarly, IBM has been substituting diagnostic technology, which the customer can activate, for personal service calls to repair mainframe computers or microcomputers. Because sufficient customers prefer personalized service, there is now a flourishing business for other firms in repairing IBM products. Third-party maintenance companies include chains like Computer Doctor Inc. and Serviceland Inc.[13]

Self-service also creates options. Nolo Press is publishing a series of books on "sue-it-yourself"—i.e., self-service legal services. Innovative technology has made it possible to provide a wide range of home health services for persons who might otherwise be hospital-bound or hospital-dependent—e.g., kidney dialysis, cancer chemotherapy, and intravenous feeding.[14] Similarly, home video rental services provide the opportunity to structure leisure time as desired, and include any home-bound persons.

Decoupling of Production from Consumption

Increasing self-service components are illustrations of a more general trend towards decoupling the production of the service from its consumption. In order to decouple effectively, the service firm needs to differentiate between the "high-contact" portion of service delivery (the points of needed interaction between producer and customer) and the "low-contact" portions that can be conducted without the customer present (Chase 1978). Any portion that can become low-contact has the potential for generating increased efficiencies and economies of scale. Most self-service gas stations are still dependent on producer-customer interaction for collecting payment; but in Switzerland, true decoupling has occurred with the introduction of gas pumps activated by credit card.

Mail-order services, as an historic example of decoupling, have made it possible for customers in rural communities to purchase the same range of products available in large metropolitan stores. Now the variety of mail-order services has mushroomed into a multimillion-dollar business, offering items ranging from general clothing merchandise to specialty gifts and labor-saving devices.[15] Toll-free "800" numbers answered by computers are making it possible to order by phone, often around the clock, without having to have staff available. The timing of order-processing can be kept separate from the placing of those orders.

"Industrialization" of Delivery

In a number of service industries, the combination of new technologies and increased business volume is making it economical to create ways in which to routinize and standardize service delivery.

Levitt (1972) was one of the first to analyze the potential savings for service operations in applying the production line approach. The method employed in the Soviet Union for performing a radical keratotomy (an operation to correct nearsightedness) is an interesting example of a "production line" approach in a field not usually thought of as appropriate.[16] An assembly line of five surgeons is used to perform various portions of the surgery, enabling the team to operate on over 100 patients in a day. While such an approach may seem dehumanizing, the negative aspect is offset by the reduction in fixed costs per operation, which makes it possible then to provide the service to a wider range of persons. The introduction of robots may further routinize and standardize such surgery.

Changes in Range

The range and variety of possible service products is limited only by our imagination. For example, new computer technology has spawned services in software design, microcomputer rental, computer lending from libraries, coin-operated computers in airports and hotels, computer-fraud insurance, and special Club Med vacation packages to become computer literate while tanning.

Service Supermarkets

One of the recent trends in Industrial economies has been toward "one-stop shopping." Just as department stores and grocery supermarkets (or hypermarkets) have traditionally brought together a wide range of goods for purchase, service supermarkets are bringing together a wide range of services under one roof. The term is most commonly used in reference to the financial supermarkets which have developed—such as the Sears financial network of stock brokers (Dean Witter), real estate (Coldwell Banker), and insurance agents (Allstate).

Other forms have developed and continue to do so. For example, integrated health services, like the health maintenance organizations (offering medical, dental, psychological, laboratory, pharmacy, and X-ray services in a coordinated package) are linking with hospitals, home health care, and medical equipment rental firms to provide one-stop health care.[17] Amusement parks can be viewed as traditional forms of a recreational supermarket, while shopping malls have become the super-supermarket.

Specialty Firms

As the complexity of economies increases and demand for a particular service grows, specialty service firms emerge. For example, there are now investment banks which do not deal in cash at all, only in electronic funds transfer. Pediatric services have begun to specialize in well-child, acutely ill, or chronically ill care. Many of the top-of-the-line specialty services depend upon referrals from generalists and thus can survive only if the volume of generalist business reaches a critical mass.

At the other extreme, we find a proliferation of discount services—discount brokers, warehouse clubs, airlines—offering "no frills" service at a reduced price. Such discount services are successful only if the lower service level is clearly offset by price savings.

Customization

A final trend in product lines is toward an increase in the service content. Wendy's advertises, "Have it your way." Firms in India, for example, have carved out a market niche in customizing standard software packages to fit the needs of their business customers. Tour buses now offer "customized" service via earphones which can be tuned to pick up taped commentary in any one of a variety of languages.

Again, technological advances offer numerous possibilities for customized service with little contact between provider and customer. Want to get really involved in the story you are reading or the movie you are watching? With the help of programmed fiction, you can try to solve a mystery within an alloted time period; and Nippon Electric has created an "interactive theater" in which the viewers determine the movie's outcome.[18] Want to get an education or some executive training? "Electronic universities", such as the U.S. TeleLearning or the Japanese Hoso Daigaku, will provide you with a wide variety of correspondence courses via telecommunications, including individual consultation with the instructor.[19]

MATCHING EXPLICIT SERVICES TO CUSTOMER NEEDS

The matching of implicit needs with explicit service components lies at the heart of successful service delivery. In Table 6.3, we can see a comparison of two airline services (People Express and Regent Air), each

TABLE 6.3
Matching Implicit Needs
with Explicit Service Components

Purchase Bundle	People Express	Regent Air
Implicit Needs	Security	Comfort Status
Implicit Service Component	No other fare lower	All comforts provided Exclusive environment
Explicit Service Component		
Availability	Reservations and terminal locations moderately inaccessible	Door-to-door service
Environment	Spartan	Luxurious, with private compartments Passengers limited to optimal number for right atmosphere
Style	Impersonal service	Personalized, attentive service
Range	Basic transport, with optional services a la carte	Transport, plus bundled services: videocassette library, business staff and equipment, phone, financial wire, barber

targeting a different portion of the market with different needs. People Express is one of a growing number of "no-frills" airlines. It has assumed that its customers' primary need is for security—getting the best price possible. Its 1984 coast-to-coast fare in the United States was under $300, with all services offered separately. Customers pay extra for refreshments and baggage handling. Overhead is kept low, with the result that reservation lines are often busy so that access is difficult. The general "stripped down" atmosphere helps reinforce the idea that People Express is not wasting money on nonessentials.

Regent Air has positioned itself quite differently, at a 1984 price of approximately $1,500 coast-to-coast in the United States. It is catering to comfort and status needs and therefore offers a full range of personalized services bundled into the ticket price. Carrying the optimum passenger number and mix in order to generate a luxurious, pampered environment is more important than selling every seat.

A variety of other examples could be given. American Express, seeing an unmet status need, introduced its gold card with a substantial premium attached. The Four Seasons, the Canadian company which entered the U.S. market in 1976, caters to persons with comfort and status needs with "an almost obsessive emphasis on customer service. Each hotel keeps meticulous guest histories, so that on a return visit a guest automatically gets his favorite view, soap, or type of pillow."[20]

THE GROWING IMPORTANCE OF FACILITATING GOODS

The *facilitating good* is the tangible representation to the customer of the service provided. It is not essential to service delivery but is a major aid in successfully marketing a service and ensuring repeat purchase. The facilitating good symbolizes the transaction for the customer—provides the visible wrapping, if you will. It is typically a physical object that the customer can keep, such as an imprinted match book, a concert program, or a consultant's printed report.

The usefulness of facilitating goods has not been fully understood or exploited. Most facilitating goods relate to the service provided in a passive manner—giving address and phone number—if at all. They may be witty, as in the case of chiropractor's pens which are bent crooked. Very few actually capture the flavor of the service delivery experience itself. Facilitating goods are like the wrapping on a package and should be used to continue the type of mood created by the explicit service components. Diplomas are an example of an effective facilitating good.

Distinguishing Facilitating Goods From Equipment

In understanding the role of physical objects in service production, a particularly important distinction to keep in mind is the difference between the tangible facilitating good representing the service and the tangible equipment used to produce that service. Airplanes, for example, are manufactured goods that are then used as equipment in providing transportation services. One's plane ticket is a facilitating good—a tangible but symbolic representation of the service purchased. Similarly, the durable goods rented to customers and the goods sold by retailers comprise the equipment and supplies used to deliver the service. Receipts of purchase, warranty contracts, or retail credit cards are all facilitating goods.

What is the difference between a physical object that is a manufactured product used as equipment and a physical object that is a service facilitating good? The answer lies in its primary purpose. If the primary purpose is the creation or production of a service, then it is equipment. If its purpose is to represent or document a service that has been or is to be provided, then it is a facilitating good. A credit card, for example, serves a symbolic function as a facilitating good. In order to use one's credit, all that is needed is the account number for reference purposes, not the card.

Facilitating Goods As Risk Reducers

In their symbolic function, facilitating goods can play an important role in helping reduce perceived risk. If you buy a refrigerator with a five-year warranty, that warranty of free maintenance service is linked to the record of sales; however, you will feel more certain that you can make use of that service if you have a written warranty for your own records. Similarly, insurance policies, educational achievements, and hotel reservations all depend upon verification in the firm's records, not simply on a written piece of paper; but customers typically feel more certain that they have received value for their money if they have written confirmation.

As more and more services are purchased from strangers, the facilitating good plays an important role in reinforcing a sense of stability and dependability. Since one does not know if the producer's word only can be trusted, written documentation provides a sense of security.

Facilitating Goods As Service Facilitators

Tangible service representations can also be used effectively to streamline service delivery. Airline boarding passes, held by the customer, both reassure the customer and speed up the loading of planes. Indian Airlines, for example, has taken this process another step by color-coding boarding passes so that passengers on each flight are readily identifiable to themselves and to the airline.

Physical credit cards, while theoretically unnecessary, decrease the likelihood of fraudulent transactions. They are now being used to facilitate a variety of other service operations. For example, pay telephones with the mechanism for "reading" an inserted credit card eliminates the need for a long-distance operator to intervene in order to handle billing. Hong Kong has pioneered the "easy pay system" where bankcards can be used to immediately debit bank accounts without needing to handle cash or write up credit card purchases.

SUMMARY

The purchase bundle is an essential model for understanding service delivery. The implicit service components link customer needs with explicit services so that the appropriate service is produced. The service offering can then be symbolized in the facilitating good(s).

As the market for services continues growing, successful companies need to continually adapt the explicit service components (availability, environment, style, and range) to fit the changing needs and expectations of consumers. Key among the changes is the trend to increase the time and place utility offered. Decoupling of production and consumption, along with increased possibilities for self-service, are providing more opportunities for economies of scale.

Firms need to be particularly conscious of avoiding changes that enhance, rather than decrease, the perceived riskiness of the purchase. Franchises that fail to capitalize on a standard physical environment and firms that make little (or inappropriate) use of facilitating goods are likely to lose their competitive positions.

NOTES

1. From J.E. Lasky and J.W. Henderson, "Luxury Hotels Are Taking Care of Business," *Republic Scene* (December 1983), pp. 10; 12.

2. The concept of the purchase bundle as presented in this chapter draws on the following published sources: W.E. Sasser, R.P. Olsen, and D.D. Wyckoff, *Management of Service Operations* (Boston: Allyn and Bacon, 1978); L. Shostack, "Breaking Free from Product Marketing," *Journal of Marketing* 41 (April 1977): 78–80. I am also indebted to Jack Burlin and his paper "A More Useful Purchase Bundle Model" which he submitted in April 1982 for my course on global service delivery.

3. See D.F. Salisbury, "Home Banking, Now Past Experimental Stage, Gains Popularity," *Christian Science Monitor* (April 3, 1985), p. 7.

4. From J. Worley, "A Class of Service," *Infosystems* (January 1985), pp. 72; 74.

5. See J.E. Daily, "One-Stop Shopping for the Woman on the Go," *Business Week* (March 18, 1985), p. 116.

6. See J.C. Casey, "Freestanding Clinics: Less Expensive, Less Crowded," *Advertising Age* (March 9, 1981), p. S-10.

7. See "Paying to Keep the Home Fires Burning," *Business Week* (March 12, 1984), pp. 84; 87; L.M. Schultze, "Busy, Busy, Busy," *INC.* (May 1984), pp. 46; 50.

8. See "The Insurers' Big Push For Home Health Care," *Business Week* (May 28, 1984), pp. 128; 130.

9. See T. Watterson, "Pinning Down Low Rate on a Home Mortgage Via Computer Clearinghouse," *Christian Science Monitor* (June 19, 1985), pp. 19–20.

10. See C.J. Sitomer, "A Glimpse Inside the Electronic Courtroom of the Future," *Christian Science Monitor* (March 22, 1985), pp. 23–24.

11. Videotext is a two-way interactive exchange, using two-way cable or phone lines to connect television screens with a central computer. Teletext is a noninteractive transmission of electronic data to television screens in the vertical blanking interval of standard television broadcasting. For brief overviews of the industry, see M.C. Inoussa, "Videotext and Teletext" in *1985 US Industrial Outlook* (Washington, D.C.: U.S. Government Printing Office, 1985); "Viewing Satellite Advertising Through a Crystal Ball," *Advertising World* (February/March 1984), pp. 18–20.

12. See N. Hashimoto, "Japan Packs Its Telephone Technology in One Trunk," *Christian Science Monitor* (January 29, 1985), p. 8; T. Murakami, "Inception of INS Experience: Model System Sets in Service," *Japan Telecommunications Review* 27 (January 1985): 3–25.

13. See A. Ramirez, "A New Industry Is Fixing to Fix Your Personal Computer," *Fortune* (March 18, 1985), pp. 150–152; 156.

14. See "The Robust New Business In Home Health Care," *Business Week* (June 13, 1983), pp. 96; 100.

15. See M.J. Williams, "Glut and Gluttony in the Mail Order Business," *Fortune* (July 9, 1984), p. 126.

16. See "The Radical Eye Operation That's Becoming Routine," *Business Week* (April 22, 1985), pp. 90–91.

17. See J.A. Sasseen, "Quality Care's Bid to Stand Out in the Crowd," *Business Week* (July 22, 1985), p. 87.

18. See P. Elmer-DeWitt, "Putting Fiction on a Floppy," *Time* (December 5, 1983), p. 76; "Japan's Expo '85 Is a Garden of Gadgets," *Fortune* (April 15, 1985), pp. 40–47.

19. See P. Osterlund, "Japan's University of the Air Beams Learning to Masses," *Christian Science Monitor* (May 3, 1985), pp. 23–24); D.F. Salisbury, "Entering the Age of the Electronic University," *Christian Science Monitor* (March 26, 1985), pp. 25–26; "A Wizard's Plan For an 'Electronic University'," *Business Week* (March 19, 1984), p. 60.

20. From "Four Seasons Finds Room in a Crowded Market," *Business Week* (April 2, 1984), p. 85.

7

THE INTERACTION OF
CULTURE AND SERVICES

... the value of one-stop [supermarket] shopping in an
LDC environment is not clear. . . . the LDC environment is
characterized by supply difficulties, high variability
in . . . quality . . . and the need for credit. . . . A consumer
may be beter off maintaining a flexibility of choice among
different types of stores, thus maximizing the opportunities
to get the best buys (Goldman 1981, p. 21).

... this Marxian concept of nonproductive work [referring
to services] has blinded many prominent people in the
Soviet Union to an understanding of the fundamental concept of . . . the productivity involved in providing a good
system of links among economic units (Ofer 1973, p. 156).

Virtually no research exists on the interaction of culture and services. Most studies of the service sector either have focused within a country, where cultural differences would be presumed not to occur, or have
focused on comparisons among countries on macroeconomic variables
generally considered to be independent of cultural considerations. Anec-
dotal data exist to underscore to the unwary the dangers of importing services to a foreign culture without any attempts to adapt to that culture's
values and customs, but they consist primarily of marketing do's and
don'ts.

In defining services initially, we highlighted the importance of the
relationship between the producer of the service and the customer. The
international production of goods occurs relatively unaffected by cultural
differences when compared with the degree of cultural sensitivity needed

151

to successfully trade in services. Cultural values determine when self-service is appropriate, from whom customers will accept services, and how much control the customer will expect to exercise in the transaction. Similarly, cultural philosophies dictate in what manner the service sector will be developed, the role played by public services, and the accessibility of services by the general populace.

The material in this chapter is intended to be suggestive rather than definitive, provocative rather than authoritative. We are still neophytes in conceptualizing global markets and economies. Who is to say which cultural differences will and should survive the rapid diffusion of cultural material around the world? Perhaps we will indeed end up with one homogenized global culture. I think not. Core beliefs and ways of thinking do not change easily. It is much more likely that practices will continue to be adapted to indigenous cultural norms, from which will come new ideas and service delivery styles to be tried in other markets.

DIMENSIONS OF CULTURAL DIFFERENCE

Cultural differences are very real, but generalizing about them is becoming more and more difficult. Few cultures are entirely homogeneous any longer. Within a given culture, value differences and dissimilar behavioral expectations exist based on gender, ethnicity, religion, social class, and geographic area (urban-rural, mountains-plains). In addition, more and more people have traveled outside their own culture or have had exposure through the media to the values and norms of other cultures. Any general cultural differences, then, will be mediated by subcultural identity, life experience, and personality traits.

In order to understand the effects of culture on service delivery, we first need to articulate a model for understanding and anticipating cultural differences. Three different kinds of cultural values research traditions—Hall (1959), Hofstede (1984), and Kluckhohn and Strodtbeck (1960)—are useful in explaining aspects of the relationship between culture and service delivery. None is definitive, especially in view of the profound changes occurring in many societies. Hall and Hofstede are particularly helpful in categorizing cultures, while the Kluckhohn-Strodtbeck model provides us with dimensions along which to describe the similarities and differences among the country groups.

Categorization of Cultures

Hall's distinction between "high-context" and "low-context" cultures, while simplistic, is nevertheless one of the most useful. High-context cultures are those in which interactions between persons depend primarily upon contextual, or nonverbal, cues rather than on explicit verbal communication. Shared values and assumptions are essential in order to interpret accurately interpersonal interactions. The guiding principle in a high-context culture is the maintenance of interpersonal relationships and group welfare; if necessary, task completion will be postponed or abandoned.

Low-context cultures are those which rely primarily on explicit verbal communication, often to the exclusion of nonverbal cues. Value is placed first and foremost on task completion, and individual ambitions are at least as important as group relations. The individuals in any interaction are often interchangeable—i.e., successful task completion does not depend upon particular interpersonal relationships.

Hofstede's work, although not explicitly linked to that of Hall, can be thought of as an expansion and explication of Hall's more basic dualism. Hofstede has ranked cultures along four dimensions: power distance (PDI), individualism (IDV), uncertainty avoidance (UAI), and masculinity (MAS). The first three will concern us here; the fourth will be discussed in Chapter 10.

The first dimension is "power distance" (PDI), or the extent to which clear hierarchies are maintained. In high PDI cultures, differences in social status and privilege are assumed and strangers are distrusted as potential disrupters of the status hierarchy. In low PDI cultures, the ideology emphasizes the minimization of inequalities in power and privilege.

The second dimension is "individualism" (IDV), or the extent to which individual versus group needs are the focus. In high IDV cultures, persons are expected to look out for themselves, and autonomy is highly valued. In low IDV cultures, individualism is seen as alienating; people are defined by kinship connections, and group welfare comes before personal interests.

The third dimension is "uncertainty avoidance" (UAI), or the degree to which ambiguous situations are tolerated. In high UAI cultures, careful observance of rules is expected and valued, and persons feel a continuing stress to perform correctly. In low UAI cultures, the pressure to conform is relatively low and rules are seen as open to interpretation rather than to be adhered to blindly.

We can combine the dimensions suggested by Hofstede with the high-/low-context continuum of Hall to give a more complex illustration of the similarities and differences among cultures (see Table 7.1). The high-context category is most similar to high PDI/low IDV while the low-context category is most similar to low PDI/high IDV. The interim category—high PDI/high IDV—corresponds to a distinction made by Laurent (1983) between "social" European cultures (in which power is based on social status) and "functional" European cultures (in which power is based on expertise). "Functional" cultures include the same group of cultures as does the low-context, high PDI/low IDV group. One implication of the chart in Table 7.1 is immediately clear—there is no one best culture. In each category, there are nations that have been successful economically.

Value Dimensions

The Kluckhohn-Strodtbeck model shown in Table 7.2 is one of the most useful in understanding the variety of dimensions, in addition to those tested by Hofstede, along which cultures differ. Their purpose was to take the themes common to all cultures and illustrate different cultural variations. We can use countries from Table 7.1 to illustrate how countries may be similar or different along each of the dimensions. For example, Sweden and the United States are quite similar in their temporal

TABLE 7.1.
Categorization of
Cultures

	Low-context		High-context
	Low Power Distance High Individualism	High Power Distance High Individualism	High Power Distance Low Individualism
Low Uncertainty Avoidance	Great Britain Sweden United States	South Africa	Hong Kong India Singapore
High Uncertainty Avoidance	Austria Germany (F.R.) Switzerland	Belgium France Spain	Brazil Greece Japan

Adapted from E.T. Hall, *The Silent Language* (New York: Doubleday and Company, 1959); G. Hofstede, *Culture's Consequences: International Differences in Work-Related Values* (Beverly Hills: Sage Publications, 1984).

TABLE 7.2
Cultural Differences
Along Value Dimensions

Value Dimension	Cultural Variations		
Relationship with Nature	Controlled by nature	In harmony with with nature	Mastery over nature
Temporal Orientation	Tradition-oriented	Situation-oriented	Goal-oriented
Activity Orientation	"Being"; experiencing	Inner development	Task accomplishment
Relationship with others	Patriarchal	Collective	Individualistic

Adapted from F. Kluckhohn and F. Strodtbeck, *Variations in Value Orientations* (Evanston, IL: Row, Peterson and Co., 1960).

orientation and valuing of change, while Japan and India have in common more of a temporal orientation towards tradition. However, the United States is more individualistic than Sweden; and Japan is more task-accomplishment oriented than India, which is more "being" oriented. So cultural similarities or differences depend upon the value dimension under consideration.

Relationship with Nature

Cultures differ in the extent to which they value a personal sense of mastery and control. The U.S. culture, for example, is founded on the premise that change is good and that virtually all circumstances can be changed through personal initiative. At the other extreme are cultures like India where circumstances are believed to be preordained and beyond human control. The Japanese share the U.S. sense that change is possible, but believe that all change should be undertaken cautiously in order not to disrupt a harmonious balance.

There are two major issues here for service industries: (1) To what extent do customers hold the service producer responsible for consequences? and (2) To what extent do customers expect to exercise control in the service delivery process? For residents of cultures in which transportation, for example, is very dependable and persons can consequently control their time schedules, the unpredictability of transportation systems in many countries may be excessively irritating. On the other hand, a slogan like Wendy's "Have it your way," can offer an unfamiliar and seemingly oppressive array of choices.

Time Orientation

Related to the degree of control one expects to exercise is the degree of urgency one experiences when expected time schedules are not met. In "goal-oriented" cultures, time is viewed as absolute (e.g., "we will meet at 3 p.m." means at 3 p.m.) and a scarce commodity. Note here an interesting paradox: While "mastery" cultures are typically also goal-oriented cultures, this time sense reflects a subjective feeling of being *controlled by* or at the mercy of an external time schedule that one is not free to change. Change itself is valued—except for changes in time schedules.

In traditional cultures, time is typically experienced as more relative (e.g., "we will meet at 3 p.m." means we will meet after all of the activities which occur before 3 p.m. are completed). One has much more the sense of taking as much time as is necessary—usually in order not to cut short interpersonal relating. Low-context service delivery styles are seen in high-context cultures as superficial and lacking in depth—too rushed. Similarly, holiday celebrations with family and friends take precedence over keeping offices open; thus, in more traditional cultures, there are likely to be more holidays on which business stops altogether.

An important concomitant of high-context cultures is a commitment to long-range vision. Service provision takes place within a historical context beyond that of the immediate relationship. Past inequities or kindnesses remain fresh in one's memory, as if they had occurred yesterday, and present behavior is always interpreted in such a historical context. Similarly, patience and perserverance in planning for the future are valued. Lasting benefits are seen to accrue over time. Decisions are not to be rushed as they must be based on mutual respect and trust, and the consequences will be binding into the future.

In low-context cultures, the time line is much more circumscribed. The focus tends to be on short-term change and short-term gain. "Let bygones be bygones" is a familiar U.S. saying. What is important is tomorrow, not yesterday. Since U.S. executives change jobs on an average of every five years, what is important to them is a short-term success that can be clearly attributed to themselves. As long as contracts exist to enforce agreements, mutual respect and trust are irrelevant, especially as the parties to the original agreement may not necessarily remain to carry it out.

Another difference in approach has to do with queuing traditions in service operations and their consequences. Many of the Western European cultures are geared to sequential service delivery—one waits one's turn, and then one gets exclusive attention. In Asian and Middle Eastern cultures, there is frequently more of a sense that time of arrival does not necessarily dictate when one is to be served and that a number of customers can be accommodated simultaneously. In low-context cultures, though, "simultaneous" production of services is often interpreted as a lack of respect for the customer. It is as though the customer owned a particular block of time and therefore could command the provider's undivided attention during that period.

Activity Orientation

A primary difference among cultures has to do with the pragmatism versus aesthetics distinction. In "doing" cultures, the focus is on getting things done as efficiently as possible. Physical environments are structured to be utilitarian, to enhance customer flow, with aesthetic considerations less important. Rapid turnover and handling high volume are crucial.

In "being" cultures, the quality of the experience is uppermost. One should not be simply a nameless customer processed through the system, but rather should be acknowledged and interacted with. The physical environment should delight the senses and create a spiritual experience. Here the difference is often expressed as "working to live" versus "living to work."

Related to the concept of activity orientation are issues involving perceived responsibility differences. Within the high-context culture, responsibility resides with the most senior person. Commitment and responsibility are very generally defined so that the superior becomes responsible for all unforeseen circumstances (see, for example, Lohr 1982). Since relationships between superiors and subordinates are nurturant/dependent (Sinha 1980), the superior assumes a parental-type authority. If the subordinate does not perform properly, blame rests with the superior for requiring the subordinate to handle a task for which he was not fully prepared. At the same time, subordinates feel guilty for embarrassing the superior if they do not perform well and are strongly motivated to please the superior. Thus, the superior is supported by the loyalty of the subordinates, all of whom feel responsible for the superior's and the firm's success.

By contrast, in low-context societies, responsibility resides with the individual directly discharging the task, not with the superior. Commitment and responsibility are limited both in time and scope to explicit contractual arrangements. If individuals do not perform well, they are disciplined or fired. The corporation, and its senior executives, are absolved of further responsibility once the blame has been fixed and the culprit dealt with. Further, relationships between superiors and subordinates are defined by the organizational chart and so are job specific and carry limited liability.

Thus, major differences exist between the two types of cultures in how responsibility is viewed and attributed. Executives in the United States, for example, will feel that once they have "taken responsibility" and given it their "best effort," nothing further is expected. They will not understand their Japanese counterpart's apparent unwillingness to assume responsibility without careful thought and consultation. Japanese executives, on the other hand, will view their U.S. counterparts as naive in their ready assumption of personal responsibility and will expect them to be held responsible *no matter what happens*. Past events remain fresh in one's memory, as if they had occurred yesterday, and present behavior is always interpreted in such a historical context.

Relations with Others

A final value dimension along which cultures differ has to do with the primary determinant of relationships with others. In the most high-context cultures, relationships are determined by one's family background and position. Personal wishes and aspirations play only a limited role. At the other extreme are low-context cultures where persons are much freer to form relationships by choice and where persons are expected to look after their own personal interests.

In relation to service delivery, probably the most crucial issue is that of the degree of differentiation made between "in-group" and "out-group." In order to be effective within a high-context society, one must move from being viewed as a stranger to being accepted into an interpersonal relationship. "In-group" members are like family. Requests for assistance on any matter—personal, social, or business—are to be honored if at all possible. Relationship commitments to "in-group" members are for life and are taken very seriously. Because the nuances of interpersonal relating are so important, nonverbal behavior takes on a crucial cueing function. In order not to offend "in-group" or potential "in-group" members by direct refusals or confrontations, negative cues can be quite subtle. By contrast, "out-group" members are neither trusted nor particularly respected. There is no obligation to behave fairly or equitably; in fact, there is no obligation at all.

Relationships in low-context cultures may appear quite superficial as they do not carry the same degree of interpersonal commitment as is present in high-context cultures. Friendships or alliances are formed if they are mutually desired and beneficial, and are allowed to lapse when no longer useful. Thus, the approach to interpersonal relationships is short-term and utilitarian. Major emphasis is placed on verbal (especially written) communication, and nonverbal nuances are largely ignored. Participants in a negotiation are expected to be direct and explicit about their desires. Fair and equitable treatment supersedes any notion of preferential treatment to "in-group" members.

In high-context cultures, customers tend to patronize businesses where they know the service producer and thus are "in-group." Purchase of services from a total stranger would be avoided if possible. Service delivery, then, is directly linked to the personal relationship. Banks give loans because they know the persons and their characters and thus can assess with accuracy the degree of risk. Retailers frequented are friends of cousins, and health care is provided by the medical or paramedical person responsible for your birth.

A major shift has been the purchase of a wide range of services from virtual strangers. In low-context cultures, personal relationships are not usually the variable used to select a service firm; rather, issues such as convenience, price, and skill in service delivery are considered.

In societies like the United States, dealing with strangers is so commonplace that it is taken for granted. In any case, part of the U.S. value structure is equality of treatment—i.e., one should treat strangers no differently than family members. As U.S. corporations have moved into global service markets they have often assumed little need to adapt to the host culture. If anything, they have assumed the existence of a competitive advantage based on respect for U.S. products.

In many other cultures, however, a very clear distinction is made between family (in-group) and stranger (out-group). In many European cultures, strangers are accorded courtesy and respect but usually as an inferior; all goes well as long as the dominance of the host culture is acknowledged. In other parts of the world, though, strangers are essentially nonpersons. No respect is required, and the stranger may be exploited in any one of a number of different ways.

CULTURAL VALUES AND
THE PURCHASE BUNDLE

Cultural values interact with the service product offering on several different levels. Most easily understood and documented are the implications for choice of facilitating good. The international marketing literature is full of examples of cultural differences in meaning—like the differences in the symbolic meanings of colors. There also exists a literature on consumer needs documenting that while the same general needs exist across cultures, the relative importance of various needs varies by culture.

We can conceptualize culture as a filter or screen through which services pass as they are produced by the service provider and purchased/consumed by the customer (see Figure 7.1). The cultural value issues that will affect the service provider are in essence the same needs that the customer weighs in service selection and evaluation. The service firm will wish to provide the service as easily and conveniently as possible—e.g., without modification by cultural setting—just as the customer wishes to receive services with as little effort expended as possible. The provider, in varying degrees, wishes to avoid uncertainty and unnecessary risks, just as the customer wishes to feel secure about the purchase. Depending upon their cultural backgrounds, providers will vary in how important relationship priorities and timely task completion are, similar to customers' differential valuing of belonging or self-actualization needs. Cultural differences in power distance or individualism likewise correspond to customer needs for status or autonomy.

The arena in which competition among service operations is most vigorous, and hence in which services need to be most culturally sensitive, is in the explicit components of the purchase bundle. A major issue for service firms is the degree to which service offerings should be adapted in various cultures. One of the key factors in reducing perceived customer risk is the availability of a standardized service product. Customers feel most comfortable and confident when they know that the Kwik-Copy or the Kentucky Fried Chicken on one side of town will give them the same quality service as they received on the other side of town.

If customers were only domestic, there would be no problem as service delivery could be standardized for the country but allowed to vary between countries. An increasing number of customers, though, are international students, tourists, or businesspersons who expect the same quality

FIGURE 7.1
The Interaction of Culture and Service Delivery

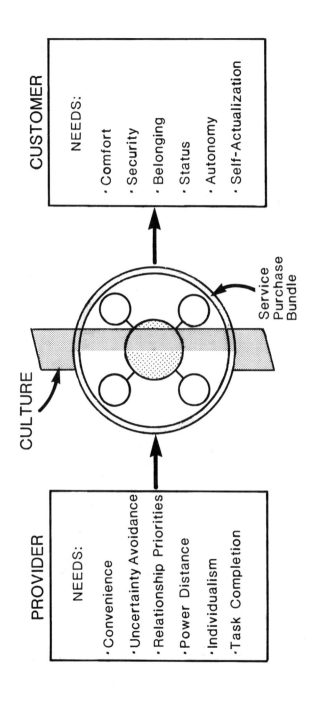

PROVIDER

NEEDS:

· Convenience
· Uncertainty Avoidance
· Relationship Priorities
· Power Distance
· Individualism
· Task Completion

CULTURE

Service
Purchase
Bundle

CUSTOMER

NEEDS:

· Comfort
· Security
· Belonging
· Status
· Autonomy
· Self-Actualization

161

of service in the host country as they received in their home country. A degree of product consistency, then, is essential; however, adaptation must also be made to the host market. Adaptation is most commonly made in the explicit components, which will be reviewed in turn.

Service Availability

Service location and hours need to be coordinated with the offerings of competitors in each market. In London, for example, postal services are available on Sunday in contrast to cities in the United States which offer services only Monday through Saturday. A firm willing and able to offer Sunday post-related services in the United States might do very well; a post-related service in London trying to maintain only Monday through Saturday hours would not be competitive. One must be cautious, however. The fact that many businesses in Moslem countries are closed on Friday does not mean that foreign firms would necessarily do a brisk business if they were open on Friday; the perceived insensitivity to religious observance might well make it impossible for the firm to stay in business.

Service availability should also take into account cultural values. IBM's commitment to 24-hour service, for example, markets nicely in a "mastery over nature" culture like the United States or a "task-accomplishment" culture like Hong Kong. In other types of cultures, though, 24-hour service can be misinterpreted as implying that the product needs continuously-available service because it is exceptionally faulty. Or the ready availability may simply not be valued. A Honeywell representative in Beijing was extremely irritated when the Chinese responded to his offer to fly in a needed technician from Hong Kong the next day with, "That is not so convenient. We will be planting trees." He had assumed rapid service was the priority.

In cultures where social class distinctions are carefully maintained (high PDI), location of facilities needs careful study. Selecting a site which is accessible to the most number of customers may also mean that it is situated between two different customer groups which would be served more effectively by separate facilities.

Service Environment

In creating the physical environment, there are a variety of factors to consider. Low-context cultures are more accepting of utilitarian office environments than are high-context cultures. If the service itself is high-contact and requires prolonged interaction between customer and provider, then the furniture and decor need to create a comfortable feeling for such interaction. Selection between traditional and modern decor will relate not only to cultural values but also to whether or not the service firm is distinguishing itself as different or "foreign." In part out of necessity, Kentucky Fried Chicken has done an excellent job of adapting its layout to the smaller retail facilities typical in Japan.

In Japan as well as in Scandinavian countries, clean lines and more subdued colors are the norm. While bright colors may be used, the overall aesthetic effect should be peaceful. In contrast, Caribbean and African cultures use more mixtures of bright colors and the visual environment is "busier"—expressing warmth and vitality.

One also needs to consider the degree of privacy customers expect. In many Latin cultures, tables placed close together in a crowded restaurant are perfectly acceptable and even facilitates interaction with acquaintances nearby. In some northern European cultures, more privacy as well as a quieter atmosphere is expected.

Service Delivery Style

The style of service delivery is most sensitive to cultural differences as the nonverbal cues communicated need to be appropriate to the cultural setting. The training of Kentucky Fried Chicken employees in Japan to hand orders to customers with both hands and a bow is quite appropriate but might cause discomfort to U.S. customers used to a more casual delivery style. In many high-context cultures, customers expect a degree of formality, including being addressed by their last name. Again, the more casual environment in the United States prompts the use of first names to convey friendliness and welcome—a practice which conveys lack of respect to persons from more formal cultural backgrounds.

Cultural values will also influence expectations about promptness and scheduling, In cultures which are not particularly time conscious ("time-driven"), waits of one-half hour or more may be quite acceptable, expecially if one can visit with others while waiting. Typically, customers then expect some social interaction time with the provider before transacting business.

In time-conscious cultures, customers became impatient if not acknowledged at least within the first few minutes. Service delivery is usually expected to be rapid and goal-directed, with little time for chit-chat. The differences in expected service delivery can manifest in a variety of ways. For example, swimming meets in the United States are highly competitive, with swimming times monitored and recorded to the hundredth of a second. U.S. swimmers work constantly to better their swimming times. In Brazil, the swim meet atmosphere is typically more geared to social recognition. Swimmers' affiliations rather than their previous time records are printed on the program. The timers may be too busy chatting to record the correct time; in any case, it is the win not the improvement over a former record which matters.[1]

While the United States is schedule and time conscious, its culture is quite informal in other ways; for example, movie theater seats are first-come-first-served. In the Netherlands, purchasing a movie theater ticket means that one also has an assigned seat so there is no competitive rush for seats.

The British are famous for understatement, and their provision style for supplemental services is typical. At a theater, snack foods are available during the intermission, and the vendor simply stands at the front of the theater or in the lobby with the food. If customers are new to the country and customs, they may miss the fact that food is available—until they see others eating. In India, vendors are much more vocal and assertive about their wares.

Finally, there is the matter of self-service. In general, having the customer participate as an unpaid laborer can be an efficient way of providing services. Two cultural issues are key: (1) Is there a prior tradition of self-service for the customer? (2) Is the customer aware of what behavior is expected? Customers not used to self-service or from tightly hierarchical societies may be insulted if asked to self-service, particularly if they are male and used to female members providing a full range of services. For example, Marriott's honor (self-serve) bar for business customers may do well in the United States but not as well in Brazil where personal attention is an expected part of the service purchased. Customers can only self-serve effectively if they know what is expected of them; for example, customers used to a library system where books are requested and then delivered by library personnel may require an inordinate amount of the librarian's time learning to use an open-stack, self-service system.

Service Product Line

Cultural expectations differ regarding the degree of customization expected in their delivery. In many high-context cultures, customers expect personal attention to their needs beyond what is usually provided. Singapore Airlines, for example, has made provision of personalized customer service one of their competitive strengths.

Expectations also differ with regard to what services are usual. Kuwait, for example, has had difficulty in keeping its medical services system from being inundated with requests for minor or routine care, since medical services are provided free of charge. In the Indian culture, there is as yet no strong tradition of preventive maintenance—repair facilities would need to market themselves with more of an educational approach than is necessary in a culture where preventive maintenance is expected.

SERVICES AND MARXIST IDEOLOGY

The political history and ideology of a country has a definite effect on the manner in which the service sector develops and the expectations which citizens have of services. For example, in some of the oil-exporting nations, citizens have come to expect a wide range of services free of charge which in most countries would be paid for. Or, as we have seen already in Chapter 2, former colonies often inherit expectations about services related to the needs of the colonial power rather than to nationalistic needs.

The set of political beliefs which has exerted the most influence on service sector development is probably Marxist economics. Marx (1913) took the position that services were nonproductive because he believed no surplus value was created in service production. Following such an ideology, the Soviet Union focused on heavy industrialization as a vehicle for economic development with little resource allocation for service sector development. It was left with productive capacity but no infrastructure to distribute the products. A comparison of a variety of socialist economies indicates that the most successful are those which have made service industries a priority.

At the time that Marx was writing, he was particularly concerned with the perceived alienating and dehumanizing effects of the Industrial Revolution. His analysis was not intended for an economic environment where technological changes had automated many of the repetitive, alienating aspects of production and where global markets had created competitive pressures which force employers to "rehumanize" the workplace.

The Soviet Union, with its initial focus on heavy industry, took Marx' analysis quite literally. It is only after some disastrous experiences with the consequences of a poor distribution system that allocation priorities have begun to change. In the 1970s, Eastern European (particularly Hungarian) economists began to point out that the service sector played a vital role in improving the quality of the labor force and hence the potential productivity of the economy as a whole (Azar and Pletnikova 1974; Komarov 1973; Szabadi 1975). Analysis of the need for infrastructure services came later.

Reporting conventions continue to exclude much of "non-material production" from the accounts so the size and growth of the service sector in Soviet countries is difficult to estimate. That it is growing rapidly is undeniable; that it is receiving more attention is also clear. Shataev (1984) outlines a detailed plan for improving personal services. Service infrastructure development in rural areas is now being used as a strategy to stem the tide of migration to urban centers and help enhance the quality of life in the countryside (Khomelyansky 1982).

The People's Republic of China has maintained a less traditional view of the service sector, to its advantage. In the recent loosening of economic controls, for example, Shanghai is being positioned to become a competitive financial market. Since 1979, China has been actively improving its tourism services, both domestic and international. Transportation and communication networks have been targeted as needing improvement, both to support manufacturing industries and to support tourism. As a result, both its domestic and its internationally-traded services have been contributing more heavily to GDP.

SUMMARY

Culture as a moderating variable in services marketing and delivery cannot be overlooked if a service firm hopes to remain competitive. Basic to an understanding of the role culture plays in services is an awareness of the variety of ways in which values and priorities differ across cultures. Differences in cultural values affect the expectations of the customer, the manner in which service delivery should be structured, and the political priority assigned to service sector development.

The service purchase bundle, explained in Chapter 6, can help us conceptualize better the specific interactions between culture and effective service delivery—especially with regard to adaptations needed in the explicit service components. Any attempt to generalize about cultural effects must keep in mind that cultures are not homogenous and that cultural values themselves change over time

NOTES

1. See C.P. Kottak, "Swimming in Cross-Cultural Currents," *Natural History* (May 1985), pp. 2–11.

PART THREE
GROWTH THROUGH SERVICES

Having seen the importance of the service sector in all economies and reviewed the kinds and effects of globalization in the service sector, we turn now to the implications of service sector growth (or lack thereof) for national economies.

In Chapter 8, we review factors contributing to comparative advantage in services, including firm-specific strategies of horizontal and vertical integration, increased differentiation of intermediary services, and the contribution of franchises. In Chapter 9, we examine the issues and approaches to negotiating the increasing protectionism in services trade, as well as the types of incentives available to encourage services trade. In Chapter 10, by way of conclusion, we discuss the consequences of service-led growth for quality of life and future economic development.

8

COMPETITIVE STRATEGIES IN THE SERVICE SECTOR

International trade, investment and monetary relations would stop abruptly if industries involved with finance, insurance, transportation or communication ceased to operate. If any one of these industries was disrupted the consequences for the economic system would be immediate and immense. By contrast, if trade in leather goods, steel, or even computers were halted the economic system could adjust without much difficulty. The unique logistical role of services in the economic system is so fundamental that it is almost never considered (quoted from Aronson 1980, in Cloney 1981, p. 14).

The increasing demand for specialized services by business has created the opportunity for business firms to exploit economies of scale inherent in many service functions. For example, a market research firm may be able to spread its research costs over several similar projects and deliver its service for much less than its clients' cost for doing the job in-house, individually. This specialization in turn has opened up the market for intermediate services to small- and medium-sized firms which were previously unable to obtain these services without great cost (US Dept. of Commerce 1985, p. 39).

A recent headline asked, "Can smokestack America rise again?" A more appropriate question would be "Should smokestack America rise again?" Switzerland, a country with very high per capita GNP and near-zero inflation, "has been helped by the absence of such basic industries

171

as steel, coal, or shipbuilding."[1] Yet the United States has steadfastly maintained that such "basic" industries must be subsidized rather than suffer the usual fate of firms not able to compete successfully in the international marketplace.

We are so used to delineating "manufacturing-driven" models of growth that almost no theoretical literature exists to guide policy planners, whether government or corporate, in visualizing a dynamic model for service sector development. This chapter is only a beginning in articulating the issues involved in service-led growth and outlining the areas where further research is needed. The discussion is intended to be provocative, not authoritative. Its purpose is to suggest competitive strategy guidelines for both governments and private enterprises.

INFLUENCES ON SERVICE
SECTOR DEVELOPMENT

Given historical attitudes toward the service sector, much of development has occurred by default. While policy planning may target particular industries—finance, health, communication—the analyses all too frequently focus on industries in isolation rather than as part of the services fabric of any functioning society. As policy planners become more conscious of the importance of services, three issues emerge: (1) What should the country's developmental focus be? (2) How can appropriate economic growth be financed? (3) What role should the government play in the development process?

Focus of Sectoral Development

In thinking about sectoral development—particularly service sector development—it is helpful to differentiate between minimal and optimal levels of development. All economies have some minimal economic activity in each of the three major sectors. In addition, physical infrastructure must be developed in each economy in order to support other productive activities. Transportation and telecommunications are essential to the functioning of any economy. The importance of infrastructure development is often overlooked as conventional cost-benefit analyses tend to underestimate the real magnitude of the benefits from infrastructure development (Mera 1984). Japan's phenomenal growth after World War II has been attributed in part to its well-developed infrastructure.

Social infrastructure development—health, education, public administration—is also crucial in providing a competent workforce and an environment in which productive activities can flourish. Both manufacturing and service operations can be undermined as much by political instability and domestic fiscal problems as by inadequate transportaton.

While inadequate public administrative structure can create problems, so too can excessive administrative control. Built-in public sector rigidities can produce

> . . . growth-destroying price distortions and investment misallocations, as well as actual theft by policymakers. These distortions and misallocations take their toll in economic inefficiency. Empirical studies indicate that price distortions from trade curbs alone are costing some countries from 4% to 10% of their gross national product.[2]

The key to effective public administration is to develop the appropriate facilitative services for economic growth and to provide a politically and fiscally stable environment, while keeping market distorting restriction to a minimum.

In selecting an optimal sectoral development strategy, economies may choose either a "leading sector" or a "balanced sector" approach. One of the characteristics of the High Growth countries referred to in Table 4.3 was the greater variability in the growth rate of the manufacturing sectors among the High Growth developing countries—i.e., some grew slowly and some grew more rapidly. Perhaps this variance difference is an indication of individually tailored development plans. All of the High Growth developing countries had dynamic service sector growth, but not all also emphasized manufacturing growth.

Developmental strategies may, of course, shift over time. Both the Federal Republic of Germany and Japan have focused heavily on manufacturing-led growth in the past and now, with increased competition from the NICs, are paying more attention to the service sector in order to provide employment stability in the future.

Growth Financing

As is to be expected, the extent to which an economy is able to finance its own development plays a major role in its ability to grow. For all four country groups, lower inflation rates and higher rates of domestic investment and savings were associated with high rates of growth in GDP and per capita GNP. Amount of external debt bore no relationship to economic productivity in the developing countries studies—except for the Low-income countries where higher levels of external debt as a percent of GNP were associated with a *lower* percentage of GDP from the manufacturing sector. Nowhere in the data is there any indication that present external funding strategies are having any direct economic impact other than to raise the debt payments required of that country.

Growth financing can come from a variety of sources—private and public, domestic and foreign. For most developing countries, international lending agencies have been a primary source of funds. But such agencies continue to be biased in favor of agricultural and manufacturing projects. The followng excerpt from the Development Assistance Committee of the OECD is typical:

> The need to increase and diversify the productive capacities of low-income countries is recognised as one of the central development priorities. While agriculture will have to remain the main engine of economic and social development in most low-income countries and hence an essential focus of development co-operation, their potential for productive investment and employment in industry will also have to be fully used (Poats 1984, p. 143).

Little awareness of the importance of the service sector in developing economies exists. The World Bank, while funding infrastructure projects, maintains an ideology that manufacturing is the engine of growth. President Clausen frequently cites countries in the Pacific Basin as manufacturing-led growth models, overlooking the substantial contributions from their large service sectors.

If countries look to private commercial lending sources, similar problems exist. Just as was true in colonial times, economies which depend upon foreign private sector capital are often at a disadvantage. In the case of Bolivia, for example: "... international creditors have financed some local manufacturing, but mainly operations that do not compete with major international industries. Multinational (nonfinancial) firms have facilitated certain industrialization by local firms, either because they chose to divest of insufficiently profitable local subsidiaries or because they stood to gain from licensing contracts" (Eckstein and Hagopian 1983, p. 90). Thus the character of the Bolivian economy has been formed based on creditors' priorities rather than those of Bolivia.

The cost of foreign direct investment (in foreign exchange) presumably is directly related to the benefit derived by the host economy.

Foreign direct investment can provide not only capital but also managerial skills and technology transfer. When we examine flows of direct foreign investment from the United States, the results are disconcerting (see Table 8.1). The proportionate level of direct foreign investment in developing countries has decreased since 1970 until, by 1981, 90 percent of U.S. foreign direct investment was in other Industrial countries. Investment has decreased most sharply in the service sector—exactly the sector most strongly associated with economic growth. The bulk of investment in developing countries has been in the extractive sector—which exhibits a negative correlation with GDP growth for all three developing country groups. Data from the Federal Republic of Germany and the United Kingdom indicate investment patterns focused on the manufacturing sector.

Until recently, investment by transnational corporations has been viewed with skepticism by host governments, and rightly so. When there were few competitors, transnational corporations were relatively free to control aspects of domestic economies. But the international environment has changed in several ways. As external debt burdens have soared, due to changes in the exchange rates, transnational corporations have become welcome as investors that can finance domestic development and generate much needed foreign exchange

> Eagerly sought for the capital, technology and jobs they provide, the [transnational] companies are being courted by developing and industrialized countries alike. . . . Until the debt crisis that began a few years ago, borrowing seemed better than foreign investment as a way to attract capital. Loans could be used for whatever the country wanted, and there were no foreigners brought in to interfere with local economics or politics. But . . . borrowing resulted in more, not less, foreign interference. For when debts could not be repaid, the banks and the International Monetary Fund virtually dictated the borrowing country's economic policies.[3]

Then, too, there are now more competitors internationally, particularly from other developing countries. And consumer activist groups have been successful in influencing transnational corporations to exercise a sense of social responsibility in their operations abroad.

Whatever the drawbacks of direct foreign investment, it holds more promise for service sector development than does funding from an intergovernmental agency. While the record in service sector investment is not as substantial as it needs to be, there is promise. International

Table 8.1
Data On U.S. Foreign Direct
Investment in Developing
Countries By Economic Sector
(percentages)

	United States	
	1970–72	1979–81
Worldwide Investment:		
Extractive Sector	34.7%	31.5%
Manufacturing Sector	43.3	30.9
Service Sector	22.1	37.6
Investment in Developing Countries:		
Extractive Sector	46.3%	50.4%
Manufacturing Sector	22.0	32.4
Service Sector	31.7	14.9
Investment in Developing Countries as % of Worldwide Total:		
Extractive Sector	39.3%	15.0%
Manufacturing Sector	42.6	27.7
Service Sector	42.2	10.4
Total Investment in Developing Countries	29.5%	26.4%

Calculations based on data from the United Nations Centre on Transnational Corporations, *Transnational Corporations in World Development* (New York: United Nations, 1983).

shipping and tourism, among other service industries in developing countries, have benefitted greatly from newer forms of investment—i.e., joint ventures, licensing agreements, franchising, management contracts, turnkey contracts, product-in-hand contracts, production-sharing contracts, risk service contracts, and international subcontracting (Oman 1984). Third-world multinationals have been particularly active in these newer forms of investment, in contrast with more traditional straight capital investment (Wells 1983).

The increasing involvement of financial intermediaries opens the way for the development of new regional sources of funding free from manufacturing bias. For example, in a 1984 report to the Council of Ministers, the Association of Southeast Asian Nations (ASEAN) determined that regional development would be enhanced by cooperative ventures in the service sector ("ASEAN trade. . ." 1984). Any of the Asian countries with major financial sectors—e.g., Hong Kong or Singapore—could become a funder of service sector projects.

Types of Government Influence

A government's involvement in the service sector can range from limited governmental administrative services to regulation of a wide range of service industries, from tightly-controlled governmental monopolies to provision of services in open competition with private sector firms. Depending on the political philosophy of the country, expectations differ as to how available or accessible social services should be. With the "revolution in entitlement" (Bell 1973)—i.e., rapidly rising expectations about standard of living—which has been taking place over the past ten years, governments have assumed more responsibility for insuring that services such as health care and education will be available throughout the population.

Regardless of the political philosophy underlying the governmental structure of an economy, governments can influence national economies in several general ways: (1) through macroeconomic policies; (2) through resource development policies; and (c) through structural policies (Schultze 1983). Macroeconomic policies are directed at overall levels of production and employment in order to increase general prosperity. While these policies are not designed to affect sectoral composition, such effects are possible. For example, the U.S. government has routinely offered investment incentives more relevant to manufacturing industries than to service industries. At a minimum, governments affect financial markets and currency availability through fiscal and monetary policies, and regulate the availability of skilled workers through immigration policies.

Resource development policies are designed to "make the economy in general more flexible, more dynamic, more productive, and more capable of adjustment to technological change" (Schultze 1983, p. 6). Such policies focus on education and training, research and development, and ridigities within the economy. Again the thrust is general, rather than sector specific. Again the consequence is often sectorally biased—e.g., What type of education? What type of research? What aspects are targeted as rigidities?

Structural policies are those aimed at creating a different sectoral and industry composition than would occur in a free market economy. Structural compostition can be affected either by "protecting the losers" or by trying to "pick the winners" (Schultze 1983). Ironically, while the United States fears that it is losing its competitive edge in relation to Japan and proposes protecting the steel and automotive industries to regain superiority, Japan is opting to phase out noncompetitive manufacturing industries and focus resources in services and service-related technology. While more centralized government structures do appear to accelerate the development of a well-balanced service sector, that success is due to the ability to implement coordinated long-term planning and general developmental incentives rather than to protectionistic practices.

In Chapter 5, we noted the worldwide trend toward the privatization of services often delivered by the public sector. Three possible approaches are open to government, in addition to supplying the service directly. First, governments may retain administrative control over service delivery while subcontracting the actual delivery to private firms. For example, in Kenya and the Dominican Republic individuals contract to maintain a particular portion of public roads for a fee paid by the government (Willoughby 1983). The advantage of such a strategy is that equitable access to services among socioeconomic groups remains under governmental control. The primary disadvantage is the continuing overhead cost for retaining such control.

Second, governments may turn over total responsibility for service delivery to the private sector. With this strategy, there are no associated overhead costs and the government can generate revenues from the sale of existing public services. The disadvantages include the lack of policy control and the potential for misallocation of services to wealthier citizens.

Third, governments may continue to provide public services directly or through subcontracting, but allow (or even encourage) private sector competition. Research has shown that such a combination can effectively put pressure on public agencies to increase efficiency (Savas 1981). On the other hand, if the private sector can provide the service effectively, duplication in the public sector may be a poor use of scarce resources.

The second option, turning service delivery over to the private sector, is an increasingly popular option, especially as countries become aware that the countries which are better off economically are those that have free markets and have welcomed competition. Privatization of public enterprises has been occurring particularly rapidly in Asia, some examples of which are given in Table 8.2.

Table 8.2
Public Sector Enterprises
Privatized in Asia

Industry	Countries	
Airlines	Bangladesh (Bangladesh Biman)	
	Malaysia (MAS)	
	Republic of Korea (Korea Air)	
	Singapore (SIA)	
	Thailand (Thai International)	
Banking	Bangladesh	Singapore
	Philippines	Taiwan
	Republic of Korea	
Container Terminals	Malaysia	
Highways	India	Malayasia
Hotels	Philippines	Singapore
Railways/Bus Services	Japan (Japan National Railways)	
	Thailand (Bangkok Bus Company)	
	Sri Lanka (Ceylon Transport Board)	
Shipping and/or Shipbuilding	Bangledesh	Sri Lanka
	Singapore	
Telecommunications	Bangladesh	Republic of Korea
	Japan	Sri Lanka
	Malaysia	Thailand

From A. Rowley, "Private Affair in Asia," *Far Eastern Economic Review* (July 25, 1985), pp. 63-64.

SOURCES OF COMPARATIVE
ADVANTAGE IN SERVICES

If governments are to feel secure about service-led growth, they must be able to believe that economic comparative advantage can be based on service sector strengths, not just the tangible attributes associated with merchandise trade. Historically, theories of comparative advantage were developed with reference to tangible goods, not intangibles. Traditional factor endowments considered included raw materials and strategic location.

Only recently have items such as human capital, capital (financial) markets, and political stability been added to the list, and the shift from static fixed-resource endowments to dynamic measures of learning-curves and economies of scale is still underway (Lodge and Crum 1985). The fact that these newer additions comprise service sector contributors has gone unnoticed.

While trade theories directly applicable to services remain to be developed, reflection suggests that service trade could well be directly related to economic growth—in which case developing a comparative advantage in services trade would lead to more rapid economic development. Certainly it is true that more rapid growth in exports is correlated with more rapid economic development (Krueger 1983). In examining data from the four country groups, eighty percent of the countries showed growth in services trade between 1977 and 1981, while 59 percent had growth in merchandise trade and 51 percent in both.

Economic Comparative Advantage

Several commonly held principles can be applied directly to trade in services. International competition can function effectively to improve the quality and price of services available to consumers. Similarly, specialization in particular services can help countries exploit natural and human resources and take advantage of economies of scale. The few persons who have written about comparative advantage in services (e.g., Hindley and Smith, 1985; Oulton, 1984; Sapir and Lutz, 1981) find no reason to believe that these economic theories cannot be extended to services. In examining the services trade experience of developing economies, physical capital appears to be directly related to comparative advantage in transportation services, while human capital appears related to comparative advantage in insurance and other services (Sapir and Lutz 1981).

Sources of comparative advantage differ by industry. Tourism, for example, may be heavily dependent on natural resource endowments, while financial services may be linked to geographical location with regard to international time zones. For the United Kingdom, the recent computerization of London's stock exchange has made it possible to capitalize on geographical location more effectively. "[By] not being tied to a trading floor . . . an early broker-dealer will be able to operate in the closing stages of the Far Eastern markets and still catch New York in the late afternoon, giving London the potential to be a 24-hour international financial center."[4]

The manner in which human capital is developed and deployed can also determine a country's comparative advantage in services. With the increasing information-handling content of occupations, a literate work force is essential. Quality of education, then, can be a determining factor. When adequate advanced training facilities are not available, education and training can be imported (much as are raw materials) and then technical expertise or consulting services can in turn be exported as a "finished product." The People's Republic of China has adopted such a strategy successfully, importing training from Japan, Europe, and North America and then exporting skilled consultants to Africa and other developing countries.

Most writers suggest that industrialized countries will continue to dominate service markets. Is this necessarily so? The dominant position of the Republic of Korea in the construction services is only one of many counterinstances which could be raised. Both Hong Kong and Singapore are taking the lead in "cashless shopping" by developing automated "easy pay" systems in which a credit card is electronically scanned and one's account debited in a matter of seconds.[5] Because of their compact size and close cooperation from the banking community, they are in a position not only to refine such services but then to export the systems worldwide.

Some intriguing data have been presented indicating that comparative advantage is industry-specific and that the European Economic Community in general demonstrates stronger comparative advantage than the United States in most services (Oulton 1984). In surveying the Industrial countries, it is clear that competitive positioning[6] in services varies by services trade category (see Table 8.3). It is conceivable, then, that different countries could carve out their own competitive niches in the global service market.

Cultural Comparative Advantage

As the volume of services exports from developing countries increases, it is interesting to speculate on possible cultural sources of advantage. The United States has been losing market share in the global service market. Could it be that in an increasingly competitive environment the low-context cultural approach of most U.S. firms has only a limited market?

The hospitality market has an increasing number of entrants from developing countries culturally versed in more high-context service delivery (Wells 1983). In a related field, Japan Airlines has been so successful in service delivery that it now holds "etiquette schools" for employees of

TABLE 8.3
Top Competitors in
Services Exports: 1980

	Category of Services Exports		
Shipping	*Other Transport*	*Travel & Tourism*	*Other Services*
Denmark	Greece	Greece	Greece
Japan	Netherlands	Spain	Belgium/Luxembourg
United Kingdom	Portugal	Portugal	Switzerland

Note: Countries listed in order of comparative advantage.

Adapted from N. Oulton, "International Trade in Service Industries: Comparative Advantage of European Community Countries" (paper presented at an international conference on Restrictions on Transactions in the International Market for Services, June 1984, Wiston House, England).

other service corporations. Regarding technology transfer, Hong Kong has postitioned itself as an intermediary between the industrial countries and the developing countries (Chen 1984). In the related area of professional services, third-world multinationals appear to be gaining an advantage in being able to work more effectively with clients.

It is vital that we develop new ways of understanding comparative advantage. Rather than thinking about economic dichotomies in terms of per capita GNP, perhaps we should think of dichotomies in terms of the value placed on human resource development (Vitro 1984). We would then have "information-rich" countries which place a high priority on human resource development, and "information-poor" countries which do not.

A recent breakthrough in computer technology is an interesting case in point. A Bolivian mathematician, Ivan Guzman de Rojas, has used Aymara (a language spoken by 2.5 million Indians) as the "bridging" language to translate back and forth among English, French, German, Portuguese, and Spanish.[7] The new language, Atamiri, can be used not only for numerous business applications but also to help increase literacy among the Aymaras.

CORPORATE COMPETITIVE STRATEGIES

As the global economy has become more interdependent, sources of competition continue to shift geographically and by industry. Service industries are inherently risky businesses since product intangibility allows competitors to replicate new service offerings virtually immediately. In order to manage producer risk and remain competitive, new potentials for economies of scale must be continually explored. As industry strategies are revised, both integration and specialization are occurring simultaneously.

Integration In Service Operations

In the United States, with the advent of deregulation in transportation has come the birth of the "supertransportation" or "intermodal" company.[8] CSX has integrated rail and trucking services, as well as expanding into air and barge services. Consolidated Freightways of Palo Alto, California, has combined trucking with air freight. The Port of Seattle (Washington) has complemented its container shipping services with warehousing, trucking, and other distributive services targeted at the small export firm.[9] In the communications arena, similar integration is occurring between previously separate service modalities to create an integrated information transmission industry.

Vertical integration possibilities are also expanding, fueled by new technology. Compugraphic Corporation, for example, anticipates introducing a composition system combining computer software and typsetting so that companies can print their own publications in-house.[10] By using software which allows secretarial staff to "typeset" documents in much the same manner that they presently type them, companies will be available to generate professional-quality publications without resorting to professional typesetting services. Compugraphics has specifically targeted technical publications—instructions, service manuals, training materials—to demonstrate the possibilities of such a system.

Another trend is the forward integration of manufacturing companies into wholesale and retail distribution and related services, described as the "shift in management's point of view from selling a product to selling the solution to a consumer's problem" (Canton 1984, p. 90). GATX has withdrawn from railcar manufacturing and moved into leasing and maintenance services, while Alco Standard has gone from manufacturing into distribution. IBM is a classic example of a manufacturing firm which not only services its products but has also recently branched into retail stores to market its microcomputer products. While IBM's retail outlets floundered at first, owing to retailing inexperience, IBM has now successfully entered the Japanese and European retail markets.

Manufacturers of mass-market products are fast becoming "worldwide storekeepers" (Barry 1984). The "shop-in-shop" concept where manufacturers lease space in a retail store to market their product has been used successfully by cosmetics manufacturers worldwide. Now we see a proliferation of "storemanufacturers" creating one-product-line stores for products which were traditionally distributed through retailers. Benetton of Italy, Laura Ashley of Britain, Esprit de Corps of the United States all have established their own worldwide network of retail outlets to promote their goods most effectively. While some retailers say that all product promotion helps, as the "storemanufacturers" increase retailers will need to reposition themselves more competitively.[11]

The key to successful integration is identifying competitive strengths and then moving into fields which capitalize on those strengths. Too many corporations try to take on operations in unrelated fields where they have little expertise, and the consequences are almost always disastrous. For example, successful "diversification for the airlines no longer means getting into... broadcasting and real estate... [but] developing revenues by finding new uses for the people, skills and equipment basic to their central business."[12] Delta Airlines has begun contract work in replacing airplane engines for other airlines. United Airlines trains flight crews for other airlines and for the U.S. Air Force. American Airlines has branched out in telemarketing, while USAir Inc. has become an aircraft broker.

Growth of Intermediate Services

The most rapid growth in the service sector has taken place in the provision of intermediary services—services provided primarily for producers of goods or services. For example, companies like Telecheck Services provide check and credit card verification for merchants worldwide. What we see happening is a twofold process: (1) an increase in the externalization and specialization of functions which were formerly provided by generalists or by specialists within the firm; and (2) an expansion of the distribution channels for service products.

Many of the professional services fall into the first category. Numerous firms have sprung up to provide businesses with accounting, advertising, public relations, or market research skills. Businesses can contract for property and equipment maintenance, supply and supervision of office staff, provision of food services, inventory control, handling of accounts receivable. The early 1980s witnessed, for example, the growth of a new industry in "employee leasing."[13] The company to which workers are leased is able to reduce its labor costs by hiring only the employees it needs at the moment. The employees, in turn, enjoy better benefits with leasing companies such as Omnistaff Inc. because the large payroll makes possible comprehensive packages which smaller firms cannot afford.

In short, there is virtually no function other than that of chief executive officer which cannot be contracted out to a third party. Such a range of intermediary services makes it possible for firms in all economic sectors to concentrate on the activities which they can perform themselves in a cost-effective manner, while taking advantage of the economies of scale possible for a specialty firm for those activities which are not cost-effective to provide in-house. Nonairline third-party vendors, such as Tymnet and Travel Scan Videotext, can provide automated reservation systems for airlines too small to maintain their own systems economically.

Frequently, new services are developed for other service producers and then offered to the final consumer when costs have decreased. Videotex, which in the U.S. market has been too expensive to enjoy widespread consumer support, has been repositioned to appeal to businesses.[14] Buick's "Salesman's Assistant" is an example; it tracks vehicles on order, computes alternate financing plans, and compares Buick products to competitors'. Hotels and airports are using videotext systems to supply customers with information about services and activities.

One consequence of the kinds of intermediary services now available is that there are increasingly complex distribution channels for services. The growth in financial wholesaling is one example. In software publishing, agents are springing up. Telemarketing is on the increase. The tailoring of computer software to the needs of a particular industry, a lucrative application of vertical marketing principles, is gaining momentum.[15] The growth of the Pacific Rim economies has stimulated the creation of Pacific Rim Advisory Council, an association of law firms from the United States, Canada, and New Zealand.[16]

Growth in Franchising

Franchising has expanded enormously since the 1940s when it was first introduced, and comprises 15 percent of the U.S. GNP or one-third of all retail sales (Wood 1985). Table 8.4 illustrates the growth of U.S. franchisors outside the United States as of 1983. Industrial countries average over 80 different franchise chains, with over 45 outlets each. In

TABLE 8.4
International Statistics
for U.S. Franchises: 1983

Region	Average Number of Franchisors	Average Outlets Per Franchisor
Industrial Countries		
Canada	217	35.8
Europe	75	58.3
Australia	61	35.0
Japan	56	90.7
United Kingdom	53	42.1
New Zealand	21	18.1
Average	80.5	46.7
Developing Countries		
Caribbean	86	8.3
Asia	65	15.9
Middle East	37	7.1
Mexico	36	13.8
Africa	30	19.8
South America	29	16.1
Central America	25	6.2
Average	44	12.5

Calculated from data in A. Kostecka, *Franchising in the Economy 1983–85* (Washington, D.C.: U.S. Government Printing Office, 1985).

developing countries, 44 U.S. franchisors are represented on the average, with over 12 outlets each.

"Franchising has been called the last and best hope for independent business in an era of growing vertical integration. It helps small businesses compete and prosper using the franchisor's know-how and trademark or servicemark; it also offers a unique opportunity to people with limited capital and experience" (Kostecka 1985, p. vi). Franchising takes one of the historical limitations of many service operations—small size—and turns it into a business asset. Its flexible structure is particularly suited to adapting rapidly to changing market conditions. Services can be added or dropped. New franchises—e.g., in computer rental and repair—can be established quickly as the prototype franchises have already been developed and tested.

Franchising makes possible the entry into new markets at decreased cost because a successful partner has already been established. The new

Burger King franchisee does not have to start from scratch in building name recognition. Business format is particularly popular as it "is characterized by an ongoing business relationship between franchisor and franchisee that includes not only the product, service, and trademark, but the entire business format itself—a marketing strategy and plan, operating manuals and standards, quality control, and continuing two-way communications" (Kostecka 1985, p. 3). The management training provided decreases considerably the likelihood of failure in the new venture.

The function of the overhead services provided in business franchising is to create and exploit economies of scale in an industry setting where small-scale establishments are the norm. Individual franchisees do not need to retain the services of an accountant, a tax lawyer, an advertising agency, etc. Instead, these professional services are provided to the corporation/franchise as a whole. Equipment and supplies can be bulk-ordered and centrally warehoused. Computerized inventory systems can be installed for the franchise network as a whole at considerably less expense than if each small establishment were to purchase its own. Employee benefits can be managed for the franchise as a whole, making possible the offering of options not possible for small independent firms.

As an increasingly popular form of distribution, franchising has had particular implications for the service sector. It is making possible the worldwide standardization of service expectations—what kind of service you will receive, how rapidly, and at what price—which is a key to reducing the perceived risk of the purchase for the customer. A number of small local retailers are able to survive and compete in global markets through "conversion" franchising, or becoming part of an international franchise network.

Capitalizing on Service Sector Cycles

In reviewing the growth of the service sector over the past 50 years, we can see some definite patterns emerging in the development of service industries. Seemingly random changes are often part of important cycles within the sector. Again, the alert service firm can be in a position to take advantage of cyclical changes as they begin.

Service Firm Life Cycles

Just as products have a predictable life cycle, so too do service firms. One of the sources of misunderstanding about services, as a matter of fact, is our tendency to focus on the first state of that life cycle—the entrepreneur—and overlook the kinds of economies of scale which are possible as service firms mature.

The vast majority of service firms are small businesses—frequently family businesses. Entry into the service sector is both easy and difficult. In many instances, small service firms can be run on a labor intensive basis with relatively little overhead, capitalizing on the provision of highly personalized service.

More and more of the new services, though, are capital intensive—albeit on a small scale. One entrepreneur, for example, has created a computer-based business switching long distance calls to the cheapest carrier and route. Funding for new service enterprises can be hard to obtain as no tangible product exists to show to potential financial backers. Indeed, undercapitalization of small service businesses has been identified as a major barrier to present growth in Subsaharan Africa (Squire 1981).

> As a rule informal sector [i.e., entrepreneurial] enterprises find the banks unhelpful and unsympathetic to their needs since, unlike their formal sector counterparts, they cannot provide the necessary collateral. In Freetown, for example, banks provide only 2% of investment funds in the informal sector, while in Kumasi only 9 out of 298 enterprises had ever obtained a loan of any kind from a formal credit institution (Sethuraman 1977, p. 345).

Entrepreneural enterprises are created by individuals who enjoy the start-up phase but who typically tire quickly of the routinization necessary for the business to develop. A key transition is from entrepreneur to professional manager. Some entrepreneurs enjoy moving from service delivery to management. Others, like the two women who started Ladies In Painting (now a national franchise in the United States), opt to remain in service delivery and bring in a professional manager.[17] Beware the entrepreneur who wishes to remain in service delivery but will not delegate managerial functions—growth will be extremely limited.

If the service enterprise is to grow, it must also find a way to provide timely and convenient service to customers beyond its initial market segment. Such expansion to new markets usually occurs through either offering the same customers a wider range of products (airlines offer hotel reservations and car rentals, laundries offer dry cleaning and alterations) or offering the same product to a wider range of customers (construction of new sites, joint ventures).

The newest turn in the service firm life cycle has been the concept of the "intrapreneur"—a corporate entrepreneur.[18] Intrapreneurs are being encouraged by corporations as they realize that the role of the professional manager is to take a more conservative and less risk-taking position than is characteristic of entrepreneurs. In service industries where competition worldwide is increasing, the successful corporation needs to link the drive of the entrepreneur to change systems and develop new service opportunities with the resources available from established product revenues and managerial structures.

The Relationship Between Goods and Services

Services go through a cycle of being self-provided through the ownership or leasing of the necessary equipment, or being provided by a service firm.[19] Transportation services, for example, were originally self-produced—literally (walking, running), or with the help of equipment (animal- or people-drawn carts). As transportation became automated, affluent consumers were able to purchase their own vehicles to produce transportation services more efficiently while less affluent consumers purchased the services provided by public or private transportation companies.

More recently, public pressure from citizens concerned varyingly about environmental pollution from motor vehicles or overcrowding of transportation routes has resulted in lifestyle changes. In some countries, such as Greece and Singapore, there are restrictions on motor traffic to alleviate congestion. Values are shifting from ownership to leasing/renting or using mass transit services. A wide variety of services are now available: one can purchase services produced either individually (chaffeur-driven) or for the mass market, one can lease or rent vehicles, or one can purchase used (recycled) vehicles. As goods recycling gains momentum, so do auxiliary services such as maintenance and repair.

Similar examples exist in other areas such as laundry (washing machines), entertainment (VCRs), education (self-study), and professional services (do-it-yourself kits). Typically, as disposable income rises, people are willing and able to purchase a wider and wider range of services. As the cost of services rises, or the convenience with which they are delivered remains low, other alternatives are sought. The most frequent outcome is purchasing some form of good in order to self-produce the service. Next we see the service firms emerging to repair and to rent out (for use at home or on the premises) such equipment. Then, often through technological innovation, service firms become able to offer a better quality product at a lower price than consumers can self-produce; once again the service is purchased externally.

The Generalist-Specialist Cycle

A final common cycle that we see recurring in the service sector is the shift from generalist (generic service provision) to various forms of specialization. Legal services, for example, used to be most commonly provided by an all-purpose family lawyer. In certain instances, specialists were retained; all arrangements, however, continued to flow through and be coordinated by the family lawyer.

As specialities begin to proliferate, the consumer assumes more and more responsibility in needs assessment and selection of the appropriate specialist for the task at hand. While the specialists are able to concentrate on doing one particular service well and most cost-effectively, consumers experience fragmentation in service delivery.

Gradually, three alternate structures usually evolve. In one instance, we see a resurgence of family lawyers (e.g., who have as a major function acting explicitly as an intermediary for the client with the various specialists). In another instance, we are seeing the development of umbrella firms, or "legal supermarkets," which bring together under one roof a variety of specialists. The client's relationship is with the firm, rather than with the individual service provider, and legal services can thus be provided in a coordinated and integrated fashion. Finally, we see much more conscious market segmentation, with firms specializing in particular types of clients—corporate, low income—and providing or coordinating a full range of services for those clients.

In the health care field, we see the same trends. The general practitioner becomes replaced for a time by a wide range of specialists. There is then a resurgence in family practice, supplemented by the growth of internists (somewhat more specialized, but still basically generalists) who can supervise and coordinate the range of health care needs. More recently, we are seeing the "medical supermarkets," of which health maintenance organizations (HMOs) are an example, and the integrated health care firms which include not only traditional outpatient and inpatient health care but also medical equipment rental and home health care. Finally, we have the specialized programs for the smoker, the alcoholic, and so forth.

SUMMARY

Whether or not services can function as an engine of growth is still being debated, but the critical role played by services is evident. In order to maximize growth potential, governments must consciously identify nation-specific development strategies, funding sources which are not biased against service sector development, and the necessary services to provide in the public sector. The recent trend toward privatization is a result of the realization that private sector provision of many services is a viable and attractive alternative.

Comparative advantage in services is a relatively new concept and one which will attract attention in the years to come. It seems clear that, while the determinants of such advantage may not be clear, countries can enjoy comparative advantage in particular service industries. It is important to include both cultural and policy, as well as economic, factors when analyzing comparative advantage in services.

As the service sector continues to grow, it also becomes more complex and differentiated. Virtually any activity can be turned into a profitable service venture, and each new service begets a range of supporting intermediary services. Some new services, such as telecommunications, grow out of technological innovations. Others, such as renting and leasing, have their impetus in the need to conserve and recycle limited resources. Still others, such as the new area of "remanufacturing"[20] (combining new and used parts to create improved products), blur the lines between goods and services production.

While many service corporations have created worldwide empires, much of service delivery still occurs in small-firm environments through face-to-face encounters. The increase in franchising demonstrates an excellent combination of small-scale firms with the economies of scale associated with large multinational corporations, as does the encouragement of intrapreneurs. Remaining competitive in the global services market depends upon an awareness of, and an ability to exploit in a timely manner, the recurring cycles and trends in the service sector.

NOTES

1. From D.R. Francis, "Swiss Economy Basks in an Ideal Balance," *Christian Science Monitor* (July 18, 1985), pp. 21–22.

2. From P.C. Roberts, "Overpopulation Is Not the Third World's Worst Threat," *Business Week* (August 6, 1984), p. 10.

3. From N.D. Kristof, "A New Welcome for Multinationals," *International Herald Tribune* (May 18/19, 1985), pp. 7; 13.

4. From L. Curry, "The Clubbiness of the City Meets High-tech," *Christian Science Monitor* (May 28, 1985), pp. 19–20.

5. See G. Murray, "Singapore Launches Two Projects in Move Toward Becoming an Electronic Society," *Christian Science Monitor* (June 5, 1985), p. 13.

6. Comparative advantage was calculated by Outlon using two methods, each giving approximately the same results: (1) Balassa's index of Revealed Comparative Advantage (country's share of category j ÷ country's share of total exports); (2) the Index of Competitiveness (country's balance in category j ÷ country's GDP).

7. See P. McFarren, "Bolivian Creates System to Translate 5 Western Tongues Simultaneously," *News-Sun* (March 5, 1985), p. C4.

8. See P. Brimelow, "Where Those Hybrid Haulers Are Headed," *Fourtune* (March 19, 1984), pp. 114–120; L.M. Schneider, "New Era in Transportation Strategy," *Harvard Business Review* 65 (2, 1985): 118–126.

9. See R. Walker, "Northwest Moves Forward As Trade Gateway," *Christian Science Monitor* (December 5, 1984), pp. 33–34.

10. See "Compugraphics: Trying to Move Typesetting From the Shop to the Office," *Business Week* (July 2, 1984), p. 89.

11. See J.W. Wilson and T. Carson, "Clothing Makers Go Straight to the Consumer," *Business Week* (April 29, 1985), pp. 114–115.

12. See "Now Airlines Are Diversifying by Sticking to What They Know Best," *Business Week* (May 7, 1984), pp. 70; 72.

13. See J. Fierman, "Employees Learn to Love Being Leased Out," *Fortune* (April 1, 1985), p. 80.

14. See D.C. Scott, "In US, Videotext Has Business Use," *Christian Science Monitor* (April 15, 1985), pp. 19–20.

15. See A.R. Field, "Software Makers Narrow Their Markets," *Business Week* (March 18, 1985), pp. 100; 104; B. Uttal, "Pitching Computers to Small Business," *Fortune* (April 1, 1985), pp. 95–96; 100; 104.

16. See L.L Castro, "Pacific Rim Services to Be Offered," *San Diego Union* (November 18, 1984), p. 3.

17. See T. Richman, "Personal Business," *INC.* (April 1985), pp. 68–72; "Two House Painters with a Woman's Touch" *Nation's Business* (January 1983). pp. 74–75.

18. See J.S. DeMott, "Here Come the Intrapreneurs"; R. Walker, "'Intrapreneurs': Sprouting New Ventures Within," *Christian Science Monitor* (January 14, 1985), pp. 19; 21.

19. Bhagwati (1984) has associated the process in which "services splinter off from goods and goods, in turn, splinter off from services" (p. 134) with a "disembodiment effect", or what is more commonly known as decoupling. He

makes the point that modifications in services, particularly through shifts from labor- to capital-intensive forms, occur continuously and demand rethinking.

20. See R. Schulman and M. Sabin, "A Growing Love Affair with the Scrap Heap," *Business Week* (April 29, 1985), pp. 69; 72.

9

STIMULATING TRADE
IN SERVICES[1]

Although average tariff rates have shown no significant increase, as much as 20 percent of OECD trade in manufactures, and 44 percent of total OECD trade might now be subject to some form of non-tariff restriction . . . [compared] with 4 percent and 36 percent respectively in 1974. This increasing dependence on non-tariff barriers is referred to as the 'new protectionism' (Greenaway 1984, p. 30).

Certain beneficial effects of international trade in goods . . . normally apply to international trade in services. For example there are the advantages we associate with the exploitation of international economies of scale, of allowing countries to specialise in the fields in which they have particular expertise, and of using international competition as an incentive to improve the quality and lower the price of the product offered to the consumer (Fielding 1983, p. 6).

Since the oil crises in 1973-74, the pendulum has swung away from trade liberalization and back toward protectionism. The forms which that protectionism has taken have increasingly been nontariff barriers to trade. In the service sector, the proliferation of nontariff barriers to trade has been geometric—an alarming trend in light of the importance of services trade at all levels of development.

By 1982, there were over 2,000 barriers "designed to protect from foreign competition the services provided by local banks, communications monopolies, insurance companies, transportation companies, data processing organizations, and other service industries. Many of these discriminatory practices strike at the heart of international business by impeding or even blocking the flow of vital management information across national borders'' (Anderson 1982, p. 16). Some of these nontariff barriers are industry-specific, such as reserve requirements for foreign banks, while others like governmental procurement policies or exchange rates are general.

Although issues of trade in goods and trade in services are intrinsically interwoven, most countries remain unconvinced that services trade plays any role of consequence in their economies. As a result, little attention has been paid to ensuring more open international trade in services. While nontariff barriers to foreign service firms have increased, little has been provided in the way of incentives for growth of new services.

Attempts to address trade issues in services have been plagued by the lack of a universally-accepted framework for understanding services trade issues. Reasons for the lack of consensus on negotiation procedures and issues have not always been clear. The discussion in this chapter is an attempt to clarify both the issues and the reasons for the dissimilar approaches taken by various countries.

FRAMEWORK FOR SERVICES TRADE ISSUES[2]

In Chapter 5, we discussed the various forms of services trade currently captured in the IMF Balance of Payments statistics. As was apparent from the few categories used, much of services trade data are either overly aggregated or simply not reported. If we wish to develop a categorization that can help us understand how best to approach negotiations regarding services trade issues, we will need to adopt a model that does not correspond directly to the categories of international data as they currently exist.

Developing such a model poses problems similar to those encountered in trying to define services initially. In order to have an adequate definition of services, we had to move away from simply listing service industries or their presumed attributes and focus instead on the common functions. Similarly for services trade, we must move away from focusing on the characteristics of individual services and focus instead on the key trade issues.[3]

While some aspects of international merchandise trade theory may apply to trade in services, a major difference exists between the two types of trade. Traditional merchandise trade theory assumes both that the factors of production (notably labor and capital) become fixed by location and that the finished product moves to the consumer. Neither of these assumptions is necessarily true in services trade, where either the production factors or the consumer can and do move across national borders.

Taken together, the alternatives of production factors and consumers either moving or not moving gives us a model with four services trade strategy alternatives (see Table 9.1). The first strategy, "across-the-border trade," is similar to trade in goods as only the product moves across borders. In the other three strategies, though, the product does *not* cross any national boundary, creating situations quite different from that of merchandise trade.

Across-the-border trade (as defined already in Chapter 5) includes transportation, communication, some rental/leasing, and a wide range of professional services. Many of the professional services, though, are traded through channels not normally monitored for traded items—for example, by telephone or mail. If enough volume of work is conducted in a particular foreign country, there may not even be an easily-tracked currency flow as payment may be made into a local bank account within the foreign country.

TABLE 9.1
Model of Services Trade
Strategy Alternatives

| | | Factors of Production | |
		Don't Move	Move
Consumers	Don't Move	Across-the-border trade	Foreign-earnings trade
	Move	Domestic-establishment trade	Third-country trade

Domestic-establishment trade encompasses the tourism and educational services for foreign nationals traditionally reported in the IMF "Travel" category. It also includes a wide range of services, not necessarily reported in the IMF statistics, which the consumer travels to the production site in order to purchase. For example, Singapore exports medical services to Malaysia and Indonesia by attracting consumers to Singapore who are in need of specialized health care. Another type of domestic-establishment trade frequently overlooked is the wide range of services, such as public utilities or sanitation, purchased locally by foreign corporations.

Foreign-earnings trade is comprised of services delivered in the consumer's country which involve the importation of factors of production. There are three general types of foreign-earnings trade: (1) foreign affiliates whose repatriated profits are commonly classified as investment income; (2) capital exports, also commonly classified as investment income; and (3) labor exports, commonly classified as workers' remittances. In the first instance, the affiliates (subsidiaries, branch offices, franchises) deliver services for the parent company. In the second instance, the customer receives financial returns (services) from investment abroad without having established an ownership position in any enterprise. In the third instance, countries export labor services, either skilled or unskilled, whose earnings are then repatriated.

Third-country trade, the fourth trade strategy, is comprised of traded services seldom discussed or captured in trade statistics. Indeed, such services are not considered traded services under the "location" definition even though both the producer and the customer are outside their native countries. If, for example, a French firm in Hong Kong purchases accounting services from a U.S. firm also located in Hong Kong, from a currency flow perspective (and from the "ownership" definition of trade) an international trade in services has occurred; however, the more traditional "location" definition would treat this transaction as a domestic service purchase. Many of the concerns of developing countries regarding revenue losses when tourists patronize primarily (or exclusively) multinational enterprises rather than domestic firms fall into this category.

Knowing that the above categories do not correspond neatly to services trade data as it is currently compiled, why might such a model be useful? The answer lies in the fact that such a model can help clarify the types of trade negotiations which need to take place in order for services trade to continue relatively unfettered by nontariff barriers.

NONTARIFF BARRIERS TO SERVICES TRADE

Nontariff barriers to trade in services exist in countries at all levels of development. They are most frequent and most severe in developing countries, but in Industrial countries their economic ripple effects are, if anything, greater. Brazil represents the protectionistic end of a continuum, with relatively unrestricted economies like Singapore at the other end.

Barriers to trade in services are difficult to tabulate and categorize. At the most general level there are restrictions which affect all types of services trade—telematics (transborder data flow) restrictions, currency restrictions, and immigration restrictions. These three general restrictions affect producers and consumers alike. Producers may have difficulty in gaining access to information needed to operate efficiently, in purchasing needed items or repatriating profits, and in moving staff across national borders. Consumers may have difficulty in obtaining information about competitive service products, in purchasing services in other currencies or countries, and in leaving their own countries or entering others.

There are also a variety of strategy-specific nontariff barriers to trade in services. The more specific barriers which have been identified to date are of several types. Some stem from general government regulation of any firm in a particular industry—public or private, domestic or foreign—so that their adverse effects on trade is accidental. Some stem from attempts to protect infant domestic service industries or to limit the outflows of foreign exchange, and thus are conscious barriers to trade. Indeed, we can think in terms of a trichotomy of nontariff barriers: (1) pure nontariff barriers, intended to protect domestic economies; (2) quasi-nontariff barriers, intended both for needed regulation and for protection; and (3) accidental nontariff barriers, intended only for legitimate market regulation but with unintended protectionistic consequences.[4]

Barriers to trade in services exist for a variety of reasons. Regarding pure nontariff barriers, two of the more usual motives include desires to insure job availability to domestic nationals (hence work permits for foreign nationals) and attempts to protect the cultural heritage of the society from excessive influence from foreign lifestyles and values. Infant industry protection is a classic example of a quasi-nontariff barrier, usually combining attempts at protection of domestic industries with industry regulation. Accidental nontariff barriers include consequences of fiscal policies intended to limit unnecessary use of foreign exchange, regulations aimed at protecting consumers from unnecessary risks, and concerns about national security.

One of the difficulties in discussing nontariff barriers is the fact that not all forms of barriers have yet been identified, nor have they been categorized in a consistent fashion. If we combine the types of services trade strategies with the concept of barriers affecting product, consumer, or production factors, we can begin to get a clearer idea of the issues involved (see Table 9.2). An analysis of the types of nontariff barriers to trade in nine services industries which affect ASEAN-Australian indicates that barriers to product movement and producer establishment each constitute approximately 44 percent of the identified barriers (see Table 9.3). Further, the economies with higher per capita GNP (Australia, Malaysia, Singapore) have significantly fewer barriers to trade than do the economies with lower per capita GNP (Indonesia, Philippines, Thailand).

Barriers to Product Movement

At the most restrictive level, countries may require local content in services and bar foreign products completely from access to the domestic market. Canada has insisted that advertisements be created and filmed within Canada. Brazil has required that all color motion pictures be reprinted in Brazil before they can be shown. Argentina and Mexico have both required that shippers of wholesale or retail goods insure the cargo with a host country firm. Even if services may enter the domestic market, they may be barred from access to needed marketing channels—as with international airlines which are denied access to domestic airline reservation systems.

Once products have gained market access, local purchase requirements may contribute to increased costs of doing business. Firms may be required to purchase equipment locally, to use local distribution networks, or to lease facilities rather than purchase outright. Or quotas may exist, as in the movie industry, that limit the number of foreign products purchased.

Restrictions on telematics, or transborder telecommunications and data transmission, affect both product movement and consumer purchase. The Federal Republic of Germany, Canada, and Sweden have all prohibited the processing of data outside the host country for use in the host country. Brazil has enacted legislation to restrict the use of foreign data communication facilities. Firms may be prohibited from connecting privately owned equipment to public communication networks. Import restrictions on foreign advertising or data communications may also make it difficult to promote domestic-establishment or third-country trade in services to consumers in their home markets.

TABLE 9.2
Types of Nontariff Barriers
to Trade in Services

	Category of Service Trade			
	"Trade"		*"Investment"*	
Barrier to:	*Across-the-border*	*Domestic-establishment*	*Foreign-earnings*	*Third-country*
Product Movement	Market access Local purchase Telematics Govt. activity[b] Technical standards Charges/taxes Intellectual property	Telematics[a]	Market access Local purchase Telematics Govt. activity Technical standards Charges/taxes Intellectual property	Market access Local purchase Telematics Govt. activity Technical standards Charges/taxes Intellectual property
Capital Movement	Currency restrictions	Currency restrictions	Currency restrictions Repatriation of profits	Currency restrictions Repatriation of profits
Human Movement: Labor Consumers	Work permits	Visas Departure tax	Work permits	Work permits Visas Departure tax
Producer Establishment			Right of establishment Access to production inputs	Right of establishment Access to production inputs

[a]In consumer's home country.
[b]Subsidies, dumping, procurement practices, regulations, monopolies.

Adapted from R.J. Krommenacker, *World-traded Services: The Challenge for the Eighties* (Dedham, MA: Artech House, 1984); R.K. Shelp, *Beyond Industrialization: Ascendency of the Global Service Economy* (New York: Praeger Publishers, 1981).

TABLE 9.3
Analysis of Nontariff Barriers
to ASEAN-Australian Services Trade: 1981

| Barrier to: | Development Category | | | | | |
| | Lower Middle[a] | | Upper Middle/ Industrial[b] | | Total | |
	Number	Percent	Number	Percent	Number	Percent
Product Movement	25	42%	18	44%	43	43%
Capital Movement	6	10	1	2	7	7
Human Movement	4	7	3	7	7	7
Producer Establishment	25	42	9	46	44	44
Totals	60	101%[c]	41	99%	101	101%

[a]Includes Indonesia, Philippines, Thailand.
[b]Includes Australia, Malaysia, Singapore.
[c]Totals may not add to 100% because of rounding.
Note: The proportion of nontariff barriers in Industrial and Upper-middle-income countries is significantly less than the proportion in Lower-middle-income countries ($z = 8.16$, $p < .001$).
Calculated from data in K. Tucker; G. Seow; and M. Sundberg, *Services in ASEAN-Australian Trade* (Kuala Lumpur and Canberra: ASEAN-Australia Joint Research Project, 1983), p. 36, Table 18.

The role of the government in hindering trade in services, apart from specific legislation enacted, is varied. It may effectively block foreign competitors by subsidizing domestic firms. For example, the Japanese government has subsidized the Japanese shipping industry through low cost loans. Conversely, it may remove the competitive advantage of a firm in domestic-establishment trade by removing subsidies—as in the case of the British government removing subsidies for foreign students studying in Britain, thus making the tuition costs prohibitively high.[5] Or it may decrease a service firm's ability to compete internationally through domestic regulations, such as the U.S. Foreign Corrupt Practices Act which is estimated to have increased the cost of doing business internationally by as much as 30 percent.

Regarding government procurement practices, it is common to restrict public sector markets to domestic national firms. "Buy American" campaigns effectively restrict foreign firms from bidding on U.S. government contracts. If firms are theoretically able to bid for service contracts, there is frequently another stumbling block in the form of absence of written procedures for the bidding process. There may be little information on government policies and procedures, and access to appropriate government officials may be difficult to obtain. Or the government may tie the awarding of government contracts to local purchase requirements regarding insurance coverage and so forth. The government may also exercise monopoly control over the market, blocking foreign competition either directly or indirectly by selling below cost.

Governments may also fail to extend national treatment to foreign firms. Japan, for example, has required that foreign shippers move their goods through a series of warehouses, while freight on Japan Airlines goes through one warehouse only. Regarding tourism, "although tourism is a vital and growing international service industry, it is inhibited from reaching its full potential because of government-imposed impediments" (Ascher 1983, p. 1).

Not infrequently, service firms are restricted through the imposition of discriminatory technical standards. Restrictions may be imposed regarding professional credentials or the type and size of equipment used (effectively eliminating foreign-manufactured equipment). Similarly, foreign service firms may be required to pay additional transaction taxes, higher income taxes, or additional charges for use of facilities (such as airports).

Finally, foreign service delivery may be effectively curtailed through lack of statutes guaranteeing protection of intellectual property rights. The issue of computer software protection has received a great deal of attention worldwide. Professional services and franchise operations are also vulnerable to the absence of patent and copyright protection.

Barriers to Capital Movement

Regulation of currency exchange, fluctuating exchange rates, and limits on the ability to repatriate earnings effect every aspect of international services trade. All but foreign-earnings trade are adversely affected by if consumers are unable to purchase services with foreign exchange, or to purchase an unrestricted volume. Unfavorable exchange rates can make the costs of a service no longer competitive either by raising the costs of doing business or by shrinking the consumer's purchasing power. The financial institutions themselves are particularly affected by currency controls as they may be unable to offer certain services such as internationally-accepted credit cards. As financial markets worldwide become increasingly integrated, barriers related capital movements will become more and more problematic.

Barriers to Human Movements

Immigration restrictions of various types also have serious consequences for international service industries. Any restrictions on the flow of labor worldwide can limit a firm in selection of staff. Even in across-the-border trade, such as professional consultation, effective service delivery may depend upon being able to hire the most skilled staff available. Just between the United States and Canada, for example, technicians which the Canadian branch of a corporation may need to repair equipment may be only a mile away but since they are on the U.S. side of the border, they may be unable to make repairs on the Canadian side of the border because of work permit regulations.

Immigration restrictions also hamper the free flow of consumers. Consumers may be unable to enter certain countries at all, or may have excessive waiting periods in order to obtain the necessary visas. Consumers may also be discouraged from leaving their home country because of excessive departure taxes. Indonesia, for example, has restricted the flow of Indonesians to Singapore for shopping by sharply increasing its airport departure tax.

Barriers to Producer Establishment

Price Waterhouse (1983) found that over two-thirds of all U.S. service corporations cited restrictions in right of establishment as the most significant barrier to trade in services, occurring in 29 of the countries with which they traded. Such restrictions range from bans on the importation of a service, to requirements regarding percentage ownership by host nationals. Australia, for example, has prohibited the establishment of foreign banking subsidiaries, while Canada has restricted the number of foreign-owned banks to a set percentage of the banks operating in Canada.

If foreign firms are able to open affiliate offices, there may still be restrictions regarding the staff composition. In addition to immigration restrictions, there are a variety of ways in which governments curtail freedom of choice in selecting employees. One is through employment bans or quotas—U.S. civil rights legislation, Malaysia's quota system—or work permits, as in Europe. In some countries, like Brazil, local education or training is required in order to practice as a professional.

SERVICES TRADE NEGOTIATION ISSUES

Nontariff barriers to trade in services have, until now, been negotiated on an industry by industry basis through organizations such as the International Telecommunications Union, the International Civil Aviation Organization, the Bank for International Settlements, or the International Maritime Consultative Organization. The Organisation for Economic Co-operation and Development (OECD) has several codes which address trade restrictions in services—e.g., Liberalisation of Current Invisible Operations and Liberalisation of Capital Movements. Similarly, the EEC Treaty of Rome provides a framework for liberalizing trade in services within the European Economic Community. Despite the availability of such forums, though, nontariff barriers to services trade have continued to increase.

The need to negotiate a multinational reduction in nontariff barriers to trade in services was raised for the first time in an international forum at the 1982 ministerial meeting of the General Agreement on Tariffs and Trade (GATT) by the United States Trade Representative, William Brock. The immediate reponse was not positive. The European countries, with the exception of the United Kingdom, were hesitant at best. Brazil led the developing countries in protesting that services were a "developed country" issue and, further, that raising service issues was an attempt on the part of the United States to sidetrack negotiations on merchandise. The initial compromise—that member nations of GATT could, if they chose, undertake a self-study on trade in services (Guest 1982)—was followed two years later by a commitment of GATT resources to review and synthesize reports coming in from member countries (Francis 1984).

Addressing nontariff barriers to trade in services in bilateral or multilateral negotiations is relatively new. Canada and the United States began discussing barriers in both banking and computer services in 1983. In 1984, the United States and Israel successfully negotiated the first international trade agreement which explicitly includes services. Such agreements, though, are slow to materialize because of a variety of differences in outlook and values between nations.

Consequences of Free Trade in Services[6]

Initial GATT discussions about trade in services have underscored national differences in perspective regarding markets for services. The United States' position has been that trade in services is a positive-sum game—i.e., there is the potential for an ever-expanding global market which is stimulated by increases in service exports. Such a perspective implies that unrestricted trade brings the best results, that domestic markets ultimately gain from foreign competition. No data have been presented as yet to either support or refute such an expanding market for services. Without concrete evidence of an expanding market for services, the U.S. position is naturally suspect as one of self-interest since its balance of trade in services has been declining.

European governments are more skeptical of a continual growth model and maintain that there is no real evidence yet that continual growth is possible or even desirable. They point out that many industries within the service sector are, and will continue to be, regulated because of governmental responsibilities for social infrastructure, consumer welfare, monetary policy, and national security. In the face of regulation, total reliance on market forces is impossible. In the absence of convincing evidence, most European governments fear that the global market for services is more likely to be a zero-sum game—and with good reason. Having control of almost half the world trade in services, they stand to lose a great deal if inappropriate liberalization occurs.

Developing nations have also questioned whether general benefits will accrue from liberalized trade in services. In part, these questions stem from a lack of awareness of the strength and vitality of their own service sectors. Many fear that by agreeing to open their own domestic markets to imports they will become passive service technology recipients. As exporters, though, they have much to gain from liberalization if in fact services are a growth market.

The most basic issue in any services trade negotiations, then, is what are the consequences of removing nontariff barriers to services trade. If continued growth in services trade can be predicted, as has been the case in merchandise trade, then benefits will certainly accrue. The question remains of how applicable merchandise trade theories are to services trade. In the absence of well-developed theories on services trade, we can assume that at least three kinds of benefits may accrue from unrestricted services trade: (1) There are the traditional gains to be had from efficient reallocation of production worldwide. (2) There are benefits to be gained from increasing the kind and quality of services available in each market through competition. (3) There is the potential for increased efficiency in domestic service firms because of the need to continually innovate in order to remain competitive with foreign firms.

The Role of Foreign Direct Investment

Even the most superficial inspection of the nontariff barriers listed in Table 9.2 will show that "investment" trade is more seriously affected by trade restrictions than are traditional forms of trade. Any services trade negotiations, then, that do not include investment issues are doomed to be ineffective in the long run.

In reviewing the international service operations already in existence, it is clear that foreign direct investment—i.e., the right of establishment in foreign markets—is a prerequisite of maximum resource allocation efficiency. Although there may be political risks for the producer establishing a service firm in the foreign market, risks to the consumer are lowered when services are locally produced and hence can be domestically regulated for consumer protection. Again, investment by foreign service firms can create the environment which stimulates domestic firms to provide better quality service. For example, in the People's Republic of China, the first joint-venture hotel (the Jianguo Hotel in Beijing) has been held up as a model of high service standards for hotels around the country.

The Appropriate Forum

When the GATT was originally formed after World War II, the available technology in transportation and communication made globally-coordinated production a virtual impossibility. It was only natural, then, that trade was assumed to take the form of exporting and that investment issues were excluded from multilateral trade negotiations. Because of the growing importance of foreign direct investment not only by Industrial country transnational corporations but also by developing country transnationals, there have been suggestions to establish a GATT on investment. A GATT on services would be a natural complement, allowing for both "trade" and "investment" issues to be addressed.

The issue of whether or not GATT, as presently constituted, is the appropriate forum for addressing service trade issues continues to be a matter of debate. Most Industrial countries agree that GATT is an appropriate vehicle for discussion on trade in services; certainly, the GATT principles are being used as a possible model by OECD in its studies of services trade issues. But the European nations, while submitting national studies on services to the GATT, have focused their discussions primarily within the European Communities and OECD.

The United States views GATT as *the* forum for negotiation, although it has participated in the work in OECD. The United States has pushed for GATT as the forum for several reasons: (1) GATT has the broadest membership of any forum in which trade issues could be negotiated. (2) Agreements within the GATT are legally binding, with a built-in mechanism for settling disputes. The Europeans have taken the position that discussions should continue until some form of consensus is reached; therefore, the internal legal mechanisms of GATT for dispute settlements are less important to the Europeans than to the United States.

Most developing countries, in contrast, would like to see service trade issues dealt with only in UNCTAD where each country has one vote—giving developing countries a clear majority. Most of the developing nations feel disenfranchised in GATT and are suspicious of the U.S.'s historical reluctance to work together in UNCTAD. The United States has viewed UNCTAD as a political forum in which the developing nations exert a disproportionate amount of power (and in which the United States wields very little power) and so has opposed discussing services in UNCTAD. Indeed, the United States underlined this opposition in November 1984 by declaring itself prepared to deal with "trade partners" but not "political blocs" (Francis 1984). Fortunately, the U.S. reversed its position in March 1985 and agreed to participate in discussions in UNCTAD on services.

The Appropriate Participants

Because of the objections raised by developing countries to consideration of services trade issues in GATT, a proposal had been made to restrict initial discussions to the Industrial nations, or even to bilateral negotiations between "like-minded parties." Certainly, the United States had indicated its intention to make such a move if it was not satisfied that sufficient progress was being made through GATT. After the November 1984 GATT ministerial meetings, U.S. Deputy Trade Representative, Michael Smith was quoted as saying: "If we do not address these emerging issues [i.e., services] in the GATT framework, some contracting parties will lose interest and they will inevitably turn to other means to pursue their national trade objectives" (Francis 1984, p. 20).

Any restriction of participants, though, would appear shortsighted in light of prior experience in merchandise trade negotiations which suggests that maximum participation in services trade negotiations is desirable. As UNCTAD's report (1984a) on services and development and the data in this book have made clear, services trade is of vital concern to developing nations. If developing countries do not participate, they may fail to reap the benefits of open access to other markets on a most-favored-nation basis for their own exported services. Further, to the extent that they are dependent on imported services, they stand to benefit from "successful efforts to liberalize world-traded services [which] would result in greater competition among suppliers of services internationally and ultimately in lower service prices" (Krommenacker 1984, p. 123).

The Appropriate Approach

Another issue is whether negotiations on services should proceed generally or on an industry-specific basis. Until now, the primary focus has been industry-specific and the consequences have not been overwhelmingly successful. The progress on merchandise trade issues made under GATT over the past 35 years has been in large part due to the multilateral establishment of general trading principles. "Trade can flourish only in a context of security, stability, and predictability. Governments provide that context by agreeing on multilateral rules of general trade policy under which all countries may benefit from international competition and may be given such essential safeguards as may be needed" (Krommenacker 1984, p. 122).

In order for progress to be made, it is essential that countries be able to identify areas of clear self-interest so that they have a stake in the outcome. Malaysia, for example, has already identified issues underlying the composition of its services trade with Japan and the United Kingdom which could become bases for negotiations.[7] Thailand has proposed that the Industrial nations consider relaxing immigration restrictions in return for better access to the domestic service markets of developing countries.

It is important to recognize that different countries will have different priorities for such negotiations—a major reason for the current lack of consensus on how to proceed. The statistics presented in Table 9.4 help clarify the kinds of differences in emphases which are occurring. If one assumes that countries would be most eager to discuss nontariff barriers to services trade in areas where they are exporting less volume than would be expected, we would expect the United States to raise issues regarding "other services" (like finance, telematics, professional consultation), the European Communities to focus on "travel and tourism," and the developing countries to focus on "transportation." That is exactly what has happened. The United States has focused on financial services and telematics, the E.C. participants at OECD helped undertake an excellent study on tourism issues, and the Asian countries are talking of forming their own shipping conference.

TABLE 9.4
Percentage Shares in Components
of Services Trade: 1981

Country/Region	Percent of Country/ Region Total			Percent of Component Total			Percent of World Total
	Transport	Travel	Other	Transport	Travel	Other	
Services Exports							
United States	39%	31%	30%	11%	12%	9%	11%
EEC	38	23	39	41	34	45	40
Japan	70	3	27	11	1	5	6
Other Industrial	31	39	30	14	24	14	17
Rest of World	31	31	38	22	29	28	26
World Total	37%	27%	36%				
Services Imports							
United States	51%	36%	13%	10%	12%	3%	8%
EEC	38	27	35	34	40	41	38
Japan	51	13	37	11	5	11	9
Other Industrial	33	34	33	10	17	13	13
Rest of World	47	22	31	35	27	32	32
World Total	43%	26%	31%				

Calculated from data in W.H. Witherall, "Liberalisation of International Trade and Investment in Services: An OECD Perspective" (paper presented at the Salzburg Seminar on New Patterns of Trade and Finance, April 1984).

Similarly, we could expect that countries would be most willing to make concessions regarding imports in areas where they are importing less than might be expected. Again, the United States has already proceeded on a bilateral basis to discuss becoming more open regarding financial and communications-related services. The E.C. is least protective about transportation services, and the developing countries are most open to discussions regarding tourism.

The Appropriate Agenda

As the leader in raising services trade issues, U.S. strategy can and does affect the outcome of services negotiations. The U.S. position that services trade issues should be handled by multilateral negotiations rather than by consensus is a clear reflection of cultural values rooted in confrontation and majority rule. In keeping with its relatively brief history, the United States has taken a rather short-term, pragmatic position which includes an adversarial and confrontational approach to international trade discussions. Thus, the United States feels impatient that services trade issues were not resolved over the two-year period between 1982 and 1984. Since 1984, the United States has been intimating that it may withdraw from service negotiations in GATT and pursue agreements with other "like-minded" nations. The 1984 trade agreement with Israel which incorporated services as a trade issue has been held up as a model for such bilateral treaties.

The Europeans, on the other hand, view the exploration of service issues as only just begun. In keeping with their centuries of international economic dealings, the Europeans have taken a long-term perspective. They hold to the traditional tenets of diplomacy—those of seeking consensus and avoiding confrontation. As the consensus process requires the creation of goodwill and a modicum of trust, it is hardly surprising that the Europeans were taken aback that they should be pressured by the United States to support a GATT study of services in 1982 while the United States was simultaneously attacking E.C. agricultural policies, applying sanctions against U.S. firms supplying equipment for the European-Soviet gas pipeline, and attempting to strengthen protection of the U.S. steel industry.

The work within OECD is an example of the differences in approach between the United States and Europe. Substantial progress has been made towards establishing a general framework for considering services trade issues (Devos 1984). While specific industry reviews have been undertaken, the priority has been given to creating a foundation and set of principles which can guide further discussions. The United States has been relatively impatient with this process, wanting to get down to industry specifics.[8]

The Appropriate Guidelines for Negotiations

In negotiating nontariff barriers to trade in services, a number of the concepts which have been used in GATT to guide negotiations regarding merchandise are being applied more or less directly to services. There remain, however, differences of opinion as to how each guideline should be carried out.

Transparency

A basic tenet of trade policy has been that a nation's regulations governing various areas of trade should be transparent or readily apparent. As long as trading partners are aware of potential barriers to trade, these can be taken into account and are subject to negotiation.

In merchandise trade, such barriers are primarily customs duties and tariffs. For services, attention needs to be given to making transparent trade obstacles other than customs tariffs as many services cannot be monitored at the border.

Since so little work has yet been done on tabulating national regulations which could affect services, transparency may be impractical in the immediate future given the existing number of regulations which would require notification. While pure nontariff barriers may be fairly readily identified, quasi- and accidental nontariff barriers will take time to articulate. A proposed compromise being considered by OECD is (1) notification of regulations that treat non-national suppliers differently and/or have an impact on international trade, combined with (2) a "counter notification procedure" under which foreign governments could ask for verification or refutation of an apparent regulatory barrier.

National Treatment

Once across the border, foreign service firms may be treated in the same manner as local service firms under an agreement of national treatment. This entails that the foreign firms accept the same obligations as a domestic firm regarding customer protection codes, treatment of employees, etc. Of course, there are forms of restriction which can be imposed which are non-discrminatory—e.g., a statute which specifies "no new firms" (foreign or domestic).

Then, too, it may be necessary to distinguish between national treatment accorded a subsidiary and "equivalent treatment" accorded foreign-based enterprises carrying on transborder trade. While national treatment under GATT has typically applied to all signatories, an initial strategy based on reciprocity (similar to retaliatory tariffs) may be more realistic. Several issues arise in applying the national treatment concept to services. Under GATT, exceptions to national treatment have historically been made in the areas of government procurement and subsidies. Since the impact of government procurement and subsidies on service firms can potentially be quite great, such exceptions require careful study.

Within the OECD, the proposed adoption of a "single instrument of protection"—i.e., an agreed percentage of the domestic market to be held by foreigners or an agreed number of foreigners who can service domestic markets—is still being debated. Such an approach is similar to the manner in which Canada has protected its banking industry—an approach which has been opposed by the United States and which has been the subject of recent trade negotiations between the United States and Canada.

Market Access

In order to have access to certain markets, service industries may need the right of establishment—either because of governmental regulations or because of the nature of the service industry. The more general question, then, of the relationship between trade in services and foreign direct investment becomes crucial. The United States has kept a very firm, though not always clear, distinction between trade and investment issues, as GATT does not address investment. The E.C. has concurred with such a distinction. Both parties, however, may need to reexamine this issue if certain aspects of services trade negotiations are to be resolved.

Nondiscrimination

The concept of nondiscrimination refers to equity in the treatment of foreign firms. Most-favored-nation status typically does not include all trade, but rather is accorded industry by industry. The major issue here is whether or not nondiscrimination should be conditional on reciprocity.

The issue of nondiscrimination is complicated for all regional communities (such as ASEAN, LAFTA, CARECOM, EEC) because of their efforts to establish an internal common market for services. There are provisions within the GATT already for distinguishing between nondiscrimination agreements for internal regional markets and nondiscrimination among external trading partners. For example, concessions given to a French firm doing business in the Federal Republic of Germany do not have to be extended to a United States firm doing business there.

Minimum Protection

A number of service industries—e.g., banking, communications, defense—have historically been heavily regulated or protected for reasons of national security. Service barriers negotiations are not intended to eliminate *all* protection; rather, they are intended to clarify the specific forms and levels of protection, industry by industry, which governments feel they must maintain. While many of the previous government monopolies are now being turned into private sector corporations, arguments still exist for some minimal level of control over "national interest" industries.

A more basic issue is that of the legitimacy of government regulation in the service sector. Protection may well be useful for infant industries—especially in new technology (Westphal 1981) and to counter international oligopolies in services. No international anti-trust legislation exists to impose competition internationally. Minimum protection is an area where empirical studies are most needed before theories developed for trade in goods are extended to trade in services.

The United States is on record opposing protectionism in services: "We must do what we can to resist protectionist solutions to current trade problems in services and to work out mutually satisfactory solutions to those problems " (Brock 1982, p. 236). While the United States may be relatively free of protectionism, it does protect certain service industries. Lack of acknowledgement of either the protectionism that exists or the role of currency exchange rates in determining terms and balance of trade detracts from the credibility of the U.S. position and makes this issue more difficult to discuss in international forums.

INCENTIVES FOR TRADE IN SERVICES

Much of the literature on services trade to date has focused on the reduction of barriers to trade rather than on the creation of incentives. In Chapter 8, we saw that it is possible for countries and firms to develop comparative advantages in services. Similarly, it is possible for countries to create an environment which attracts desired service operations in order to complement areas of national comparative advantage.

One common strategy is that of free-trade zones—zones in which taxing and other regulations are effectively suspended—extended beyond retailing operations. Open-registry shipping is a historic example of the creation of incentives to attract service sector activity. Off-shore banking is another example which has been expanding. Bahrain, for example, has positioned itself to attract major international banks, offering the attractions of proximity to oil-exporting nations and time-zone location (Gerakis and Roncesvalles 1983).

Governments can also offer investment incentives to encourage the growth of desired service industries. Most commonly such incentives have been offered in tourism, particularly to multinational hotel corporations willing to provide hospitality management services. France has offered assistance to services willing to locate outside of the Paris basin (OECD 1978). Others have experimented with incentives to health services willing to serve rural, rather than urban, areas.

Another type of incentive which can be offered is that of unrestricted and well-developed telematics infrastructures. In the face of rising concern about the negative effects of restricted international data flow, an OECD panel has recommended free flow of data across borders.[9] The U.S. Council for International Business has taken a similar stand: "Telecommunication plays a central role in the international trade of all information-based services, because it is the primary distribution channel for these services. The efficient and effective use of telcommunications has become a driving force behind world competition in service industries" (1985, p. I-7).

SUMMARY

Services trade encompasses not only trade in which a product moves across national borders, but also trade in which consumers move across borders (tourism) or production factors themselves move (subsidiaries, franchises). Four types of services trade have been identified: (1) across-the-border trade; (2) domestic-establishment trade; (3) foreign earnings trade; and (4) third-country trade.

Nontariff barriers to services trade have been steadily increasing. They include general barriers (restrictions on telematics, currency, and immigration) as well as barriers which are trade-type or industry specific. The most rapid proliferation of barriers has occurred in restrictions on general market access for a service product and on the right of establishment. The latter issue is traditionally viewed as an investment, rather than a trade, issue; but such a dichotomy has become artificial in services. "It may take a break in established patterns of thought to include relevant investment and immigration regulations in a program of trade liberalization, but this would appear to be essential in dealing with protectionism in services" (Frank 1981, p. 45).

If we assume that increased liberalization in services trade is in the common interest, we have the dual problem of identifying and reducing existing barriers, as well as ensuring that further restrictions are not instituted. A variety of issues must be resolved before services trade liberalization is possible. The most pressing one is the most effective forum in which to proceed. With the beginning in 1984 of the submission of national studies on services trade to the GATT, using the GATT as a major negotiating forum seems likely. However, the GATT as presently constituted does not address investment issues which are vital to the service sector. Once the forum issue has been resolved, other strategy issues regarding focus, participants, and general framework remain.

It is to be hoped that all parties involved will recognize the mutual advantage of multilateral negotiations. " ... [T]he same considerations of increased efficiency, growth, and employment, which ... [flow] from increased international trade in goods, can apply to trade in services; and ... barriers lead to similar costs and inefficiencies" (Golt 1982, p. 125). As the potential positive ripple effects of active international trade in services become more apparent, we can expect more focus on proactive incentives to attract multinational service corporations, rather than simply reactive negotiations to lower trade barriers.

NOTES

1. Much of the material for this chapter was first developed in D.I. Riddle and B. Springer, "Conflicting Perspectives on Trade in Services: Negotiating Non-tariff Barriers to Trade through GATT" (Paper presented at the annual meeting of the International Studies Association, March 1985, Washington, D.C.).

2. The model developed in this section assumes an "ownership" rather than a "location" definition for determining traded services (see Chapter 5 for a discussion of the difference between the concepts).

3. I am indebted to G.P. Sampson and R.H. Snape (1985) for the concepts underlying the model in Table 9.1 as they were the first to focus on the issue of whether or not factors of production move across borders.

4. See I. Walter, "Non-Tariff Barriers and the Free Trade Option," *Banca Nazionale del Lavoro Quarterly Review* (March 1969), cited in Gray (1983).

5. See A. Denton, "British Education Fees Discourage Overseas Students," *New Straits Times* (May 23, 1985), p. 10.

6. The types of issues to be negotiated have been modeled on the categories proposed by Gray (1983).

7. Speech given by Tun Ismail bin Mohamed Ali, Chairman, Council on Malaysian Invisible Trade, at the Seminar on Malaysian-British Invisible Trade Links, July 1984; Y.B. Tan Sri Thong Yaw Hong, "Malaysia-Japan Trade: Partners in Development" (speech given at the eighth joint JAWECA/MAJECA annual conference, April 1985).

8.   The United States has declared itself dedicated to free market principles; however, its request for exemption from compliance with portions of the OECD *Code of Liberalisation of Current Invisible Operations,* notably with regard to shipping (1980, p. 33) undermines its credibility as an objective free-trade advocate.

9.   See "OECD Panel Backs Free Int'l Data Flow In Developing World," *Communications Weekly* (April 8, 1985), pp. 29; 36.

10

SERVICES AND QUALITY OF LIFE

Productivity gains in farming and manufacturing, which created more goods with less labor, have freed workers to provide services that a poorer society could not afford—more education, more health care, more financial services, more travel, more professional sports, more eating out. Business's quest for greater efficiency and quality has encouraged contracting out of services once supplied in-house—everything from menial tasks like cleaning and maintenance to top-notch legal and public relations advice to the latest in computer and communications services (Kirkland 1985, p. 38).

Private and voluntary organizations (PVOs) are entering the business world. Technology brokering—serving as go-between for small and medium-sized firms in the U.S. and developing countries—is one field where PVOs are starting to make an impressive dent.[1]

The roles played by the service sector have been largely taken for granted and hence been invisible—like much of domestic work. Service industries make available the food most of us eat, the clothes we wear, the appliances we use, the books we read—in short, the many goods we consume. Service industries ensure that raw materials reach manufacturers, and that manufactured goods reach businesses. Service industries provide transportation and communications services, financial services, leisure and recreation services. The service sector is responsible for the coordination and provision of public services, including judicial,

217

legislative, and national security. Were the service sector to disappear, we would be left with a fragmented economy in which all households would have to be self-sufficient.

The comparison of the service sector to domestic housework is intentional. In many ways, the service sector is the "housekeeper" of the world economy. The range of supportive activities provided in the service sector globally mirror the activities engaged in by numerous housewives in individual households. The housewife transports family members, relays messages, lends money, cares for the sick, instructs the young, cleans house, provides meals, plans and implements recreational activities, settles disputes, sets guidelines, and in general ensures the well-being of the family. In spite of all this work, she gets little recognition and is most usually referred to as "not working." Without all of these tasks being provided, however, life would grind to a halt—-just as is the case for businesses were services to become unavailable.

Economically, we have seen that the service sector plays a vital and critical role at all levels of development. Domestically and in international trade, services are directly linked to economic growth. But what effect does service sector growth have on the lives of citizens within an economy? Have people's daily lives improved or deteriorated as the service sector has expanded? If we expect the service sector to continue to expand, are there any concerns we must address regarding the social consequences of service-led growth?

SERVICES AND THE PHYSICAL QUALITY OF LIFE

At the most basic level, we need to know if people have a greater chance of functioning effectively in the context of service-led growth. Three indicators have traditionally been used to assess physical quality of life—literacy rate, infant mortality rate, and average life expectancy. From the data in Table 10.1, we can verify the fact that the three measures are interrelated. For the developing countries, these three indicators improve simultaneously. For the Industrial countries, literacy rates are so close to 100% and the infant mortality rates are so low that little additional improvement is possible.[2] It is interesting to note that while each of the indicators improves by development level none of the indicators is consistently correlated with per capita GNP (see Table 10.2). These three physical quality-of-life indicators indeed seem to be measuring a construct separate from personal income.

TABLE 10.1
Physical Quality-of-Life
Indicators: 1981

Variable	Development Category			
	Low Income	Lower Middle	Upper Middle	Industrial
Averages for:				
Literacy Rate (%)	35.3%	56.6%	76.5%	98.9%
Infant Mortality[a] (per '000)	127.1	94.2	45.4	10.5
Life Expectancy (years)	49.5	56.9	67.4	74.8
Correlation between:				
Literacy & Infant Mortality[b]	−.71**	−.74**	−.76**	−.15
Literacy & Life Expectancy	.49*	.77**	.78**	.25
Infant Mortality & Life Expectancy	−.75**	−.83**	−.90**	−.78**

*$p < .05$
**$p < .01$
***$p < .001$

[a]Note that a higher infant mortality rate has negative implications as it means more infants are dying.

[b]Note that a negative correlation with infant mortality has a positive meaning—i.e., that infant deaths per thousand are decreasing.

Calculated from data in the World Bank, *World Development Report 1983* (New York: Oxford University Press, 1983).

What about the relationship between quality-of-life indicators and sectoral emphasis? As the service sector increases in importance, is there any correlation between service sector focus and quality-of-life indicators? While GDP from services is independent of quality-of-life indicators for all but the Upper-middle-income group, employment in the service sector is clearly related to longer life expectancy in developing countries (see Table 10.3). Either the working conditions in the service sector or the fact that certain services are being provided enhances physical health and well-being.

If we are concerned about enhanced physical quality of life, then, service sector focus is crucial. Service-led growth incorporates the expansion of the health and education industries vital to increased physical quality of life while fostering a work environment characterized by greater life expectancy and increased opportunities for literate workers. If national development priorities are focused instead in extraction or manufacturing as "leading" sectors, there is no similar guarantee that

TABLE 10.2
Relationships between Quality-of-Life
Indicators and Per Capita GNP: 1981

Variable	Development Category			
	Low Income	Lower Middle	Upper Middle	Industrial
Average for:				
Per Capita GNP (US$)	$284	$916	$2,809	$10,684
Growth in Per Capita				
GNP (1970–81)	1.1%	4.7%	4.0%	3.2%
Correlation between				
Per Capita GNP and:				
Literacy Rate	.19	.46	.36	.59*
Infant Mortality[a]	−.33	−.49*	−.47	−.43
Life Expectancy	.34	.60**	.60	.55
Correlation between				
Growth in Per Capita				
GNP and:				
Literacy Rate	.04	−.20	.04	−.20
Infant Mortality[a]	−.18	.24	−.23	−.31
Life Expectancy	.34	−.14	.04	.23

*$p < .05$
**$p < .01$
***$p < .001$

[a]Note that a negative correlation with infant mortality has a positive meaning—i.e., that infant deaths per thousand are decreasing.

Calculated from data in the World Bank, *World Development Report 1983* (New York: Oxford University Press, 1983).

quality of life will benefit as no positive correlations occurred between quality-of-life variables and employment or GDP in either the extractive or manufacturing sectors.

SERVICES AND THE QUALITY OF WORK LIFE

A major reservation frequently expressed about employment shifts to the service sector is that such a shift may signal a decrease in quality of work life. Service sector employment has been stereotyped as low-status, low-wage with little opportunity for advancement. Related concerns include the possible disappearance of the middle class and the growing

TABLE 10.3
Relationships between Quality-of-Life
Indicators and Service
Sector Percentages: 1981

Variable	Development Category			
	Low Income	Lower Middle	Upper Middle	Industrial
Correlation between Service Sector Percent of GDP and:				
Literacy Rate	.17	–.15	.44	.21
Infant Mortality[a]	–.12	.32	–.52*	–.31
Life Expectancy	.35	–.15	.50*	.37
Correlation between Service Sector Percent of Employment and:				
Literacy Rate	.11	.18	.38	.56*
Infant Mortality[a]	–.48	–.36	–.31	–.34
Life Expectancy	.71**	.50*	.50*	.48

*p < .05
**p < .01
***p < .001
[a]Note that a negative correlation with infant mortality has a positive meaning—i.e., that infant deaths per thousand are decreasing.

Calculated from data in the World Bank, *World Development Report 1983* (New York: Oxford University Press, 1983); *World Tables*, 3rd ed. (Baltimore, MD: Johns Hopkins University Press, 1983).

number of part-time positions.[3] It is true that, in the United States, manufacturing jobs are (thanks to union negotiations) better paid than service jobs. Does this necessarily imply that service positions are poorly paid? Given the relative sizes of the two sectors, there are at least as many service sector workers who make as much as the average manufacturing position pays as there are workers in the entire manufacturing sector. The greater proportion of part-time positions in services is a more realistic cause for concern (Kirkland 1985); however, manufacturing shows the same trend toward "variable labor costs."

Research indicates that the actual structural shifts in employment which are occurring in the United States are a decrease in low-wage manufacturing jobs and an increase in middle to high-wage service occupations (Benz 1984). While the volume of new jobs may be in areas such as building custodians, the most rapid increase is occurring in skilled, information-related positions (Kirkland 1985).

Some economists question whether, with fewer new manufacturing jobs being created, the service sector can grow fast enough to make up the difference. In the United States, for example, economists have argued that the service sector cannot be a growth leader because (1) growth in business services drops when manufacturing growth slows; and (2) service jobs do not pay as well as manufacturing jobs and hence have a smaller per worker ripple effect throughout the economy.[4]

Several erroneous assumptions are embedded in such reasoning. The first is that growth in GDP from manufacturing is necessarily correlated with growth in manufacturing jobs; indeed, the new technologies available would suggest that manufacturing output could continue to grow while employment figures remained constant or even fell. The second is that business services are tied primarily to manufacturing (as opposed to extractive or service industries); in fact, service industries are the primary purchases of intermediary business services. The third is that lower wages will result in slower GDP growth. It is just as likely that lower wage scales could create less inflationary pressure; and research indicates that average per capita GNP is unlikely to be affected. In the United States, concerns about potential slowdowns in the economy could be more profitably addressed from the perspective that protectionism and strong dollar have undermined the competitiveness of U.S. manufactured goods in the world market. The obvious solution, then, would be a combination of revising monetary policies, dismantling protectionism of unprofitable "smokestack" manufacturing enterprises, and encouraging the growth of competitive goods and services.

In order to address the traditional concepts of job satisfaction, job stress, and job level in relation to service sector employment, we need to examine the kinds of changes taking place in the workplace which are relevant to the service sector. It is clear that, given the strides being made in robotics, we can anticipate both a continuing shift of workers from the manufacturing sector to the service sector and continuing changes in the composition of service sector occupations as aspects of service delivery become automated. The issue, then, is one of continual retraining for positions created by the changes occurring.

Examples abound regarding the possible stimulus for, and direction of, initial retraining programs. Television is just entering Nepal, offering a wide array of new job possibilities for those adequately trained in TV program creation, wholesaling and retailing of equipment, and maintenance and repair.[5] India is about to computerize its governmental functions, displacing workers but again creating employment opportunities in computer programming and maintenance.[6] France has already begun to address the retraining issue by authorizing Club Med's founder, Gilbert Trigano, to set up "thousands of local workshops to teach the jobless how to use the computer."[7]

Satisfaction in service sector employment will depend not only on holding the appropriate job skills in order to be employable, but also on equity in the workplace. For women in particular, service sector employment has always been associated with job discrimination. Touted as eminently fitted for service sector work by virtue of early socialization in interpersonal skills, women are overrepresented in the service sector; however, they are consistently underpaid, promoted less rapidly, and more frequently hired into "dead end" jobs with few advancement opportunities (Springer and Riddle 1985).

The negative consequences of service sector employment for women are simply a reflection of a more fundamental problem in recognizing the economic role of women and the range of productive activities for which they are traditionally responsible in an economy. Many of the services purchased in market economies—e.g., water provision, goods transport, domestic services—are provided "free" by women in subsistence societies. In non-mechanized agricultural settings, women are the producers and traders of commodities; however, industrial development programs typically focus on training men, relegating women (who are often heads of households) to small-scale trading, farming, or other areas of traditional women's work.[8] Sufficient capital is even more difficult for women entrepreneurs to obtain than it is for their male counterparts.

All too frequently, women end up doing at the office the same kinds of supportive tasks which they perform at home. While the roots of gender inequity lie embedded in cultural ideologies and socialization patterns, there is some potential for service-led growth to contribute to lessening the imbalance. As service multinationals strive to enter new markets, they create employment opportunities for educated women in those domestic markets who might be barred from employment in local firms due to prejudice.[9] There is evidence, too, that to the extent that service sector growth is responsible for general economic expansion, women benefit from that expansion.[10]

In general, workers prefer employment in the service sector to that in other sectors (Singelmann 1978). Problems in job satisfaction have historically stemmed primarily from the pressure created in high-contact service positions. The "emotional labor" involved in interacting with customers has several consequences (Hochschild 1983): (1) The employee is required to display a particular emotional state and to induce an emotional state (pleasure, gratitude, fear) in the customer. (2) The supervisor has the authority to supervise and control the employee's emotional activites. We should note that women typically outnumber men two to one in jobs requiring emotional labor.

In response to emotional labor concerns, two different developments have occurred. First, attention has been focused on "burn-out" as a consequence of sustained emotional labor. Most of the remedies proposed, however, suggest various forms of job enhancement or enrichment, assuming that the primary problem is lack of intrinsic interest in the work rather than an overabundance of overly-controlled human interaction. In high-contact positions, and certainly in instances where burn-out has become severe, job enhancement can simply be an additional stressor. What is needed is relief from interaction with customers—a retreat to low-contact tasks over which the employee can exercise more direct control (Riddle 1985a).

The second development—that of decoupling many service functions—has been primarily a consequence of using new technology to increase productivity. With the telematics capabilities already in existence, it is possible for much of the service support work to be done anywhere at any time. The positive consequences of "homework" are multiple and include employment possibilities for the homebound, flexible work scheduling, and a sense of personal autonomy. The negative consequences of being an "invisible worker" are also multiple and include diminished visibility for promotion and physical isolation from colleagues and daily socializing (M. Mills 1984).

One of the characteristics of the service sector in the United States has been minimal labor union involvement. As awareness about the service sector increases and the wage and benefit disparities between services and manufacturing become more apparent, union efforts are likely to be more successful.[11] It is to be hoped that those unions will address not only financial benefits but also the quality of work life issues related to emotional labor requirements.

SERVICES AND THE GLOBAL QUALITY OF LIFE

A recent study in the Republic of Korea (Shin and Snyder 1983) documented the fact that economic growth does not necessarily lead to enhanced general well-being. Quality of interpersonal interaction and a sense of satisfaction with life as a whole are as important, if not more important, than job satisfaction. The service sector will continue to play an important role in both creating time for leisure activities and supplying a wide range of activities in which to participate.

Changes in information-related technologies and telematics will have far-reaching effects on people's daily lives. New competitors in the international communications market make it likely that the cost of global communications will drop dramatically in the forseeable future.[12] By 1990, both France and Japan plan to have their entire countries wired for interactive communications. "Smart" buildings, which have talking elevators, heat and motion sensors, automatic lighting, and shared tenant telematic equipment are proliferating and creating a "bundled services" product to compete with the ordinary "no frills" business rental space. Similarly, "smart houses" are being designed that not only monitor and control applicances and utilities but also incorporate internal voice communications and telematic links.

As the rationale for gender-based task distinctions disappears in the upsurge of information-skill-based, rather than physical-strength-based, occupations, cultural values need reexamining. Hofstede (1984) has compiled some fascinating data on the "masculinity" of national cultures— the rigidity of sex role distribution with emphasis on assertiveness rather than nurturance. Traditionalists might argue that the kind of assertiveness and independence characteristic of "masculine" cultures is a prerequisite for economic success. In that light, it is interesting to compare the countries at the extremes and find that there was no significant difference in their average annual economic growth between 1970 and 1982 (see Table 10.4). There was, however, a significant difference between the two groups with regard to 1982 per capita GNP; the *least* "masculine" cultures had a higher average personal income. The findings suggest that a move toward more androgynous values, in addition to benefitting women (through more equitable task division), also benefits society.

CONSEQUENCES OF SERVICE-LED GROWTH

There is no doubt that the vitality of the service sector will determine how effectively an economy will function. Drawing on the service purchase bundle as an analogy, the conceptual shift proposed by acknowledging the reality of service-led growth is that of focusing on customer/citizen

TABLE 10.4
"Masculinity" and Economic
Performance Indicators (US $)

Countries	Masculinity Score[a]	Per Capita GNP[b] (1982)	Average GDP Growth[c] (1970-82)
High Masculinity			
Japan	87	$10,080	4.6%
Austria	75	9,880	3.3
Ireland	74	5,150	3.8
Greece	73	4,290	4.1
Italy	72	6,840	2.8
Average	76.2	$ 7,248	3.7%
Low Masculinity			
Sweden	6	$14,040	1.7%
Norway	10	14,280	4.3
Denmark	22	12,470	2.1
Chile	26	2,210	1.9
Portugal	32	2,450	4.5
Average	19.2	$ 9,090	2.9%

[a]Country Masculinity Index Score, controlling for percentage of women.
[b]Mann-Whitney U test between groups for per capita GNP: U = 3, p = .028.
[c]Mann-Whitney U test between groups for GDP growth: U = 5, p = .075.

Data from G. Hofstede, *Culture's Consequences* (Beverly Hills, CA: Sage Publications, 1984), p. 189; World Bank, *World Development Report 1984* (New York: Oxford University Press, 1984).

needs rather than on the tangible equipment which can be created to provide services. Dependence on manufacturing-led growth implies that consumer demand for new goods must be stimulated or induced so that more tangible products can be sold. Some of the concerns nations have about the negative consequences of an interdependent global economy center around the artificial stimulation of consumer demand for imported consumer goods, diverting funds needed for family nurturance and domestic economic development to foreign coffers. In addition, lifestyle changes occur in adapting to those goods which may lead to a homogenization of world culture that undermines key traditional cultural values.

Service-led growth focuses instead on meeting consumer needs for enhanced quality of life. Manufacturing goods are then developed for, and primarily marketed to, the firms responsible for meeting those needs. Service-led growth is the logical extension of present business trends from selling to marketing, and from consumer marketing to industrial marketing.

Economies of scale in goods production demand a certain degree "homogeneity" of world markets as customized goods production can become quite expensive. Standardized service delivery can have benefits in both customer reduction and in efficiency of service production; however, both cultural value differences and specific customer needs frequently dictate customization of service delivery in various cultural settings. Franchising has led the way in allowing for cultural adaptation of the service purchase bundle while making possible overhead economies of scale and a minimal level of standardized expectations.

For the labor force, the service sector offers a wide range of jobs from which to choose. For example, some of the entry-level positions in the fast foods industry, which are frequently maligned as underpaid and lacking in career opportunities, serve the useful purpose of providing "first job" opportunities in economies where prior work experience is necessary for most positions. Nations can target particular service industries as purposely labor-intensive in order to generate employment, though technology can also be integrated. Also, nations can promote particular segments of the labor force in the world market, as India and People's Republic of China have done with professional consulting services in other developing countries. Barbados and Jamaica have followed a similar strategy in promoting their "literate English-speaking" workers to corporations with the telematics potential to utilize decentralized support staff.

As global markets become more integrated, new opportunities are possible. For example, a hospital in California is managing excess capacity in heart transplant surgery by marketing to potential patients in Mexico and Central and South America.[13] The package deal includes airfare and accomodations for a relative to accompany the patient. Telecommunication links are making it possible to present financial trading bids to a worldwide audience.[14]

We should keep in mind that growth can be occurring in the service sector (along with productive consequences) even though policy planners remain unaware of that fact. Hong Kong is an excellent illustration of an economy which promotes itself as a manufacturing-driven economy when in fact only 22 percent of GDP originated in the manufacturing sector in 1983, with 77 percent originating in services.

Although traditionally service products have been viewed as low in value-added, increased focus on services industries actually means moving up into higher value-added economic activities. Again, data from Hong Kong illustrate the differences in value-added among the economic

TABLE 10.5
Percentage of Value-Added by
Economic Sector (Hong Kong):
1977 and 1982

Economic Sector	1977	1982
Extractive Sector	47.4%	44.3%
Manufacturing Sector	29.9	28.9
Service Sector	**	57.8
Infrastructure Services	**	45.9
Trade Services	61.2	56.7
Business Services	**	78.1
Social/community Services	**	62.1

**Data incomplete or not available.

Calculated from data in the Census and Statistics Department, *Estimates of Gross Domestic Product: 1966-1984* (Hong Kong: Government Printer, 1985).

sectors (See Table 10.5). Of course, a corollary frequently is that the skill level of the workforce must also continue to be upgraded.

Can the service sector exhibit positive growth indefinitely? More important, is continual rapid growth necessarily the goal? "Bigger is better" in manufacturing has been largely replaced by the notion that "small is beautiful."[15] Does a drop for Singapore from an annual growth rate of over 8 percent to one of 5 percent mean that the economy is in trouble, as most analysts assume?[16] When many perfectly effective economies have annual growth rates of under 5 percent, and when Singapore's inflation remains at less than 1 percent, isn't it possible that the problem lies in our assumptions? Perhaps Singapore is going through a process of needed internal structural change. Perhaps 5 percent growth is a comfortable expansion rate while the higher growth rates were unrepresentative and could no longer be sustained without negative consequences. Or perhaps Singapore is indeed having economic difficulties because of its persistence in assuming that it is primarily a manufacturing economy. From the data in Table 10.6, it is clear that while growth in the manufacturing sector slowed during the 1970s, growth in the service sector increased, particularly in infrastructure services. In the area of transportation and communications, the growth rate from 1970 to 1981 was double that of the previous decade.

Whatever the optimal rate of growth is considered to be, services must play a vital role. Data from the Industrial countries suggest that there may be an optimal size for the service sector in its present form, after which continued growth would be contingent on opening new markets as is happening

TABLE 10.6
Sectoral Growth Rates
for GDP (Singapore):
1960-81

Economic Sector	1960-70	1970-81
Extractive Sector	4.5%	3.5%
Manufacturing Sector	14.5	10.8
Service Sector	8.3	9.4
Infrastructure Services	9.8	12.0
Transportation and Communication	7.4	14.3
Trade and Business Services[a]	8.9	10.4
Total Economy	9.2%	9.2%

[a]Data not disaggregated.
Calculated from data in the World Bank, *World Tables*, 3rd ed. (Baltimore, MD: Johns Hopkins University Press, 1983).

in space exploration.[17] Negative consequences from service-led growth are possible but would stem from a lack of careful planning and analysis of sectoral interdependencies. In that case, the answer would be not a reversion to manufacturing-led growth, but rather a rethinking of sectoral balance.

SUMMARY

Service industries are the housekeepers of the world. We might ask if it is not this very similarity to domestic functions which has led to the discounting of the service sector. As "family functions" are increasingly performed contractually by strangers, such activities frequently have been denigrated as marginal to the economy or as unimportant attempts to absorb excess labor. What has been overlooked is the fact that, with the "industrialization" of domestic functions, family members—in particular, women—are increasingly free to choose how they spend their time—and have free time over which to exercise control. The implications are far-ranging, and we are only beginning to glimpse them.

The service sector holds the key to our economic future. A healthy, vital service sector facilitates the flow of goods and information, provides the financial markets necessary, and contributes to a quality labor force. Developed wisely, services stimulate productivity in the other two sectors. May we not be blinded by the tangible output of the manufacturing sector to the vital networks of intangible services necessary for that production to occur. And may we learn to recognize and foster the synergistic leadership role which the service sector is already exerting at all levels of economic development.

NOTES

1. See A.B. Deolalikar, "Private Voluntary Organization Goes for Brokering" *Horizons* (Summer 1984, pp. 8-9).

2. Very high literacy rates and low infant mortality rates do not mean that there is not room for improvement. In a number of the Industrial countries, health and educational benefits are distributed unevenly throughout the society, resulting in subcultures where literacy and infant mortality rates continue to be problems.

3. See "Myth of the Vanishing Middle Class," *Business Week* (July 9, 1984), pp. 83, 86; D. Wise and A. Bernstein, "Part-time Workers: Rising Numbers, Rising Discord," *Business Week* (April 1, 1985), pp. 62-63.

4. See K. Pennar and E. Mervosh, "Why Service Jobs Can't Keep Stoking the Economy," *Business Week* (July 8, 1985), pp. 62; 66.

5. See A. Unger, "TV Coming to the Fairy-tale Kingdom of Nepal," *Christian Science Monitor* (April 5, 1985), pp. 23-24.

6. See "India Reveals Massive Plan to Computerise State-run Bodies," *Asian Computer Monthly* (July 1985), p. 16.

7. See F.J. Comes, "Does Club Med's Chief Have an Antidote for Unemployment?" *Business Week* (January 14, 1985), p. 45.

8. See S.E.M. Charlton, *Women in third world development* (Boulder, CO: Westview Press, 1984); D.K. Willis, "Meet an African Farmer . . . and Her Husband," *Christian Science Monitor* (July 5, 1985), pp. 9; 11.

9. See B.K. Martin, "Women Play Bigger Role at IBM Japan," *Asian Wall Street Journal* (July 16, 1985), p. 3; L. Wright, "Goodbye Kimono," *Time* (December 12, 1983), p. 46.

10. See G.S. Becker, "How the Market Acted Affirmatively for Women," *Business Week* (May 13, 1985), p. 16.

11. See D.T. Cook, "Unions March on in Service Industries," *Christian Science Monitor* (September 7, 1983), p. 9.

12. See S. Payne, "Calling Overseas: The New Battle of the Atlantic," *Business Week* (February 4, 1985), pp. 92; 94.

13. See R. Dalton, "Hospital to Offer Latin Heart-Surgery Package," *San Diego Union* (March 10, 1985), pp. A-1; A-10.

14. See "Electronic Markets and Information Systems" *International Management* (September 1983).

15. See J.H. Dobrzynski; J.P. Tarpey; and R. Aikman, "Small Is Beautiful," *Business Week* (May 27, 1985), pp. 88-90; "Small Is Beautiful Now in Manufacturing," *Business Week* (October 22, 1984), pp. 152–153; 156.

16. See J. Young and P. Zach, "Singapore's Deepening Slump," *Newsweek* (July 15, 1985), p. 19.

17. See M. Ingwerson, "Private Enterprise Sees Profit in Space," *Christian Science Monitor* (October 18, 1983), p. 6.

APPENDIX

APPENDIX A.
METHODOLOGICAL NOTES
ON SAMPLE COMPOSITION

In analyzing the data reported in this volume, three different kinds of country samples have been used, all based on the per capita GNP groupings in the 1984 *World Development Report* published by the World Bank. Only four of the per capita GNP groupings of the World Bank were used: Low-income economies, Lower-middle-income economies, Upper-middle-income economies, and Industrial (Market) economies. The five High-income oil-exporting economies were excluded as being too small a group and atypical of the usual development process. The Eastern European nonmarket economies were excluded because of insufficient data on all variables.

Economic Data Sample

The most frequently reported sample consisted of all countries in each of the four groups for which sufficient domestic and international trade data could be obtained. The groups consisted of the following countries, listed in ascending order by per capita GNP:

Low-income (n = 17): Bangladesh, Ethiopia, Mali, Upper Volta, Uganda, India, Tanzania, Somalia, Haiti, Central African Republic, China (PRC), Sri Lanka, Togo, Ghana, Pakistan, Kenya, Sierra Leone.

Lower-middle-income (n = 28): Sudan, Liberia, Yemen Arab Republic, Bolivia, Indonesia, Zambia, Honduras, Egypt, El Salvador, Thailand, Papua New Guinea, Philippines, Zimbabwe, Nigeria, Morocco, Cameroon, Nicaragua, Ivory Coast, Guatemala, People's Republic of Congo, Costa Rica, Peru, Dominican Republic, Jamaica, Ecuador, Turkey, Tunisia, Colombia.

Upper-middle-income (n = 18): Syrian Arab Republic, Jordan, Malaysia, Republic of Korea, Panama, Chile, Brazil, Mexico, Algeria, Portugal, Uruguay, South Africa, Yugoslavia, Venezuela, Greece, Israel, Singapore, Trinidad and Tabago.

Industrial (n = 18): Ireland, Spain, Italy, New Zealand, United Kingdom, Austria, Japan, Belgium, Finland, Netherlands, Australia, Canada, France, Federal Republic of Germany, Denmark, United States, Sweden, Norway.

This sample was used to analyze average economic trends at various levels of development between 1965 and 1981.

Extreme Case Sample

Sometimes, rather than having information on group averages, it is more useful in policy planning to understand what makes the difference between a country which exhibits rapid economic development and a country which exhibits slow development.[1] In order to examine such extreme cases, a subsample from the four groupings used in the Economic Data Sample was selected, based on the following criteria: (1) countries having the highest or lowest per capita GNP growth rate; (2) among the low-growth countries, countries with either a decrease in per capita GNP or no more than 50 percent increase between 1970 and 1981; (3) among the high-growth countries, countries in which per capita GNP at least doubled between 1977 and 1981. The resulting subsample consisted of five low-growth countries (Bolivia, Central African Republic, Ghana, Haiti, Jamaica) and five high-growth countries (Algeria, Colombia, Egypt, Republic of Korea, Paraguay).

As we can see, there is tremendous geographical and political diversity in this sample. Such diversity was considered a strength in terms of the potential for generalizing any significant findings beyond this sample. Several key variables were checked to make sure that any mean differences were not due to extraneous differences (see Table A.1). The only significant differences found were on the variables which should distinguish the groups—1981 per capita GNP and GDP growth. It should be noted that in the 1979 *World Development Report,* based on 1977 data, Haiti and Central African Republic were in the Low-income economies group; by 1981, Ghana was also classified as a Low-income economy.

Pacific Basin Sample

The Pacific Basin has been heralded as the area of most rapid growth in the 1980s. More trade now flows across the Pacific Ocean than across the Atlantic. Some analyses, therefore, were performed on the major developing Asian economies in the Pacific region to highlight the role of the service sector in that growth. The countries included were Hong Kong, Indonesia, Malaysia, Philippines, Republic of Korea, Singapore, Taiwan, and Thailand.

TABLE A.1
Demographic and Economic Variables:
Extreme Sample Case

Variable	Low Growth Sample		High Growth Sample		t	p
	Mean	S.D.	Mean	S.D.		
1977 per capita GNP	$538	373.99	$ 740	282.93	.97	> .10
Country size (km²)	400	462.05	1005.4	879.54	1.37	> .10
Population density (per km²)	93.4	103.11	93.6	164.06	.00	> .10
Urbanization rate	38.6%	8.56	51.2%	11.02	2.10	> .05
1981 per capita GNP	$574	436.50	$1640	613.66	3.07	< .05
GDP growth (1970-81)	5.9%	5.92	15.3%	6.60	2.38	< .05

NOTES

1.   For a discussion of the rationale for analyzing extreme cases, see T.C. Miller, "Conclusion: A Design Science Perspective." In *Public Sector Performance: A Conceptual Turning Point*, edited by T.C. Miller, 251-268. Baltimore, MD: Johns Hopkins University Press.

APPENDIX B.
INTERNATIONAL CLASSIFICATION
SYSTEMS

International Standard Industry Classification (ISIC), used by the United Nations:
1. Agriculture, hunting, fishing, and forestry
2. Mining and quarrying
3. Manufacturing
4. Electricity, gas, water, sanitary
5. Construction
6. Wholesale and retail trade, restaurants and hotels
7. Transport, storage, and communication
8. Finance, insurance, real estate and business services
9. Community, social and personal services

Service sector categories used by the Organisation for Economic Co-operation and Development:
1. Transport, storage, communication
2. Wholesale and retail trade
3. Banking, insurance, real estate
4. Ownership of dwellings
5. Public administration and defense
6. Other: community, business, recreation, personal

Categories used by the World Bank *World Development Report*:
1. Agricultural (agriculture, forestry, hunting, fishing)
2. Industry (mining, manufacturing, construction, utilities)
3. Manufacturing [reported separately]
4. Services

Categories used by the World Bank *World Tables*:
1. Agriculture
2. Mining
3. Manufacturing
4. Construction
5. Electricity, gas and water
6. Transport and communication
7. Trade (wholesale and retail)
8. Banking, insurance, real estate
9. Public administration and defense
10. Ownership of dwellings
11. Services

APPENDIX C.
PRINCIPAL COMPONENTS
ANALYSES

Principal components analyses were performed on the Economic Data Sample for both 1977 and 1981 data. The variables included the following:

Quality of Life Variables:	Literacy rate (%)
	Infant mortality rate (per 1,000)
	Life expectancy (years)
Demographic Variable:	Urban population as percent of total population
Labor force Variables:	Percent population of working age (15–64 years)
	Percent employed in Extractive Sector
	Percent employed in Manufacturing Sector
	Percent employed in Service Sector
Economic Variables:	Per capita GNP
	Average annual growth of per capita GNP (1960–77; 1970–81)
	Average annual growth of GDP (1960–77; 1970–81)
	Inflation rate (1960–77; 1970–81)
	Gross domestic investment as percentage of GDP[1]
	Gross domestic savings as percentage of GDP[2]
	Percentage GDP from Extractive Sector
	Percentage GDP from Manufacturing Sector
	Percentage GDP from Service Sector
Trade Variables:	Services Credits/Exports (million US $)
	Service Debits/Imports (million US $)
	Merchandise Credits/Exports (million US $)
	Merchandise Debits/Imports (million US $)

239

Debt Variables: External public debt, disbursed, % of GNP[3]

Debt payments as percent of GNP[4]

The data reported below and referred to in the text are from the SPSSPC FACTOR program, Varimax rotation. Factors were selected using a minimum eigenvalue of 1.0 and scree plots. Final statistics for eigenvalues and percentage of total variance explained are given in Table C.1; factor loadings are given in Tables C.2 through C.5. Given the sample sizes, only factor loadings of .50 or higher are statistically significant; smaller loadings have not been reported. Multiple regression analyses were not performed because of significant correlations among the independent variables.

NOTES

1. "Domestic investment" refers to the gross "outlays for fixed assets of the economy, plus changes in the net value of inventories" (World Bank 1983a, p. 205).

2. "Domestic saving" refers to "the amount of gross domestic investment financed from domestic output. Comprising public and private saving, it is gross domestic investment plus the net exports of goods and nonfactor services" (World Bank 1983a, p. 205).

3. "External debt" refers to the amount of public and publicly guaranteed loans that has been disbursed, net of repayments of principal and write-offs at year end" (World Bank 1983a, p. 208).

4. "Debt payments" refers to "the sum of interest payments and repayments of principal on external public and publically guaranteed debt" (World Bank 1983a, p. 208).

TABLE C.1
Principal Components Analysis (Varimax Rotation)
Sigenvalues and Percentage of
Variance Explained by Factors

| | Development Category | | | | | | | |
| | Low Income | | Lower Middle | | Upper Middle | | Industrial | |
Factor	Eigen-value	Percent variance	Eigen-value	Percent variance	Eigen-value	Percent variance	Eigen-value	Percent variance
Domestic Economic Data: 1977								
1	4.6	27.3%	4.6	27.1%	4.8	28.1%	4.6	30.6%
2	3.4	20.0	2.7	15.8	3.2	18.7	3.5	23.4
3	1.9	11.5	2.1	12.3	2.6	15.5	2.4	15.9
4	1.9	11.2	1.5	8.7	2.1	12.4	1.2	8.2
5	1.5	8.8	1.4	8.2	1.3	7.6		
6	1.1	6.4	1.2	6.9				
Total Variance Explained		85.2%		79.0%		82.3%		78.1%
Domestic Economic Data: 1981								
1	6.1	35.8%	4.7	27.9%	4.8	28.1%	5.1	33.9%
2	3.7	21.6	2.8	16.7	3.0	17.5	3.6	23.7
3	1.9	11.1	2.3	13.3	2.7	15.9	2.9	19.3
4	1.5	8.8	1.6	9.6	1.7	9.7	1.2	7.8
5	1.0	6.1	1.3	7.9	1.4	8.4		
6			1.2	6.8	1.2	6.8		
Total Variance Explained		83.4%		82.2%		86.4%		84.7%
International Economic Data: 1977								
1	4.6	27.1%	4.2	24.8%	5.3	31.4%	5.5	36.6%
2	3.6	21.1	3.1	18.5	3.3	19.4	3.2	21.3
3	2.9	16.9	2.6	15.1	2.2	13.1	2.7	17.8
4	1.8	10.3	1.7	10.1	1.9	11.4	1.2	8.2
5	1.4	8.1	1.3	7.6	1.3	7.6		
6			1.2	7.0				
Total Variance Explained		83.5%		83.1%		82.9%		83.9%
International Economic Data: 1981								
1	6.0	35.2%	4.3	25.6%	4.9	29.1%	5.4	36.0%
2	3.9	23.1	3.9	23.1	2.9	17.3	4.0	26.5
3	2.8	16.2	1.9	11.1	2.6	15.2	2.1	14.0
4	1.3	7.7	1.4	8.4	1.3	11.5	1.8	11.7
5	1.1	6.3	1.3	7.6	1.3	7.6		
6			1.1	6.7	1.0	5.9		
Total Variance Explained		88.5%		82.5%		86.6%		88.2%

TABLE C.2.
Principal Components Analysis (Varimax Rotation)
Factor Loadings for Domestic Economic Data: 1977

Development Category

Factor 1

Low Income — Growth		Lower Middle — Manufacturing		Upper Middle — Manufacturing		Industrial — Personal Income	
Services % GDP	.92	Manufacturing % GDP	.86	Domestic Saving % GDP	-.79	Per Capita GNP	.86
Domestic Investment % GDP	.84	Extractive % GDP	-.85	Domestic Investment % GDP	-.79	Extractive % Employed	-.84
Extractive % GDP	-.83	Literacy Rate	.76	Manufacturing % GDP	.71	Inflation Rate	-.81
Change in Per Capita GNP	.81	Per Capita GNP	.75	Manufacturing % Employed	.55	Services % Employed	.78
Change in GDP	.58	% Urbanization	.72	Inflation Rate	.52	Extractive % GDP	-.77
Debt Payments/GDP	.55					Literacy Rate	.60
						Manufacturing % GDP	.57

Factor 2

Low Income — Employment		Lower Middle — Employment		Upper Middle — Quality of Life		Industrial — Investment	
Extractive % Employed	-.95	Extractive % Employed	-.95	Life Expectancy	.93	Domestic Investment % GDP	.87
Services % Employed	.73	Services % Employed	.73	Per Capita GNP	.80	Domestic Saving % GDP	.78
Manufacturing % Employed	.72	Manufacturing % Employed	.72	Extractive % GDP	-.64	% Urbanization	-.66
Inflation Rate	.57	Domestic Saving % GDP	.57	Literacy Rate	.63	Change in GDP	.65
				Services % GDP	.52	Change in Per Capita GNP	.55

Factor 3

Low Income — Quality of Life		Lower Middle — External Debt		Upper Middle — Services		Industrial — Services GDP	
Literacy Rate	.86	External Debt % GDP	.86	Extractive % Employed	-.93	Services % GDP	.85
Domestic Saving % GDP	.84	Debt Payments % GDP	.84	Services % Employed	.75	Manufacturing % GDP	-.75
Life Expectancy	.62			% Urbanization	.62	Change in Per Capita GNP	-.64
				Services % GDP	.61	Literacy Rate	.55
				Extractive % GDP	-.58		

4 External Debt

External Debt/GDP		Investment		Growth	
Per Capita GNP	.90	Domestic Investment % GDP	.84	Change in GDP	.90
Inflation Rate	-.76	Inflation Rate	-.56	Change in Per Capita GNP	.82
				Inflation Rate	-.69

				Quality of Life	
				Life Expectancy	.76
				Manufacturing % Employed	-.73

5 Urbanization

% Urbanization	.93	**Growth**		**External Debt**	
		Change in GDP	.72	External Debt % GDP	.96
		Change in Per Capita GNP	.66	Debt Payments % GDP	.90
		Life Expectancy	-.54		

6 Manufacturing

Manufacturing % GDP	.98	**Inflation**	
		Inflation Rate	.84
		Services % GDP	-.59

TABLE C.3.
Principal Components Analysis (Varimax Rotation)
Factor Loadings for Domestic Economic Data: 1981

			Development Category	
Factor	Low Income	Lower Middle	Upper Middle	Industrial
1	**Growth**	**Services Employment**	**Quality of Life**	**Personal Income**
	Change in Per Capita GNP .94	Extractive % Employed -.92	Life Expectancy .90	Extractive % Employed -.88
	Change in GDP .87	Services % Employed .91	Literacy Rate .89	Per Capita GNP .86
	Inflation Rate -.86	Manufacturing % GDP .78	Extractive % GDP -.81	Inflation Rate -.83
	Extractive % GDP -.78	Domestic Saving % GDP .60	Per Capita GNP .58	Literacy Rate .82
	Domestic Investment % GDP .77	Manufacturing % Employed .55	Services % GDP .56	Services % Employed .69
	Services % GDP .73			Extractive % GDP -.54
	Debt Payments % GDP .58			
2	**Employment**	**Growth**	**Growth**	**Investment**
	Extractive % Employed -.97	Change in GDP .90	Change in Per Capita GNP .89	Domestic Investment % GDP .87
	Services % Employed .91	Change in Per Capita GNP .86	Change in GDP .85	Domestic Saving % GDP .87
	Manufacturing % Employed .85	Domestic Investment % GDP .60	Domestic Investment % GDP .84	Change in GDP .78
	% Urbanization .65		Inflation Rate -.77	% Urbanization -.71
	Life Expectancy .56			Extractive % GDP .58
3	**Quality of Life**	**Quality of Life**	**Services Employment**	**Services**
	Literacy Rate .83	Literacy Rate .91	Extractive % Employed -.94	Manufacturing % Employed -.95
	Domestic Saving % GDP .79	Life Expectancy .87	Services % Employed .82	Manufacturing % GDP -.93
	Life Expectancy .67	Per Capita GNP .50		Services % GDP .87
				Services % Employed .61

4 **External Debt**
External Debt % GDP .79
Manufacturing % GDP −.73

External Debt
Debt Payments % GDP .92
External Debt % GDP .82

External Debt
Debt Payments % GDP .95
External Debt % GDP .94

Growth
Change in Per Capita GNP .77
Life Expectancy .58

5 **Personal Income**
Per Capita GNP .89

Services GDP
Extractive % GDP −.88
Services % GDP .87

Services GDP
Manufacturing % GDP −.94
Services % GDP .67

6 **Inflation**
Inflation Rate .77
Manufacturing % Employed .62

Manufacturing Employment
Manufacturing % Employed .76
Domestic Saving % GDP .72

245

TABLE C.4.
Principal Components Analysis (Varimax Rotation)
Factor Loadings for International Economic Data: 1977

Factor	Low Income		Lower Middle		Upper Middle		Industrial	
	Development Category							
1	**Trade**		**Trade**		**Trade**		**Trade**	
	Services Exports	.98	Services Imports	.98	Services Imports	.92	Merchandise Exports	.97
	Merchandise Exports	.98	Merchandise Imports	.95	Merchandise Exports	.88	Merchandise Imports	.97
	Services Imports	.97	Merchandise Exports	.90	Merchandise Imports	.87	Services Imports	.92
	Merchandise Imports	.95	Services Exports	.56	Manufacturing % Employed	.52	Services Exports	.90
	Domestic Saving % GDP	.56						
2	**Services GDP**		**GDP**		**Services**		**Services Employment**	
	Services % GDP	.89	Extractive % GDP	.89	Extractive % Employed	-.96	Services % Employed	.87
	Change in Per Capita GNP	.85	Manufacturing % GDP	.85	Extractive % GDP	.81	Per Capita GNP	.84
	Extractive % GDP	-.84	Services % GDP	-.84	Services % GDP	.65	Extractive % Employed	-.80
	Change in GDP	.69	Per Capita GNP	.69	Services % Employed	.60	Extractive % GDP	-.78
	Debt Payments % GDP	.59			Per Capita GNP		Inflation Rate	-.75
3	**Employment**		**Employment**		**Growth**		**Growth**	
	Extractive % Employed	-.96	Extractive % Employed	-.83	Change in Per Capita GNP	-.95	Change in Per Capita GNP	.89
	Services % Employed	.75	Services % Employed	-.82	Change in GDP	.82	Change in GDP	.89
	Manufacturing % Employed	.72	Manufacturing % Employed	.81	Inflation Rate	.81	Domestic Saving % GDP	.69
	Inflation Rate	.55		.70	Services Exports			
				.64				

4 Personal Income

		External Debt		Manufacturing		Manufacturing	
Per capita GNP	.89	Debt Payments % GDP	.90	Domestic Saving % GDP	-.84	Services % GDP	-.72
External Debt % GDP	-.76	External Debt % GDP	.90	Manufacturing % GDP	.76	Manufacturing % Employed	.72
Inflation Rate	.61			Manufacturing % Employed	.56	Manufacturing % GDP	.66

5 Manufacturing

		Growth		External Debt	
Manufacturing % GDP	.85	Change in GDP	.86	Debt Payments % GDP	.96
Debt Payments % GDP	-.51	Change in Per Capita GNP	.71	External Debt % GDP	.95

6 Inflation

Inflation Rate	.82
Domestic Saving % GDP	-.58

TABLE C.5.
Principal Components Analysis (Varimax Rotation)
Factor Loadings for International Economic Data: 1981

Development Category

Factor	Low Income	Lower Middle	Upper Middle	Industrial
1	**Trade** Services Exports .98 Merchandise Exports .97 Services Imports .97 Merchandise Imports .95 Domestic Saving % GDP .74	**Service Employment** Services % Employed .92 Extractive % Employed -.91 Manufacturing % GDP .81 Domestic Saving % GDP .63 Per Capita GNP .52	**Trade** Merchandise Imports .91 Services Imports .88 Services Exports .86 Merchandise Exports .83 Domestic Saving % GDP .53	**Trade** Merchandise Exports .97 Merchandise Imports .97 Services Exports .94 Services Imports .89
2	**Growth** Change in Per Capita GNP .89 Inflation Rate -.88 Change in GDP .85 Extractive % GDP -.79 Services % GDP .72	**Trade** Merchandise Exports .89 Services Imports -.88 Merchandise Imports .85	**Personal Income** Extractive % GDP .95 Per Capita GNP .95 Services % Employed .93	**Personal Income** Extractive % Employed -.90 Per Capita GNP .86 Inflation Rate -.84 Services % Employed .72 Extractive % GDP -.64
3	**Employment** Extractive % Employed -.98 Services % Employed .91 Manufacturing % Employed .87	**Growth** Change in Per Capita GNP -.98 Change in GDP .91 Services Exports .87	**Growth** Change in Per Capita GNP .89 Change in GDP .84 Inflation Rate .56	**Manufacturing** Manufacturing % GDP .92 Manufacturing % Employed .92 Services % GDP -.89 Services % Employed -.63

4 Personal Income
Per Capita GNP .79
Debt Payments % GDP .72
Domestic Saving % GDP .50

External Debt
Debt payments % GDP .91
External Debt % GDP .77

External Debt
Debt Payments % GDP .93
External Debt % GDP .83

5 External Debt
External Debt % GDP .76
Manufacturing % GDP -.60

Services GDP
Services % GDP .89
Extractive % GDP -.86

Manufacturing
Manufacturing % GDP .82
Services % GDP -.74
Domestic Saving % GDP .57

6

Inflation
Inflation Rate .83
Manufacturing % Employed .57
Per Capita GNP .56

Manufacturing Employment
Manufacturing % Employed .86

Growth
Change in GDP .95
Domestic Saving % GDP .81
Change in Per Capita GNP .76

BIBLIOGRAPHY

Abegglen, J. C. 1984. *The strategy of Japanese business.* Cambridge, MA: Ballinger Publishing Company.

Adam, E. N., Jr.; Hershauser, J. C.; and Ruch, W. A. 1978. *Measuring the quality dimension of service productivity.* National Science Foundation Grant No. APR 76-07140.

Ahluwalia, M. S.; Carter, N. G.; and Chenery, H.B. 1979. Growth and poverty in developing countries. *Journal of Development Economics* 6 (September): 299–341.

Alexander, A. N. 1982. "Invisibles" move into international trade spotlight. *Business America*, November 1, pp. 2–5.

Alexander, C. P. 1983. The new economy. *Time*, May 30, pp. 62–70.

Alter, J. 1982. Precarious prosperity: The siren song of the service sector. *The Washington Monthly*, December, pp. 34–36.

America rushes to high tech for growth. 1983. *Business Week*, March 28, pp. 84–90.

America's hidden problem: The huge trade deficit is sapping growth and exporting jobs. 1983. *Business Week*, August 29, pp. 66–71.

America's trade trouble-shooter William Brock wants a new GATT round of talks on freeing invisible trade. 1982. *The Economist*, February 12, p. 63.

Ammer, C., and Ammer, D. S. 1984. *Dictionary of business and economics.* New York: The Free Press.

Ammons, D. N., and King, J. C. 1983. Productivity improvement in local government: Its place among competing priorities. *Public Administration Review* 43 (2): 113–120.

Anderson, W. S. 1982. How to stem the rising protectionism. *Business Week*, March 8, p. 16.

Andreasen, A. R. 1982. Nonprofits: Check your attention to customers. *Harvard Business Review* 60 (3): 105–110.

Arndt, H. W. 1981. Economic development: A semantic history. *Economic Development and Cultural Change* 29: 457–466.

Aronson, J. D. 1980. Industrial structure, surplus capacity and the international monetary system. The role of the service sector in the world economy. Paper presented at the annual meeting of the American Political Science Association.

Ascher, B. 1984. Obstacles to international travel and tourism. *Journal of Travel Research* 22 (3): 2–15.

ASEAN trade, industry links found lacking. 1984. *Asian Wall Street Journal*, February 27, pp. 1; 18.

Azar, V., and Pletnikova, I. 1974. On the question of the classification and full assessment of services in personal consumption. *Problems of Economics* 17 (2): 52–64.

Bacon, R., and Eltis, W. 1978. *Britain's economic problem: Too few producers.* 2nd ed. London: Macmillan.

Baer, W., and Samuelson, L. 1981. Toward a service-oriented growth strategy. *World Development* 9 (6): 499–514.

Balassa, B. 1979. A "stages approach" to comparative advantage. In *Economic growth and resources*, Vol. 4, edited by I. Adelman. London: Macmillan.

———. 1978. Exports and economic growth: Further evidence. *Journal of Development Economics* 5 (2): 181–189.

Ball, D. A. 1971. Permanent tourism: A new export diversification for less developed countries. *International Development Review*, pp. 20–23.

Ballance, R. H., and Sinclair, S. W. 1983. *Collapse and survival: Industry strategies in a changing world.* London: George Allen & Unwin.

Bannock, G.; Baxter, R. E.; and Rees, R. 1972. *The Penguin dictionary of economics.* Harmondsworth, Middlesex, England: Penguin Books, Ltd.

Barker, T., and Gimpl, M. L. 1982. Differentiating a service business: Why and how. *Journal of Small Business Management* 20 (April): 1–7.

Barry, M. E. 1984. A new global export strategy: manufacturers as worldwide storekeepers. Paper presented at the annual meeting of the European International Business Association, December, Rotterdam.

Bauer, P. T., and Yamey, B. S. 1951. Economic progress and occupational distribution. *Economic Journal* 61 (December): 741–755.

Baumol, W. J. 1967. Macroeconomics of unbalanced growth: The anatomy of urban crisis. *American Economic Review* 57: 415–426.

Bell, D. 1973. *The coming of the post-industrial society: A venture in social forecasting.* New York: Basic Books.

Benz, S. F. 1984. High-technology occupations lead growth in services employment. *Business America*, September 3.

Berle, A. A. and Means, G. 1968. *The modern corporation and private property.* Rev. ed. New York: Harcourt, Brace and Jovanovich.

Berry, L. L. 1980. Services marketing is different. *Business* 30 (May-June): 24–29.

Bessom, R. M. 1973. Unique aspects of marketing services. *Arizona Business Bulletin* 20 (9): 8–15.

Bessom, R. M., and Jackson, D. W. 1975. Service retailing: A strategic marketing approach. *Journal of Retailing* 51 (2): 75–84.

Belgium: National study on trade in services. 1985. Brussels: Government of Belgium (for submission to the GATT).

Bhagwati, J. N. 1984a. Splintering and disembodiment of services and developing nations. *World Economy* 7 (2): 133–143.

———. 1984b. Why are services cheaper in the poor countries? *The Economic Journal* 94: 279–286.

Bhalla, A. S. 1973. A disaggregate approach to employment in LDC's. *Journal of Development Studies* 10 (1): 50–65.

———. 1970. The role of services in employment expansion. *International Labour Review* 101: 519–539.

Bistline, S. M. 1982. Service corporations: The profit side of nonprofits. *Association Management* 34 (August): 74–79.

Bjur, W. E. 1981. Coproduction in human services administration. *International Journal of Public Administration* 3 (4): 389–404.

———. 1975. The international manager and the third sector. *Public Administration Review* 35: 463–467.

Blades, D. W.; Johnston, D. D.; and Marczewski, W. 1974. *Service activities in developing countries.* Paris: OECD.

Bleuel, W. H., and Patton, J. D., Jr. 1978. *Service management: Principles and practices.* Research Triangle Park, NC: Instrument Society of America.

Blois, K. J. 1984. Productivity and effectiveness in service firms. *The Service Industries Journal* 4 (3): 49–60.

———. 1974. The marketing of services: An approach. *European Journal of Marketing* 8 (2): 137–145.

Bohme, H. 1978. *Restraints on competition in world shipping.* London: Trade Policy Research Centre.

Booms, B. H., and Bitner, M. J. 1981. Marketing strategies and organization structures for service firms. In *Marketing of services,* edited by J. H. Donnelly and W. R. George, 47–51. American Marketing Proceedings Series.

———. 1978. Marketing services by managing the environment. *The Cornell H.R.A. Quarterly,* May, pp. 35–39.

Bowles, J. 1983. The search for a new engine of growth. *Business Week,* January 17, p. 10.

Boyer, E. 1983. The recovery is reshaping the economy. *Fortune,* October 3, pp. 60–65.

Brink, J. W., and Morton, S. W. 1981. The "invisible" exports that service companies generate. *Harvard Business Review* 59 (6) 36–40.

Brock, W. E. 1982. A simple plan for negotiating trade in services. *The World Economy* 5 (3): 229–240.

Brooks, H. 1983. Technology, competition, and employment. *The Annuals of the American Academy of Political and Social Science* 470 (November): 115–122.

Browning, H. C., and Singelmann, J. 1978. The emergence of a service society and its sociological implications. *Politics and Society* 8 (3–4).

———. 1975. *The emergence of a service society: Demographic and sociological aspects of the sectoral transformation of the labor force in the U.S.A.* Springfield, VA: National Technical Information Service.

Brudney, J. L., and England, R. E. 1983. Toward a definition of the coproduction concept. *Public Administration Review* 43 (1): 59–65.

Bryant, B. E., and Morrison, A. J. 1980. Travel market segmentation and the implementation of market strategies. *Journal of Travel Research* 18 (Winter): 2–8.

Bryant, W. K., and Gerner, J. L. 1982. The demand for service contracts. *Journal of Business* 55: 345–366.

Buntz, C. G. 1981. Problems and issues in human service productivity improvement. *Public Productivity Review* 5: 299–320.

Burger, A. 1970. *Economic problems of consumers' services*. Budapest: Akademia Kiado.

Canadian national study on trade in services. 1984. Ottawa: Government of Canada (for submission to the GATT).

Canton, I. D. 1984. Learning to love the service economy. *Harvard Business Review* 62 (3): 89–97.

Caporaso, J. A. 1981. Industrialization in the periphery: The evolving global division of labor. In *World system structure: Continuity and change*, edited by W. L. Hollist and J. N. Rosenau, 140–171. Beverly Hills, CA: Sage Publications.

Carter, R. L., and Dickinson, G. M. 1979. *Barriers to trade in insurance* (Thames Essay no. 19). London: Trade Policy Research Centre.

Center for Strategic and International Studies. 1982. *Services and U. S. trade policy*. Washington, D. C.: Georgetown University.

Channon, D. E. 1978. *The service industries: Strategy, structure, and financial performance*. London: Macmillan.

Chase, R. B. 1979. A strategy for improving service operations. *Arizona Review* 28 (Second Quarter): 16–21.

_____. 1978. Where does the customer fit in a service operation? *Harvard Business Review* 56 (6): 137–142.

Chase, R. B., and Tansik, D. A. 1983. The customer contact model for organization design. *Management Science* 29: 1037–1050.

Chen, E. K. Y. 1984. Hong Kong. *World Development* 12: 481–490.

Chenery, H. B. 1983. Interaction between theory and observation in development. *World Development* 11: 853–861.

_____. 1967. Patterns of industrial growth. *Economic Development and Cultural Change* 15: 174–182.

_____. 1960. Patterns of industrial growth. *American Economic Review* 50: 624–654.

Chenery, H., and Syraquin, M. 1975. *Patterns of development: 1950–1970*. New York: Oxford University Press.

Chilcote, R. H. 1984. *Theories of development and underdevelopment*. Boulder, CO: Westview Press.

Chittum, J. M. 1985. Operations and maintenance services. *Business America*, February 18, 21.

Choi, K. 1983. *Theories of comparative economic growth*. Ames: The Iowa State University Press.

Chow, G. C. 1985. *The Chinese economy*. New York: Harper and Row.

Christopher, M.; Schary, P.; and Skjott-Larsen, T. 1979. *Customer service and distribution strategy*. New York: Wiley.

Clark, C. 1940. *The conditions of economic progress.* London: Macmillan.

Clark, L. H., Jr. 1982. How to shoot yourself in the foot, internationally. *The Wall Street Journal,* October 26, p. 29.

Cloney, G. J. II. 1982. *A review of problems relating to trade policy: Use of balance of payments data describing trade in services.* Background paper prepared for the International Chamber of Commerce Commission on Obstacles to Trade in Services, Paris.

_____. 1981. *The composition and role of trade in services.* Background paper prepared for the International Chamber of Commerce Rountable on Liberalization of Trade in Services, June, Paris.

Commission of the European Communities. 1984. *Seventeenth general report of the activities of the European Communities.* Brussels: Commission of the European Communities.

Committee on Definitions of the American Marketing Association. 1960. *Marketing definitions: A glossary of marketing terms.* Chicago: American Marketing Association.

Committee on Invisible Exports. 1980. *World invisible trade.* London: Committee on Invisible Exports.

Cook, J. 1983a. Service City, U. S. A. *Forbes,* April 25, pp. 78–79.

_____. 1983b. You mean we've been speaking prose all these years? *Forbes,* April 11, pp. 142–149.

_____. 1982a. The molting of America. *Forbes,* November 22, pp. 161–167.

_____. 1982b. So, what's wrong with a service economy? *Forbes,* August 30, pp. 62–67.

Corbet, H. 1977. Prospect of negotiations on barriers to international trade in services. *Pacific Community* 8 (April): 454–469.

Cowell, D. W. 1983. International marketing of services. *The Service Industries Journal* 3 (3): 308–328.

Czepiel, J. A.; Solomon, M. R.; and Surprenant, C. F. eds. 1985. *The service encounter: Managing employee/customer interaction in service businesses.* Lexington, MA: Lexington Books.

Dale, R. 1984. Is the US already a debtor nation? *The Banker* 134 (December): 8–9.

Datta-Chaudhuri, M. 1980. Infrastructure and location. In *Policies for industrial progress in developing countries,* edited by J. Cody et al. Oxford: Oxford University Press.

Dave, U. 1984. US multinational involvement in the international hotel sector: An analysis. *The Service Industries Journal* 4 (1): 48–63.

Davis, K., and Golden, H. H. 1954. Urbanization and the development of pre-industrial areas. *Economic Development and Cultural Change* 3 (October): 6–26.

Deane, P. 1979. *The first industrial revolution.* Cambridge: Cambridge University Press.

Denison, E. F. 1973. The shift to services and the rate of productivity change. *Survey of Current Business* 53 (October): 20–35.

Denmark: National study on trade in services. 1984. Copenhagen: Government of Denmark (for submission to the GATT).

Dervis, K.; de Melo, J.; and Robinson, S. 1982. *General equilibrium models for development policy.* Cambridge: Cambridge University Press.

Devos, S. A. 1984. Service trade and the OECD. *Journal of Japanese Trade and Industry* No. 4: 16–19.

Dhrymes, P. J. 1963. A comparison of productivity behaviour in manufacturing and service industries. *Review of Economics and Statistics* 45: 64–69.

Dickinson, G. M. 1980. Insurance and the balance of payments. *Proceedings of International Insurance Seminars Meeting,* Paris.

_____. 1978. International insurance transactions and the balance of payments In *Essays in the economic theory of risk and insurance.* Geneva: Association Internationale Pour L'Etude de L'Economie de L'Assurance.

Donnelly, J. H. Jr. 1976. Marketing intermediaries in the channel of distribution for services. *Journal of Marketing* 40 (1): 55–57.

Eckstein, S., and Hagopian, F. 1983. The limits of industrialization in the less developed world: Bolivia, *Economic Development and Cultural Change* 32: 63–95.

Economic and Social Committee for Asia and the Pacific. 1985. *Economic and social survey of Asia and the Pacific 1984* (E.85.II.F.1). Bangkok: United Nations.

_____. 1984a. *Economic and social survey of Asia and the Pacific 1983* (E.84.II.F.1). Bangkok: United Nations.

_____. 1984b. *Statistical yearbook for Asia and the Pacific 1982* (E/F84.II.F.8). Bangkok: United Nations.

El-Ansary, A. I., and Kramer, O. E., Jr. 1973. Social marketing: The family planning experience. *Journal of Marketing* 37 (July): 1–7.

Elias, V. 1978. Sources of economic growth in Latin American countries. *Review of Economics and Statistics* 50: 362–370.

Ellis, H. B. 1982. Trying to stem the tide of protectionism in world trade. *The Christian Science Monitor,* November 18, p. 3.

Emi, K. 1978. *Essays on the service industry and social security in Japan* (Economic Research Series No. 17). Institute of Economic Research, Hitotsubashi University.

_____. 1971. The structure and its movements of the tertiary industry in Japan. *Hitotsubachi Journal of Economics* 12 (June): 22–32.

England, G. W. 1978. Managers and their value systems: A five-country comparative study. *Columbia Journal of World Business,* Summer, pp. 35–43.

English, E. H. 1973. The service sector: US and Canadian. *Conference Board Record* 10 (June): 59–61.

Etzioni, A. 1980. Rebuilding our economic foundations. *Business Week,* August 25, p. 16.

European Communities: Study on international trade in services. 1984. Brussels: Commission of the European Communities (for submission to the GATT).

Ezekiel, H., and Pavaskar, M. 1976. *Second India Studies: Services.* New Delhi: Macmillan Company of India, Ltd.

Fabricant, S. 1972. Productivity in the tertiary sector. *National Bureau Report Supplement* No. 10 (August):1–10.

Feder, G. 1982. On exports and economic growth. *Journal of Development Economics* 12 (1–2): 59–73.

Federal Republic of Germany: National study on trade services. 1984. Bonn: Government of the Federal Republic of Germany (for submission to the GATT).

Fielding, L. 1983. The development of a Community view on trade in services. Speech delivered at the Conference of the Chambers of Commerce of the North Sea Ports, October 21, London.

Files, L. A. 1981. The human services management task: A time allocation study. *Public Administration Review* 41: 686–692.

Finland: National study on trade in services. 1984. Helsinki: Government of Finland (for submission to the GATT).

Fisher, A. G. B. 1954. Tertiary production: A postscript. *Economic Journal* 64 (September): 619–621.

———. 1952. A note on tertiary production. *Economic Journal* 62 (December): 820–834.

———. 1939. Production, primary, secondary, and tertiary. *Economic Record,* 15 (June): 24–38.

———. 1935. *The clash of progress and security.* London: Macmillan.

Fisher, C. 1980. *International negotiation: A cross-cultural perspective.* Chicago: Intercultural Press.

Fletcher, J., and Snee, H. R. 1982. The service industries and input-output analysis. *The Service Industries Journal* 2 (1): 51–78.

Foote, N. N., and Hatt, P. K. 1953. Social mobility and economic advancement. *American Economic Review* 43: 364–378.

Francis, D. R. 1984. World takes small step toward freer trade in services. *Christian Science Monitor,* December 3, pp. 19–20.

Frank, I. 1981. *Trade policy issues for the developing countries in the 1980s* (World Bank Staff Working Paper No. 478). Washington, D. C.: World Bank.

Fuchs, V. R. 1980. *Economic growth and the rise of service employment.* New York: National Bureau of Economic Research.

———. 1968. *The service economy.* New York: National Bureau of Economic Research.

———. 1965. *The growing importance of the service industries.* New York: National Bureau of Economic Research.

Fuchs, V. R., ed. 1969. *Production and productivity in the service industries.*
New York: National Bureau of Economic Research.

Fuchs, V. R., and Wilburn, J. A. 1967. *Productivity differences within the service
sector* (Occasional Paper No. 102). New York: National Bureau of
Economic Research.

Gainsley, K. 1981. Developing hotel computer based systems to enhance customer service. *The Service Industries Journal* 1 (2): 36–61.

Galenson, W. 1963. Economic development and the sectoral expansion of
employment. *International Labour Review* 87: 505–519.

Gartner, A., and Riessman, L. 1974. *Service society and the consumer vanguard.*
New York: Harper and Row.

Gemmell, N. 1982. Economic development and structural change: The role of the
service sector. *Journal of Development Studies* 19 (1): 37–66.

George, W. R. 1977. The retailing of services: A challenging future. *Journal of
Retailing* 53 (3): 85–98.

George, W. R. and Barksdale, H. C. 1974. Marketing activities in the service
industries. *Journal of Marketing* 38 (4): 65–70.

George, W. R. and Berry, L. L. 1981. Guidelines for the advertising of services.
Business Horizons 24 (August): 52–56.

Gerakis, A. S., and Roncesvalles, O. 1983. Bahrain's offshore banking center.
Economic Development and Cultural Change 31: 271–293.

Germidis, D., and Michalet, C. A. 1984. *International banks and financial
markets in developing countries.* Paris: OECD.

Gerner, J. L., and Bryant, W. K. 1980. The demand for repair services during
warranty. *Journal of Business* 53: 397–414.

Gershon, R. A. 1985. The Maitland Commission report: A policy review. *Telecommunications,* March, pp. 86; 89; 97.

Gershuny, J. I. 1983. Is Europe becoming a post-industrial society: Deindustrialization and the future of the service sector. In *European economy in
the 1980s,* edited by H. -G. Braun, H. Vaumer, W. Leibfritz, and H. Sher-
man. London: Gower.

———. 1982. Goods replacing services: Some implications for employment. In
Changing value patterns and their impact on economic structure, edited by
Y. Kogane, 103–127. Tokyo: University of Tokyo Press.

———. 1978. *After industrial society? The emerging self-service economy.*
London: Macmillan.

Gershuny, J. I., and Miles, I. 1983. *The new service economy: The transformation
of employment in industrial societies.* New York: Praeger Publishers.

Gersuny, C., and Rosengreen, W. I. 1973. *The service society.* Cambridge, MA:
Schenkman Publishing Company.

Ghali, M. A. 1976. Tourism and economic growth: An empirical study. *Economic
Development and Cultural Change* 24 (April): 527–538.

Gitlow, H. S. 1978. Abortion services: Time for a discussion of marketing
policies. *Journal of Marketing* 42 (2): 71–82.

Goh, K. S. 1984. Public administration and economic development in LDCs. *World Economy* 7: 229–243.

Goldman, A. 1981. Transfer of a retailing technology into the less developed countries: The supermarket case. *Journal of Retailing* 57 (2): 5–29.

Golt, S. 1982. Towards freer trade in services? *The Banker* 132 (May): 115–125.

Gorostiaga, X. 1984. *The role of the international financial centres in underdeveloped countries.* London: Croom Helm.

Gray, H. P. 1983. A negotiating strategy for trade in services. *Journal of World Trade Law* 17 (5): 377–388.

Green, R. T.; Langeard, E.; and Favell, A. C. 1974. Innovation in the service sector: Some empirical findings. *Journal of Marketing Review* 11: 323–326.

Greenaway, D. 1984. Multilateral trade policy in the 1980s. *Lloyds Bank Review,* January, pp. 30–44.

Greenfield, H. I. 1966. *Manpower and the growth of producer services.* New York: Columbia University Press.

Greenwald, D., ed. 1982. *Encyclopedia of economics.* New York: McGraw-Hill Book Company.

———. 1973. *The McGraw-Hill dictionary of modern economics: A handbook of terms and organizations.* New York: McGraw-Hill Book Co.

Griffiths, B. 1975. *Invisible barriers to invisible trade.* London: Trade Policy Research Centre.

Gronroos, C. 1980. Designing a long range marketing strategy for services. *Long Range Planning* 13 (April): 36–42.

Guest, I. 1982. GATT pulls trade back from the brink. *The Christian Science Monitor,* November 30, p. 1.

Gummesson, E. 1981. Marketing cost concept in service firms. *Industrial Marketing Management* 10 (July): 175–182.

Hall, E. T. 1976. *Beyond culture.* New York: Doubleday.

———. 1966. *The hidden dimension.* New York: Doubleday.

———. 1959. *The silent language.* New York: Doubleday.

Hamer, A. 1985. Urbanization patterns in the Third World. *Finance and Development,* March, pp. 39–42.

Hanke, J. E., and Reitsch, A. G. 1981. *Business forecasting.* Newton, MA: Allyn and Bacon.

Hartwell, R. M. 1973. The service revolution: The growth of services in modern economy. In *The Fontana economic history of Europe: The Industrial Revolution,* edited by C. M. Cipolla, 359–396. London: Collins Clear-Type Press.

Hasan, P. 1982. *Growth and structural addjustment in East Asia* (World Bank Staff Working Papers No. 529). Washington, D. C.: World Bank.

Hatch, S., and Mocroft, I. 1979. The relative costs of services provided by voluntary and statutory organizations. *Public Administration* 57: 397–405.

Havrylyshyn, O., and Wolf, M. 1983. Recent trends in trade among developing countries. *European Economic Review* 21: 333–362.

Heaton, H. 1977. *Productivity in service organizations.* New York: McGraw-Hill.

Hershman, A. 1983. How to hone the U.S. competitive edge. *Dun's Business Month,* July, pp. 38–42.

Higgs, H. 1952. *The Physiocrats.* New York: Langland Press.

Hill, T.P. 1977. On goods and services. *Review of Income and Wealth* Series 23: 315–338.

Hindley, B. 1982. *Economic analysis and insurance policy in the Third World.* London: Trade Policy Research Centre.

Hindley, B., and Smith, A. 1985. Comparative advantage and trade in services. *World Economy* (forthcoming).

Hochschild, A.R. 1983. *The managed heart: Commercialization of human feeling.* Berkeley, CA: University of California Press.

Hofstede, G. 1984. *Culture's consequences: International differences in work-related values.* Beverly Hills, CA: Sage Publications.

Hofstede, G. 1983. The cultural relativity of organizational practices and theories. *Journal of International Business Studies* 14 (2): 75–89.

Hollander, S.C. 1979. Is there a generic demand for services? *MSU Business Topics* 27 (Spring): 41–46.

Holliday, G.D. 1984. *East-West technology transfer: II. Survey of sectoral case studies.* Paris: OECD.

Hopkins, M. 1983. Employment trends in developing countries, 1960–80 and beyond. *Internatinal Labour Review* 122 (4): 461–478.

Hopkins, T.K., and Wallerstein, I. 1981. Structural transformations of the world-economy. In *Dynamics of world development,* edited by R. Rubinson, 233–261. Beverly Hills: Sage Publications.

Hostage, G.M. 1975. Quality control in a service business. *Harvard Business Review* 53 (4): 98–106.

How American Express measures quality of its customer service. 1982. *AMA Forum,* March, pp. 29–31.

Hughes, J.T. 1974. The service sector. *Scottish Journal of Political Economy* 21: 317–322.

Humphrey, D.B. 1981. Scale economies of automated clearing houses. *Journal of Bank Research,* Summer, pp. 71–81.

Indonesia aborts its push for heavy industry. 1983. *Business Week,* June 20, pp. 48–49.

Industrial policy: Is it the answer? 1983. *Business Week,* July 4, pp. 54–57; 61–62.

International Labour Office. 1983a. Employment structure changing in developing world. *ILO Information* 11 (2): 1; 5.

———. 1983b. *Yearbook of labour statistics.* Geneva: ILO.

International Monetary Fund. 1977. *Balance of payments manual.* 4th ed. Washington, D.C.: IMF.

International toll-free numbers boost US firms' foreign business. 1984. *Communications News,* August, pp. 36–37.

Is free trade dead? 1982. *The Economist*, December 25, pp. 75–93.

Italy: First national study on trade in services. 1984. Rome: Government of Italy (for submission to the GATT).

Japan: National study on trade in services. 1984. Tokyo: Government of Japan (for submission to the GATT).

JETRO. 1984. *Softnomics: The service-oriented economy of Japan.* Tokyo: JETRO (Now in Japan Publication No. 35).

Johansen, L. 1960. *A multisectoral study of economic growth.* Amsterdam: North-Holland.

Judd, R.C. 1964. The case for redefining services. *Journal of Marketing* 28 (1): 58–59.

Kaldor, N. 1966. *Causes of the slow rate of economic growth of the United Kingdom.* Cambridge: Cambridge University Press.

Katouzian, M.A. 1970. The development of the service sector: A new approach. *Oxford Economic Papers* 22 (November): 362–382.

Katrak, H. 1983. Multinational firms' global strategies, host country indigenisation of ownership and welfare. *Journal of Development Economics* 13 (3): 331–348.

Kelley, L.J. 1985. Services data: Expanding our understanding. *Business America*, March 4, p. 6.

Khomelyansky, B.N. 1982. Stabilising the USSR's rural population through development of the social infrastructure. *International Labour Review* 121: 89–100.

Kichen, S., and Bornstein, P. 1983. New wave? *Forbes*, May 23, pp. 184–185.

Killing, J.P. 1982. How to make a global joint venture work. *Harvard Business Review* 60 (3) 120–128.

Kim, J-I. 1984. Need for the developing countries to play their part in GATT. *World Economy* 7: 245–252.

Kirkland, R.I., Jr. 1985. Are service jobs good jobs? *Fortune*, June 10, pp. 38–43.

Kluckhohn, F., and Strodtbeck, F. 1960. *Variations in value orientations.* New York: Row, Peterson.

Komarov, V. 1973. The service sphere and its structure. *Problems of Economics* 16 (3): 3–21.

Kostecka, A. 1985. *Franchising in the economy: 1983–85* (1985-461-105/10192). Washington, D.C.: U.S. Government Printing Office.

Kotler, P., and Conner, R.A., Jr. 1977. Marketing professional services. *Journal of Marketing* 41 (1): 71–76.

Kotler, P., and Levy, S.J. 1969. Broadening the concept of marketing. *Journal of Marketing* 33 (1): 10–15.

Kotler, P., and Murray, M. 1975. Third sector management: The role of marketing. *Public Administration Review* 35: 467–472.

Kotler, P., and Zaltman, G. 1971. Social marketing: An approach to planned social change. *Journal of Marketing* 35 (7): 3–12.

Kravis, I.B. 1983. *Services in the domestic economy and in world transactions.* New York: National Bureau of Economic Research.

————. 1970. Trade as the handmaiden of growth: Similarities between the nineteenth and twentieth centuries. *The Economic Journal* 80: 850–872.

Kravis, I.B.; Heston, A.; and Summers, R. 1982. *World product and income: International comparisons of real gross product.* Baltimore, MD: Johns Hopkins University Press.

Krommenacker, R.J. 1984. *World-traded services: The challenge for the eighties.* Dedham, MA: Artech House, Inc.

Krueger, A.O. 1983. *Trade and employment in developing countries.* Chicago: University of Chicago Press.

Kutscher, R.E., and Mark, J.A. 1983. The service-producing sector: Some common perceptions revisited. *Monthly Labor Review*, April, pp. 21–24.

Kuznets, S. 1971. *Economic growth of nations: Total output and production structure.* Cambridge, MA: Harvard University Press.

————. 1966. *Modern economic growth: Rate, structure, and spread.* New Haven: Yale University Press.

————. 1957. Quantitative aspects of the economic growth of nations, II: Industrial distribution of national product and labor force. *Economic Development and Cultural Change* 5 (July Supplement): 14–22.

————. 1938. *Commodity flow and capital formation*, Vol. 1. New York: National Bureau of Economic Research.

Kuznets, S.; Moore, W.E.; and Spengler, J.J. 1955. *Economic growth: Brazil, India, Japan.* Durham, NC: Duke University Press.

Lall, S. 1982. The emergence of third world multinationals: Indian joint ventures overseas. *World Development* 10: 127–146.

Langer, W.L. 1968. *An encyclopedia of world history.* Boston: Houghton Mifflin Company.

Laurent, A. 1983. The cultural diversity of management conceptions. *International Studies of Management and Organization* 13 (1–2): 75–96.

Layton, R.A. 1984. Trade flows in Australia, 1974–75: An assessment of structural change. *Journal of Macromarketing* 4 (1): 62–73.

Lederer, E.P.; Lederer, W.,; and Sammons, R.L. 1982. *International services transactions of the United States: Proposals for improvement in data collection.* Report prepared for the Departments of State and Commerce and the Office of the United States Trade Representative.

Lengelle, M. 1966. *The growing importance of the service sector in member countries.* Paris: OECD.

Leontief, W.W. et at. 1977. *The future of the world economy.* New York: Oxford University Press.

Leung, J. 1983. Recession reveals fundamental flaws in Singapore's economic structure. *Asian Wall Street Journal*, August 8, p. 4.

Lenin, V.I. 1978. *Collected works.* Moscow: Progress Publications.

Levitt, T. 1983. The globalization of markets. *Harvard Business Review* 61 (3): 92–102.

_____. 1981. Marketing intangible products and product intangibles. *Harvard Business Review* 59 (3): 94–102.

_____. 1976a. The industrialization of service. *Harvard Business Review* 54 (5): 63–74.

_____. 1976b. Management and the 'post-industrial' society. *The Public Interest* 44 (Summer): 69–103.

_____. 1972. Production-line approach to service. *Harvard Business Review* 50 (5): 41–52.

Lewis, R. 1973. *The service society.* London: Longman.

Lewis, W.A. 1955. *Theory of economic growth.* London: Allan and Unwin.

_____. 1954. Economic development with unlimited supplies of labor. *Manchester School of Economics and Social Studies* 22 (May): 139–191.

Lindbeck, A. 1984. Industrial policy as an issue in the economic environment. *World Economy* 7: 391–405.

Linden, F. 1974. The consumer's view of value received. *Conference Board Record* 11 (November): 48–53.

Lodge, G.C., and Crum, W.C. 1985. U.S. competitiveness: The policy tangle. *Harvard Business Review* 63 (1): 34–52.

Lohr, S. 1982. Tokyo air crash: Why Japanese do not sue. *The New York Times*, March 10, p. 1.

Long, F.A. 1984. Potential contributions of Western business to the service sector of LDCs. In *Public-private partnerships*, edited by H. Brooks, L. Liebman, and C.S. Schelling, pp. 319–337. Cambridge, MA: Ballinger Publishing Company.

Lovelock, C.H. 1984. *Services marketing.* New York: Prentice-Hall.

Lovelock, C.H., and Quelch, J.A. 1983. Consumer promotions in service marketing. *Business Horizons*, May-June, pp. 66–75.

Lovelock, C.H., and Young, R.F. 1979. Look to consumers to increase productivity. *Harvard Business Review* 57 (3): 168–178.

_____. 1977. Marketing's potential for improving productivity in service industries. In *Marketing consumer services: New insights.* Cambridge, MA: Marketing Science Institute.

Magdoff, H., and Weintraub, D. 1940. The service industries in relation to employment trends. *Econometrica* 8: 289–311.

Malthus, T.R. 1951. *Principles of political economy* [1836]. New York: Basil Blackwell.

Manufacturers move into the services. 1974. *Industry Week*, April 8, pp. 25–34.

Manufacturing is in flower. 1984. *Time*, March 26, pp. 50–52.

Mark, J.A. 1982. Measuring productivity in services. *Monthly Labor Review* 105 (6): 3–8.

Marshall, A. 1961. *Principles of economics*, vol. 1. Edited by C.W. Guillebaud. Cambridge: Macmillan.

Marx, K. 1913. *Capital: A critique of political economy* [1887]. Edited by F. Engels. Chicago: Charles Kerr.

Maslow, A. 1954. *Motivation and personality.* New York: Harper and Bros.

Masuda, Y. 1982. The conceptual framework of information economics. In *Changing value patterns and their impact on economic structure,* edited by Y. Kogane, 151–171. Tokyo: The University of Tokyo Press.

Matteis, R.J. 1979. The new back office focuses on customer service. *Harvard Business Review* 57 (2): 146–159.

McAleer, L.J., and Levine, S.J. 1984. Service marketers should weigh levels of customer satisfaction. *Marketing News* 18 (April 27): 9.

McDermott, D.R. 1978. Mass transit issues from a marketing perspective. *Transportation Journal,* Fall, pp. 28–35.

McGranahan, D. 1972. Development indicators and development models. In *Measuring development: The role and adequacy of development indicators,* edited by N. Baster, 91–102. London: Frank Cass.

Mera, K. 1984. *Measuring economic contributions of infrastructure in cities of developing countries* (No. WUDD 54). Washington, D.C.: World Bank.

Mera, K., and Shishido, H. 1984. A cross-sectional analysis of urbanization and socioeconomic development in the developing world (No. UDD 40). Washington, D.C.: World Bank.

Michell, P. 1979. Infrastructure and international marketing effectiveness. *Columbia Journal of World Business* 91 (Spring).

Miller, T.C. 1984. Conclusion: A design science perspective. In *Public sector performance: A conceptual turning point,* edited by T.C. Miller, 251–268. Baltimore, MD: Johns Hopkins University Press.

Mill, J.S. 1936. *Principles of political economy* [1871]. Edited by W.A. Ashley. London: Longmans.

Mills, M.K. 1984. Teleconferencing: Managing the "invisible worker." *Sloan Management Review,* Summer, pp. 63–67.

Mills, P.K. 1984. The socialization of clients as partial employees. Paper presented at symposium, "Managing employee and client involvement in the creation of service." Annual meeting of the Academy of Management, August, Boston.

Mills, P.K., and Margulis, N. 1980. Toward a core typology of service organizations. *Academy of Management Review* 5: 255–265.

Minter, A. 1982. Why have the service industries been ignored? *The Service Industries Journal* 2 (3): 65–71.

Mokhov, N. 1981. The economics, planning, and organization of culture. *Problems of Economics* 24 (3): 36–54.

Mundel, M.E. 1975. *Measuring and enhancing the productivity of service and government organizations.* Tokyo: Asian Productivity Organization.

Murakami, T. 1985. Inception of INS experience: Model system sets in service. *Japan Telecommunications Review* 27 (1): 2–25.

Nader, D., and Lawler, E. 1983. Quality of work life: Perspectives and directions. *Organizational Dynamics*, Winter, pp. 20–30.

Naisbitt, J. 1982. *Megatrends: Ten new directions transforming our lives.* New York: Warner Books.

The Netherlands: National study on trade in services. 1984. Amsterdam: Government of the Netherlands (for submission to the GATT).

Neubauer, J. 1982. The service industry: Maintaining the competitive edge. *Vital Speeches of the Day*, June 15, pp. 528–532.

Niemi, A.W., Jr. 1975. *U.S. economic history: A survey of the major issues.* Chicago: Rand McNally.

Nishimizu, M., and Robinson, S. 1984. Trade policies and productivity change in semi-industrialized countries. *Journal of Development Economics* 16 (1–2): 177–206.

Norway: National study on trade in services. 1984. Oslo: Government of Norway (for submission to the GATT).

Nukazawa, K. 1979. *Implications of Japan's emerging service economy* (Keindanren Paper No. 8). Tokyo.

Nurkse, R. 1970. *Problems of capital formation in underdeveloped countries.* New York: Oxford University Press.

Obstacles to international trade in services: Banking. 1984. *OECD Observer* No. 128 (May): 21–24.

Obstacles to international trade in services: Insurance and tourism. 1984. *OECD Observer* No. 126 (January): 13–15.

O'Donnell, T., and Kichen, S. 1982. Strong-arming the recession. *Forbes,* July, pp. 99–106.

Ofer, G. 1976. Industrial structure, urbanization, and the growth strategy of socialist countries. *Quarterly Journal of Economics* 90: 219–244.

_____. 1973. *The service sector in Soviet economic growth: A comparative study.* Cambridge, MA: Harvard University Press.

_____. 1967. *The service industries in a developing economy: Israel as a case study.* New York: Praeger Publishers.

Oman, C. 1984. *New forms of international investment in developing countries.* Paris: OECD.

Organisation for Economic Co-operation and Development. 1984a. *Development co-operation.* Paris: OECD.

_____. 1984b. *External debt of developing countries.* Paris: OECD.

_____. 1984c. *Maritime transport: 1983.* Paris: OECD.

_____. 1983a. *An exploration of legal issues in information and communication technologies.* Paris: OECD.

_____. 1983b. *Investing in developing countries.* Paris: OECD.

_____. 1980. *Code of liberalisation of current invisible operations.* Paris: OECD.

_____. 1978. *Regional policies and the service sector.* Paris: OECD.

_____. 1977. *Policies for innovation in the service sector: Identification and structure of relevant factors.* Paris: OECD.

_____. 1976. *Code of liberalisation of capital movements.* Paris: OECD.

_____. 1974. *Service activities in the developing countries.* Paris: OECD.

Osborne, D. 1985. Business in space. *Atlantic Monthly* 255 (5): 45.

Oshima, H.T. 1971. Labor-force "explosion" and the labor-intensive sector in Asian growth. *Economic Development and Cultural Change* 19 (2): 161–183.

Oulton, N. 1984. International trade in service industries: Comparative advantage of European Community countries. Paper presented at an international conference on "Restrictions on Transactions in the International Market for Services" (convened by Wilton Park and the Trade Policy Research Centre), June, Wiston House, England.

Palmer, R.R., and Colton, J. 1971. *A history of the modern world to 1815.* 4th ed. New York: Alfred A. Knopf.

Partel, F.J., Jr. 1984. What the American consumer wants and what the responsive banking institution can do about it. *Journal of Retail Banking,* Spring/Summer, pp. 1–7.

Patrick, H.T. 1966. Financial development and economic growth in underdeveloped countries. *Economic Development and Cultural Change* 14 (1): 174–189.

Pearce, D.W. 1981. *The dictionary of modern economics.* Cambridge, MA: The MIT Press.

Penchansky, R., and Thomas, J.W. 1981. The concept of access: Definition and relationship to consumer satisfaction. *Medical Care* 19 (2): 127–140.

Peterson, J.M., and Gray, R. 1969. *Economic development of the United States.* Homewood, Ill.: Richard D. Irwin.

Pine, A. 1982a. GATT meeting communique isn't likely to have much influence on world trade. *The Wall Street Journal.* November 30, p. 2.

_____. 1982b. Common market balks at support of trade pledge. *The Wall Street Journal.* November 23, p. 33.

_____. 1982c. Threat of a trade war rises as recession spurs competition, nations impose curbs. *The Wall Street Journal,* November 17, p. 56.

_____. 1982d. Ministers mull world trade Nov. 24: GATT parley clouded by protectionist mood. *The Wall Street Journal,* November 16, p. 31.

_____. 1982e. U.S. worries that Nov. 24 GATT parley will increase protectionism, not trade. *The Wall Street Journal,* November 5, p. 34.

_____. 1982f. GATT talks face problems as negotiators fail to agree on any big issue on agenda. *The Wall Street Journal,* October 25, p. 6.

Pipes, R. 1970. *Europe since 1815.* New York: Harper & Row.

Poats, R.M. 1984. *Development co-operation.* Paris: OECD.

Porter, G. 1973. *The rise of big business, 1860-1910.* Arlington Heights, Ill.: AHM Publishing Corporation.

Possett, R.W. 1980. Measuring productive costs in the service sector. *Management Accounting* 62 (4): 16-24.

Power, K. P. 1983. Now we can move office work offshore to enhance output. *Wall Street Journal,* June 9, p. 26.

Price Waterhouse. 1983. *Business views on international trade in services.* Report prepared for the U.S. Department of Commerce.

Prottas, J.M. 1981. The cost of free services: Organizational impediments to access to free services. *Public Administration Review* 41: 526-534.

Pryor, F.L. 1968. *Public expenditures in communist and capitalist nations.* Homewood, IL: Richard D. Irwin.

Rathmell, J.M. 1974. *Marketing in the service sector.* Cambridge, MA: Winthrop Publications.

_____ . 1966. What is meant by services? *Journal of Marketing* 29 (10): 32-36

Regan, W.J. 1963. The service revolution. *Journal of Marketing* 27 (3): 57-62

Reinert, J. 1983. You can't measure my work. *Journal of Methods-Time Management* 10 (1): 20-23.

Richta, R. 1977. The scientific and technological revolution and the prospects of social development. In *Scientific-technological revolution: Social aspects,* edited by R. Dahrendorf et al., 25-72. Beverly Hills: Sage Publications.

Riddle, D.I. 1985a. Public sector productivity and role conflicts. In *Promoting productivity in the public sector: Problems, strategies, and prospects,* edited by R.M. Kelly (forthcoming).

_____ . 1985b. Services: Parasitic or dynamic? *Policy Studies Review* 4 (3): 467-474.

_____ . 1984a. Models of the international service sector. Paper presented at the tenth annual meeting of the European International Business Association, December, Rotterdam.

_____ . 1984b. Services in global perspective: Myths and realities. Invited address for conference, Managing the Service Sector, March University of Lethbridge, Alberta, Canada

Riddle, D.I., and Sours, M.H. 1985. Service-led growth in the Pacific Basin. In *The environment of international business: A Pacific Basin perspective,* edited by W.C. Kim and P.K.Y. Young. Ann Arbor, MI: UMI Research Press.

_____ . 1984a. The role of services in ASEAN. In *The proceedings of the annual conference of the Administrative Sciences Association of Canada: International Business Division,* edited by B.M. Wolf, 5 (8): 143-152.

_____ . 1984b. Service industries as growth leaders in the Pacific Rim. *Asia Pacific Journal of Management* 1 (3): 190-199.

_____ . 1984c. Service industries in the Pacific Basin: The role of managerial assumptions. Paper presented at the Pan-Pacific Conference: A Business, Economic and Technological Exchange, March, Honolulu.

Riddle, D.I., and Springer, B. 1985. Conflicting perspectives on trade in services: Negotiating non-tariff barriers to trade through GATT. Paper presented at the annual meeting of the International Studies Association, March, Washington, D.C.

Riedel, J. 1983. *Trade as the engine of growth in developing countries: A reappraisal* (World Bank Staff Working Paper No. 555). Washington, D.C.: World Bank.

Robinson, S. 1971. Sources of growth in less developed countries: A cross-section study. *Quarterly Journal of Economics* 85: 391-408.

Rodgers, G., and Standing, G. 1981. Economic role of children in low-income countries. *International Labour Review* 120 (1): 31-47.

Rosen, B.C. 1982. *The industrial connection: Achievement and the family in developing societies.* New York: Aldine Publishing Company.

Rosenberg, N. 1982. *Inside the black box: Technology and economics.* Cambridge: Cambridge University Press.

Rostow, W. 1971. *Stages of economic growth.* 2nd ed. Cambridge: Cambridge University Press.

Rothman, M.B. 1980. A new look at services. *Stores* 62 (May): 56-57

Rutgaizer, V. 1974. Methodological problems in assessing the population's need for services. *Problems of Economics* 17 (2): 35-51.

_____ . 1973. A comprehensive plan for the development of the service sector. *Problems of Economics* 16 (5): 41-59.

Ryan, P. 1977. Get rid of the people, and the system runs fine. *Smithsonian,* August, p. 140.

Sabolo, Y. 1971. A structured approach to the projection of occupational categories and its application to South Korea and Taiwan. *International Labour Review* 103 (February): 131-135.

Sabolo, Y. (assisted by J. Gaude and R. Wery). 1975. *The service industries.* Geneva: International Labour Office.

Sampson, G.P., and Snape, R.H. 1985. International trade in services: A framework for identifying the issues. *The World Economy* (forthcoming).

Sapir, A. 1982. Trade in services: Policy issues for the eighties. *Columbia Journal of World Business,* Fall, pp. 77-83.

Sapir, A., and Lutz, E. 1981. *Trade in services: Economic determinants and development-related issues* (World Bank Staff Working Paper No. 480). Washington, D.C.: The World Bank.

Sasser, W.E. 1976. Match supply and demand in service industries. *Harvard Business Review* 54 (6): 133-140.

Sasser, W.E.; Olsen, R.P.; and Wyckoff, D.D. 1978. *Management of service operations.* Boston: Allyn and Bacon.

Saunders, R.J.; Warford, J.J.; and Wellenius, B. 1983. *Telecommunications and economic development.* Baltimore, MD: Johns Hopkins University Press.

Savas, E.S. 1981. Intracity competition between public and private service delivery. *Public Administration Review* 41:46-52.

Say, J.B. 1984. *A treatise on political economy* [1880]. New York: A.M. Kelly.

Scherer, R. 1982. US asked to reduce goals for next GATT meeting. *The Christian Science Monitor,* October 5, p. 10.

Schultze, C.L. 1983. Industrial policy: A solution in search of a problem. *California Management Review* 25 (4): 5-15.

Seashore, S. Defining and measuring the quality of working life. In *The quality of working life,* edited by L. Davis and A. Cherns, 105-118. New York: Free Press.

Sengupta, J.K. 1958. On the relevance of the sectoral concept in the theory of economic development. *Indian Economic Journal* 6 (July): 50-61.

Seow, G. F-H. 1981. The service sector and economic growth. Unpublished manuscript. National University of Singapore, Economic Research Centre.

_____. 1980. *The service sector in Singapore's economy: Performance and structure* (ERC Occasional Paper Series No. 2). Singapore: Chopmen Publishers.

Service break. 1984. *The Economist,* January 28, p. 48.

Sethuraman, S.V. 1977. The urban informal sector in Africa. *International Labour Review* 116(3): 343-352.

Shataev, I. 1984. The economics and organization of personal services. *Problems of Economics* 27 (8): 55-70.

Shelp, R.K. 1985. Entrepreneurship in the information society. Paper presented to The Heritage Foundation Conference on Entrepreneurship in the American Economy, April, Washington, D.C.

_____. 1984. US already a service economy. *Financier* 8 (1): 29-33.

_____. 1983. The service economy: Implications for policy and economic analysis. *Vital Speeches of the Day* 50 (4): 119-122.

_____. 1981. *Beyond industrialization: Ascendency of the global service economy.* New York: Praeger Publishers.

Shelp, R.K.; Stephenson, J.C.; Truitt, N.S.; and Wasow, B. 1984. *Service industries and economic development: Case studies in technology transfer.* New York: Praeger Publishers.

Sherbiny, N.A. 1984. Expatriate labor in Arab oil-producing countries. *Finance and Development,* December, pp. 34-37.

Shin, D.C., and Snyder, W. 1983. Economic growth, quality of life, and development policy: A case study of South Korea. *Comparative Political Studies* 16 (2): 195-213

Shostack, G.L. 1978. The service marketing frontier. In *Review of marketing 1978,* edited by G. Zaltman and T.V. Bonoma. Chicago: American Marketing Association.

_____ . 1977. Breaking free from product marketing. *Journal of Marketing* 41 (April): 73-80.

Sibatani, A. 1980. The Japanese brain: The difference between East and West may be the difference between right and left. *Science*, December, pp. 24-26.

Siegel, S. 1956. *Nonparametric statistics for the behavioral sciences.* New York: McGraw-Hill Book Company.

Singelmann, J. 1978. *From agriculture to services: The transformation of industrial employment.* Beverly Hills, CA: Sage Publications.

Singer, P. 1971. Forca de trabalho e emprego no Brasil: 1920-1969. *Caderno CEBRAP* 3, Sao Paulo, CEBRAP. [Cited in J. Singelmann. *From agriculture to services: The transformation of industrial employment.* Beverly Hills, CA: Sage Publications, 1978.]

Sinha, J.B.P. 1980. Dynamics of power relationships. Paper presented at the fifth annual conference of the International Association for Cross-Cultural Psychology, December, Bhubaneswar, India.

_____ . 1978. Power in superior subordinate relationship. *Journal of Social and Economic Studies* 6: 205-218.

Skolka, J.V. 1976. The substitution of self-service activities for marketed services. *Review of Income and Wealth,* Series 22, pp. 287-304.

Smith, A. 1904. *An inquiry into the nature and causes of the wealth of nations* [1776] (Vol 1, Book 2, Chapter 3). Edited by E. Cannan. New York: Modern Library.

Smith, A.D. 1973. *The measurement and interpretation of service output changes.* London: National Economic Development Office.

Solomon, M.R. 1985. Packaging the service provider. *The Service Industries Journal* 5 (1): 64-72.

Spellman, J. 1983. Barriers multiply to trade in services. *Europe,* No. 204 (November-December): 15-17.

Spero, J.E. 1983. Trade in services: Removing the barriers. *PS,* Winter: 17-24.

Springer, B., and Riddle, D.I. 1985. Women in the service sector: E.C.-U.S. comparison. Paper presented at the annual meeting of the Western Political Science Association, March, Las Vegas.

SPSSPC.

Squire, L. 1981. *Employment policy in developing countries: A survey of issues and evidence.* New York: Oxford University Press.

Stacey, B. 1982. Women in banking. *The Service Industries Journal* 2 (2): 56-65.

Stanback, T.M., Jr. 1981. *Services, the new economy.* Montclair, NJ: Allanheld, Osmun.

_____ . 1979. *Understanding the service economy: Employment, productivity, location.* Baltimore: Johns Hopkins University Press.

Steel, W.F. 1981. Female and small-scale employment under modernization in Ghana. *Economic Development and Cultural Change* 30 (1): 153-169.

Stiger, G.J. 1956. *Trends in employment in the service industries.* Princeton: Princeton University Press.

Swedish national study on trade in services. 1984. Stockholm: Government of Sweden (for submission to the GATT).

Swinyard, W.R. 1977. Market segmentation in retail service industries: A multiattribute approach. *Journal of Retailing* 53 (1): 27-34.

Switzerland: National study on trade in services. 1984. Geneva: Government of Switzerland (for submission to the GATT).

Szabadi, B. 1975. Relationship between the level of economic development and the services. *Acta Oeconomica* 15: 343-364.

Taniike, H. 1985. The CAPTAIN system and its services. *Japan Computer Quarterly* 61 (March): 10-41.

Tansik, D.A. 1984. The customer-server interface: Implications of job design. Paper presented for symposium, Managing employee and customer involvement in the creation of service. Annual meeting of the Academy of Management, August, Boston.

Thomas, D.R.E. 1978. Strategy is different in service businesses. *Harvard Business Review* 56 (4): 158-165.

Towards a GATT for services. 1982. *International Services Update* 1 (5): 1-2.

Trade in services: The UK's national examination. 1984. London: Government of the United Kingdom (for submission to the GATT).

Triantes, S.G. 1953. Economic progress, occupational redistribution, and international terms of trade. *Economic Journal* 63 (September): 627-637.

Tsurutani, T. 1976. Japan as a postindustrial society. In *Politics and the future of industrial society,* edited by L.N. Lindberg, 100-125. New York: David McKay.

Tucker, K.A. 1977. The nature and size of the service sector. In *Economics of the Australian service sector,* edited by K.A. Tucker. London: Croom Helm.

Tucker, K.A.; Seow, G.; and Sundberg, M. 1983. *Services in ASEAN-Australian trade* (ASEAN-Australia Economic Papers No. 2). Kuala Lumpur and Camberra: ASEAN-Australia Joint Research Project.

Tugendhat, C. 1985. Opening up Europe's financial sector to intra-Community competition. *The Banker* 135 (January): 21-24.

Umoh, P.N. 1984. Nigeria's rural banking scheme: A case study in financial development. *The Banker,* September, pp. 75-81.

United Nations. 1983. *Statistical yearbook: 1980/81.* New York: United Nations.

_____. 1983. *Yearbook of national account statistics: 1981.* New York: United Nations.

_____. 1971. *Indexes to the International Standard Industry Classification of all economic activities* (Series M No. 4, rev. 2, add. 1). New York: United Nations.

United Nations Centre on Transnational Corporations. 1983. *Transnational corporations in world development* (ST/CTC/46). New York: United Nations.

United Nations Conference on Trade and Development Secretariat. 1984a. *Services and the development process* (No. T/B1008). Geneva: UNCTAD.

_____ . 1984b. *Services and the development process: Summary and conclusions* (No. TD/B/1008: Summary). Geneva: UNCTAD.

_____ . 1983a. *Handbook of international trade and development statistics* (E/F83.II.D.2). New York: United Nations.

_____ . 1983b. *Protectionism and structural adjustment: Production and trade in services, policies and their underlying factors bearing upon international services transactions* (No. TD/B/941). Geneva: UNCTAD.

U.S. Council for International Business. 1985. *Statement of the U.S. Council for International Business on a new round of multilateral trade negotiations: Recommended U.S. business objectives.* Submitted to the Office of the U.S. Trade Representative.

U.S. Department of Commerce. 1985. *1985 U.S. industrial outlook: Prospects for over 300 industries* (No. 1985-451-632:20611). Washington D.C.: U.S. Government Printing Office.

_____ . 1984. *1984 U.S. industrial outlook: Prospects for over 300 industries* (No. 1984-429-530). Washington D.C.: U.S. Government Printing Office.

_____ . 1980. *Current developments in U.S. international service industries.* Washington, D.C.: U.S. Government Printing Office.

_____ . 1976a. *Study of service industries and their relation to domestic and international trade.* Washington, D.C.: U.S. Government Printing Office.

_____ . 1976b. *U.S. service industries in world markets: Current problems and future policy development.* Washington, D.C.:U.S. Government Printing Office.

_____ . 1975. *Service industries trends and prospects.* Washington, D.C.: U.S. Government Printing Office.

_____ . 1957. *Historical statistics of U.S. colonial times.* Washington, D.C.: U.S. Government Printing Office.

U.S. International Trade Commission. 1982. *The relationship of exports in selected U.S. service industries to U.S. merchandise exports* (USITC Publication No. 1290). Washington, D.C.: USITC.

U.S. national study on trade in services (No. 455-773-20145). 1984. Washington, D.C.: U.S. Government (for submission to the GATT).

Upah, G.D. 1980. Mass marketing in service retailing: A review and synthesis of major methods. *Journal of Retailing* 56 (3): 59-76.

Urquhart, M. 1981. The sevices industry: Is it recession-proof? *Monthly Labor Review* 104 (October): 12-18.

Veil, E. 1982. The world current account discrepancy. *OECD Occasional Studies,* June, pp. 46-63.

Vitro, R.A. 1984. The information engine. *Managing International Development* 1(1): 24-39.

Wanhill, S.R.C. 1983. Measuring the economic impact of tourism. *The Service Industries Journal* 3 (1): 9-20.

Wells, L.T., Jr. 1983. *Third world multinationals.* Cambridge, MA: MIT Press.

Westphal, L. 1981. *Empirical justification for infant industry protection* (World Bank Staff Working Paper No. 445). Washington, D.C.: World Bank.

Whitaker, G.P. 1980. Coproduction: Citizen participation in service delivery. *Public Administration Review* 40 (3): 240-246.

White, J.W. 1984. Multilevel network connects worldwide stations. *Telecommunications,* August, pp. 41-45.

Wilkins, M. 1970. *The emergence of multinational enterprises: American business abroad from the colonial era to 1914.* Cambridge: Harvard University Press.

Willoughby, C.R. 1983. Infrastructure: Doing more with less. In *Economic development and the private sector.* Washington, D.C.: World Bank.

Witherall, W.H. 1984. Liberalisation of international trade and investment in services: An OECD perspective. Paper presented at the Salzburg Seminar on New Patterns of Trade and Finance, April, Salzburg.

Witz, A., and Wilson, F. 1982. Women workers in service industries. *The Service Industries Journal* 2 (2): 40-55.

Wojnilower, A.M. 1985. Foreign aid: A way to save the smokestack industries. *Business Week,* April 29, p. 16.

Wolfe, M. 1955. The concept of economic sectors. *The Quarterly Journal of Economics* 69 (3): 402-420.

Wood, D.B. 1985. The rise of franchises, the homogenizing of America. *Christian Science Monitor,* April 2, p. 37; 42; 44.

World Bank. 1984. *World development report 1984.* New York: Oxford University Press.

———. 1983a. *World development report 1983.* New York: Oxford University Press.

———. 1983b. *World tables,* 3rd edition. Baltimore, MD: Johns Hopkins University Press.

———. 1979. *World development report 1979.* New York: Oxford University Press.

World trade profile: Brant W. Free. 1983. *American Import Export Management,* April, pp. 16-18.

Worthy, J.C. 1984. Managing the "social markets" business. In *Public-private partnerships,* edited by H. Brooks, L. Liebman, and C.S. Schelling, 221-240. Cambridge, MA: Ballinger Publishing Company.

Zhuravleva, G., and Mirskova, L. 1977. The price of trade services. *Problems of Economics* 20 (5): 38-50.

INDEX

ABOUT THE AUTHOR

DOROTHY I. RIDDLE is an Associate Professor of International Studies at the American Graduate School of International Management, Glendale, Arizona. Since 1982, she has been teaching a graduate course on the international service sector and seminars on both the management of international nonprofit organizations and program evaluation and operations efficiency in services.

Dr. Riddle's work on public sector productivity has been published in the *Public Policy Review,* while her work on services in the Pacific Basin has appeared in the *Asia Pacific Journal of Management.* Her research on international services has been presented at annual meetings of the Academy of International Business, the Academy of Management, the European International Business Association, the International Studies Association, and the American Political Science Association. She was also an invited speaker at the first conference on services in Canada.

Dr. Riddle holds a B.A. from the University of Colorado, an M.B.A. from the University of Arizona, and a Ph.D. from Duke University.